LAN Times Guide to Networking
Windows 95

About the Authors...

Brad Shimmin is a technical editor for *LAN Times* magazine. He lives in Salt Lake City with his loving wife, Alice.

Eric Harper is a reviews editor for *LAN Times* magazine. He currently works in the *LAN Times* Testing Center in Provo, Utah, evaluating and writing about Windows, Windows NT, DOS, Unix, and network management products.

LAN Times Guide to Networking Windows 95

Brad Shimmin
and
Eric Harper

Osborne **McGraw-Hill**

Berkeley New York St. Louis San Francisco
Auckland Bogotá Hamburg London Madrid
Mexico City Milan Montreal New Delhi Panama City
Paris São Paulo Singapore Sydney
Tokyo Toronto

Osborne **McGraw-Hill**
2600 Tenth Street
Berkeley, California 94710
U.S.A.

LAN Times Guide to Networking Windows 95

1234567890 DOC 9987

ISBN 0-07-882086-3

Publisher
Brandon A. Nordin

Editor in Chief
Scott C. Rogers

Acquisitions Editor
Jeff Pepper

Project Editor
Mark Karmendy
Cynthia Douglas

Copy Editor
Dennis Weaver

Indexer
Richard Shrout

Computer Designer
Jani Beckwith

Illustrator
Rhys Elliott

Series Design
Lance Ravella

Quality Control Specialist
Joe Scuderi

Cover Designer
EM Design

Contents at a Glance

Contents

Introduction

ownsizing. Rightsizing. Whatever you want to call it, with local area networks becoming more and more prevalent, using a computer has become almost synonymous with using a computer on a network. If connecting your Windows clients has scared you—either from an end-user or from an administrative standpoint, this book will help you become familiar with the new networking tools included with Windows 95. It will help you learn how to use the networking tools that let you customize your system and minimize the confusion.

We set out to create a book that would help anyone who works with Windows 95 in a network environment. Nowadays this includes everyone from large companies to small homes where anyone can benefit from connecting their computers to share some files or a printer. Windows 95 includes all the software you need to perform the simple and complex tasks of networking. If you have ever wondered about hooking up a couple computers but didn't know how, this book will guide you through the steps—whether you decide to install ethernet cards or use a serial cable to hook up your systems.

If you are wondering which networking protocols are best for your environment, we will help you decide by telling you the benefits and limitations of each. If you need to know how to best manage a large group of Windows 95 users for whom the interface is as foreign as can be, we will introduce you to the many management tools this product provides and teach you how to use them. If you want to customize your own Windows 95 environment or the environment of the company PCs that you manage, we will teach you what you need to do. If you are wondering how to connect your Windows 95 clients to network servers running NetWare, Windows NT, or UNIX, we will show you how it's done.

Before long, you will learn that Windows 95 is a very flexible operating system. You can control many of the networking and interface aspects of the environment and manage them remotely. You can also learn how to use your applications in a way that makes you more productive and more comfortable.

Windows 95 is the best client operating system for the hardware that is hitting the market. With Plug and Play, Windows 95 users will have no problems adding a new network card or modem. And with a full understanding of how users work with the new notebook computers on the market, Windows 95 demystifies the PCMCIA confusion and makes mobile computing as easy as it can be.

Next to the new user interface, the networking features of Windows 95 are the most obvious enhancements the operating system has to offer. Microsoft obviously recognizes the importance of local area networks (LANs) since all of their operating systems, both current and future, have networking capabilities built in. Since networking is becoming more and more simple, it's also becoming more and more prevalent. With Windows 95 it's going to be hard to distinguish the operating system from the network operating system. Knowing how to use a computer used to be enough of a skill to help you immensely in the job market. Now you need to know how to use a computer on a network to be truly marketable. We hope this book shows you how to get these skills and become proficient.

Chapter One

Getting Connected

"You can't say civilization isn't advancing;
in every war they kill you in a new way."
              —Will Rogers

The idea of running Windows on a network is certainly not a new one. On many local area networks (LANs) Windows has played an important part. But before Windows 95, networking was not considered a key component of the operating system—it was always an add-on. Windows for Workgroups led the way in showing the importance of the Windows client and server. With built-in peer-to-peer networking, Microsoft intended for this product to be the standard operating system anywhere a network was present. However, it suffered from many of the problems of its ancestors, such as system failures when the network connection went down and configuration files that were hard to, well, configure.

Windows 95 brings networking functionality to the forefront. Not only is it easier to connect to other PCs than ever before, it is also easier to connect to larger LAN systems like Windows NT, NetWare, and Banyan Vines. Accessing the resources on another machine can be just as easy as browsing through the files on your own hard drive.

A Brief History of Windows Networking

It is interesting to follow the history of Windows networking as a networking resource. It went from a slow, unstable toy, to a real tool that people would use to be more productive. It was a gradual process, but Windows has really changed the way people compute. Since Windows has caught on, the industry itself has experienced a transformation. All but gone are the days where DOS-based applications rule. Windows is now the norm on both home and business systems, and the main reason is ease of use.

Windows 95 gives the term "ease of use" new meaning both in standalone and network environments. But before we dive in, let's take a look at a few of the ancestors of Windows 95 and learn what got us this far.

Windows 3.0

Windows 3.0 was really the first version of Windows that had mass-market appeal. Consequently, it was the first version of Windows to find its way onto many LANs. Unfortunately, Windows 3.0 was pretty awful at networking. Network managers called it a nightmare; it wasn't exactly stable. Users learned to save their work often because the system would often crash several times a day, without warning and without apparent reason. Obviously, people on the network were not too happy about losing the last hour's worth of work.

Since it was the network managers' job to support all these angry users, they were happier when users did not have Windows at all. And since there were still many DOS programs out there for the users to work with, they did not really need Windows anyway. In fact network managers had a saying, "People don't use

Windows, they just play with Windows," and for the most part, they were right. After all, the most famous Windows program for a long time was Solitaire.

In addition, Windows 3.0 was slow. A lot of people still had old XT's with their slow 8-bit architecture. Most folks at this time were buying 286s with 1 megabyte of RAM, and 386s were only for power users. Windows 3.0 ran in three modes:

- Real mode (running DOS or Windows 2.0 applications)
- Standard mode (task-switching DOS and Windows applications)
- Enhanced mode (multitasking on 80386 or higher systems)

If you were running Windows on an XT, getting your work done wasn't a priority. The 286 users could run Windows in standard mode. At least they had task switching and a larger memory base to run programs in. The power users with their 386s could run in Enhanced mode. With this, they had the ability to multitask—actually run two programs at once—a relatively new concept for DOS PC users.

With all of its faults, however, Windows 3.0 was a success because of what it offered the computer user, a way to avoid DOS. DOS is confusing to many people with its monochrome appearance and cryptic commands. Windows was a shot at smoothing out the rough edges. With Windows, the screen was colorful. With a little effort, people could learn to place a pretty picture of their favorite flower in the background as they worked on their word processor. Instead of memorizing nasty DOS commands, people could use a comfortable little unit called a mouse and click the buttons on pretty little icons that would start their programs. With all of its problems, Windows was too interesting (and escaping from DOS was too appealing) to pass up.

Windows 3.1

With Windows 3.1, things changed, and not just on the networking side (although that was vastly improved). Windows 3.1 was much more stable. Network managers felt a lot better about putting it on their users' machines. And a whole slew of new applications started pouring out into the marketplace. Pretty soon, Windows programs really were easier to use than their DOS counterparts. The predominant machine that people were buying was the 386—although 486s were becoming very common. A standard computer had 4 megabytes of RAM, which was usually enough for most of the applications people needed.

Gone from Windows 3.1 was the Real mode. Hopefully, XT computer owners upgraded their hardware or gave up on trying to run Windows, because the support was no longer there. But this was no big loss; they weren't running Windows well anyway.

The improvements in Windows 3.1 networking were fairly substantial. There wasn't much the user could see, but several hundred bugs were fixed that made the system more stable. Microsoft added some setup options to simplify network installation. Network administrators could automatically take care of the most tedious setup tasks by typing **SETUP /A**. When used, this switch expanded the compressed

Windows files, copied them to the network directory, then flagged them "read-only." The user at the workstation could run SETUP from a shared network directory and easily install the program to his or her hard drive.

Connecting to network resources was made easier too. File Manager was the focus of most of the network functions. Through this utility you could not only attach to servers, you could map drives, and actually make those mappings a permanent resource each time you entered Windows. It became a "Windows only" mapping, not affecting your login script in any way.

Windows for Workgroups 3.1

Windows for Workgroups 3.1 was the first version of Windows built with networking as a priority. It was not an initial commercial success, but it was an important step in Microsoft's understanding of how Windows reacts in a network environment. Some of the new features included a built-in Mail client and a group scheduling program called Schedule+. A chat program was added, along with some management tools called WinMeter and NetWatcher. WinMeter gave you a graphical representation of how many of your system's processor cycles were used by network clients and how many were spent on local applications. NetWatcher let you keep track of who was logged into your machine and what files they had open.

The File Manager had some important improvements too. A toolbar was added with icons used for mapping drives and sharing your own directories for use on the network. A shared directory was represented by an icon of a hand presenting the folder. The Print Manager in Windows for Workgroups also got a toolbar. The icons looked similar to the File Manager's icons, but in Print Manager they were for sharing your printer or redirecting your print jobs to a network printer.

For sharing data with other users on the network, Windows for Workgroups incorporated an enhanced clipboard, called the ClipBook. Anything you cut or copied in your application went to the clipboard as usual. But items from the clipboard could be copied to pages of the ClipBook and shared with other network users. The ClipBook could also serve as a personal collection of objects and text for users.

Windows for Workgroups 3.11

Windows for Workgroups 3.11 was kind of a trial run for many of the networking components that eventually ended up in Windows 95. It had a lot of neat features, such as native support for IPX/SPX and TCP/IP, and network access was based on a 32-bit architecture rather than the 16-bit found in previous versions.

Another important feature of Windows for Workgroups 3.11 was the addition of the remote access service (RAS). This utility made it possible for clients to dial in via modem to a remote access server and, over the phone line, gain access to network resources. In this version, however, there were some limitations such as the inability to connect IPX or TCP/IP networks. These limitations were fixed in Windows 95. The new RAS software you see in Windows NT 3.5 and Windows 95 uses the point-to-point protocol (PPP) to make the connections. It is a standard, flexible remote-access solution that allows users to access all types of networks, including NetBIOS, IPX, and TCP/IP.

Enter Windows 95

You can tell from the preceding section that Microsoft has been making a concentrated effort at making Windows run better on networks. That's because the need to connect computers has moved past the point of convenience. The computer industry is approaching the era where hooking machines together, whether in an office or in a home, is more the norm than the exception. Windows 95 has made this simpler than ever before.

There are a number of reasons Windows 95 is so much better on a network than its predecessors. First of all, Windows 95 is generally easier to use than previous Windows products. From an overhauled user interface to support of the Plug and Play standards, users and network managers alike will appreciate the improvements Microsoft has made. Second, Windows 95 handles networking well because of its architecture. You have 32-bit network and file access, much improved multitasking, and better protocol support.

The third reason Windows 95 works well on a network is because of its new messaging client. This feature provides users with the means for sharing information easily, but also provides developers with the tools they need to write network-aware applications. Fourth, Windows 95 provides improved remote access. One of the challenges of computing in the 90s is the ability to stay connected while away from the office. As more people stay home to work or take their work on the road, network managers are noticing a larger need to provide users with remote access to critical data.

Finally, Windows 95 provides network administrators with an operating system that can be easy to manage. With a hardware and software database housed in Windows 95 Registry, administrators have access to all the data they need to see what people are using and how they have it configured. Built-in simple network management protocol (SNMP) support means that administrators will have the tools to find out how each system on the network is performing.

As we explore each of these features in detail, you will see how well-suited Windows 95 is for networking.

Ease of Use

As you look at the history of Windows over the last five years, you will notice that not much changed to make Windows easier for users. Microsoft added a toolbar here and there as a shortcut to common tasks, but the interface stayed relatively the same. During those same five years, other operating systems like Macintosh and OS/2 have shown what can be done with an intuitive interface. The more popular these products became, the more criticism earlier versions of Windows received for using the Program Manager and File Manager approach to launching applications and managing the file system.

Responding to that criticism, Microsoft invested a great deal of time and money into usability testing to really understand where new users were having problems and where experienced users were getting frustrated. Their goal was to provide a new interface that met three criteria:

- Easy to learn for beginners
- Powerful for experienced users
- Compatible for people upgrading from Windows 3.1

Making something easier to use while at the same time making it more powerful was a real challenge. Microsoft knew that in order to meet the goal, Windows 95 had to be customizable. The new features that made performing a task easier for new users could not get in the way of the experienced user's need for efficiency and flexibility.

New Interface

The result of all this testing and planning is the Windows 95 interface. With the program manager and file manager now out of the picture, experienced PC users have finally got what they have been clamoring for and what Macintosh users had all along—a desktop and windowing system where directories are represented by folders and files by document icons. In earlier versions of Windows, when you moved an icon from one group to another, it was a symbolic move—nothing happened at the file system level. With Windows 95, if you move a file icon from one folder to another, the file is moved as well.

If you're a new user, you'll benefit from utilities like the Taskbar, which you can use to quickly start or switch to an application; the My Computer icon that makes browsing through the files on your PC or attached servers easy; and the Network Neighborhood that makes browsing networks as easy as looking at your local computer's files. Users can explore the whole network without having to worry about the correct syntax for attaching to servers and mapping drives.

A few other features that make Windows 95 easier to use is the long-file-names feature, a new help engine, and Wizards. The long-file-names feature means users can name a document whatever they want. Instead of limiting the file name to the old 8-dot-3 convention (eight characters, a period, and three more characters), users now have the ability to give a file a more meaningful name. Instead of naming a document, say, JOHN-LET.DOC, one could call it "Letter to John." Initially, not every application that runs under Windows 95 will recognize long file names. It may take some time for applications to recognize long file names, but when they do, it will be more and more difficult to misplace files.

The online help tools of Windows 95 have been improved by simplifying the interface, making the help messages more meaningful and easier to understand, and keeping the messages short. The Wizards feature helps users complete complex tasks by taking them step by step through a given process. That process may be adding a printer, setting up a system for RAS, or adding a new device to the system. Tasks that have intimidated or confused users now become easy.

Plug and Play

Improving the user interface to make it easy to use was an important goal of the Windows 95 developers. It solved a lot of the problems users had with installing and configuring software. However, another problem remained. Installing and configuring hardware could be just as daunting. New and experienced users alike sometimes struggle with installing a new piece of hardware in a PC. Because of the bus architecture of Intel-based systems, there are many things to contend with—interrupt conflicts, port address conflicts, memory address conflicts, and driver incompatibility to name a few.

Another hardware problem is what to do for those users who take their computers with them on the road. Under earlier versions of Windows, notebook users had to write numerous batch files so they could load only the software they needed. If they were connected to the network, they would need to load their network drivers. When they disconnected from the network to attend a meeting in another location, they would have to unload the drivers, then load them again at the new site. If their notebook was hooked in to a docking station, it might have access to a SCSI device (like a CD-ROM) and a sound card, both requiring specific drivers. When users take the notebook out of the docking station to leave for home, how can they ensure those drivers don't load when the notebook is turned on away from the docking station?

The solution to both of these hardware problems can be found in the Plug and Play solution. Plug and Play automatically assigns the interrupts, port addresses, and memory addresses for a new piece of hardware when you install it. Additionally, it senses what devices are available and dynamically loads and unloads specific drivers as needed. All this is accomplished by three components working together. First of all, the computer has to be Plug and Play aware. This is possible through updates in the system's BIOS. Most of the new machines sold will contain support for Plug and Play at a minimal cost.

The second component is a unique identifier in the hardware card that can communicate with the system. As Plug and Play catches on, more and more devices will have this support. Finally, you need an operating system that supports Plug and Play, and Windows 95 is such an operating system. Windows 95 has the means to automatically sense when a new device has been added to the system, and it can tell when devices have been disconnected. With Plug and Play, computers can potentially be as simple to use as any other appliance in your house.

Network administrators benefit because they are usually the ones responsible for installing new hardware on everyone's machine on the network. Instead of wasting time at each machine trying to decipher the hardware configuration, they will just plug in the card and move on. Or perhaps they can even let users install their own cards, saving time for more pressing tasks.

Windows 95 has made software and hardware easy to use and configure. This means less stress for network administrators whose job it is to manage the machines on the LAN.

Powerful Architecture

Windows 95 has been designed as a fully integrated 32-bit protected-mode operating system. It provides preemptive multitasking and multithreading of 32-bit applications and even improved cooperative multitasking of 16-bit applications. It has a new 32-bit file system called VFAT that allows for long file names and provides better system performance. It has 32-bit device drivers delivering not only better performance, but more orderly memory use.

Windows 95 has also improved on the management of applications. With earlier versions of Windows, sometimes when an application terminated it wouldn't free up the resources or memory it was using. Windows 95 ensures that this happens, making the operating system more stable and reliable.

Messaging

Windows 95 includes an integrated messaging client that provides users the means to exchange information across the network. It is integrated with the Mail client and uses the mail transport protocols for exchanging information. A message delivered by the integrated messaging client appears in an Inbox folder. The Inbox acts like other folders—copying information to another folder on the system is a simple drag-and-drop procedure.

The mail client has some other features that make it a powerful tool on the network. It provides support for object linking and embedding (OLE) and it gives you the ability to view faxes as they come in. You also have the ability to attach a file to your messages. Additionally, you can assign rules to your mailbox. These rules define how the messaging client handles new messages. If, for example, you want all messages except those with "private" in the subject box forwarded to an assistant, the rules can accommodate.

The messaging client also has some unique features that make it particularly useful on remote or mobile systems. If you like, you can store messages in your Inbox and Outbox. That way you can wait to read messages until you are on the road. Then you can respond to the ones that require your attention, and when you are reconnected to the network, they will automatically be sent.

As more large workgroup-based applications become prevalent on LANs, the messaging system becomes even more important. Microsoft supports the messaging application programming interface (MAPI) standard, which separates the underlying messaging system from the workgroup applications. This means that application vendors can write their programs without concerning themselves with the transport mechanisms.

The use of MAPI also implies that other components like message stores and address books can be developed to work with any MAPI-compliant application. With a MAPI application, it doesn't matter if your message is going to other users on your local network, to a user on the Internet, or to someone's fax machine. The address is resolved and the message is sent to the appropriate messaging system. The application used to create the message would be the same and Windows 95 would handle the fundamentals of getting the message there.

Remote Access

Mobile users solve their remote access problems by one of two ways: remote node or remote control. There is some confusion in the industry about which is best, and the simple answer is, "It depends...". The two are not really competitors, nor are they mutually exclusive. Instead, they complement each other.

A remote node is a workstation attached via a modem to a LAN. It is just like any other node on the network. All the processing is done on the remote machine, so if a remote user wants to run an application from the network, the entire executable file and supporting files must traverse the phone lines. Remote control, on the other hand, requires a host and a remote computer. The remote computer dials into a host computer on the network and actually takes control of that machine. All processing is done by the host computer—only screen and keyboard data have to traverse the wires.

RAS uses the remote node method. It uses the PPP to make the remote connections. It is a standard, flexible remote-access solution that allows users to access all types of networks, including NetBIOS, IPX, and TCP/IP. And since RAS uses PPP, clients can also connect to any non-Microsoft remote access PPP server. In addition, any non-Microsoft PPP client can access a RAS server.

However, RAS can provide a lot more than remote access for mobile users. You can use RAS to establish a wide area network (WAN) connection with a remote office. In addition to standard modems and modem pools, RAS supports ISDN and X.25 links. These solutions, providing much better performance than a standard phone line, make setting up a WAN connection between two network servers a breeze. (At least, installing the software should be a breeze. Getting the phone company to install your ISDN link may not be.)

Additionally, RAS works over RS-232C null modem links, so you can use it to set up a small network, connecting machines by serial cable. It may not be the fastest network in town, but for a home or small company it's the cheapest way to connect two computers. RAS is a flexible and worthwhile way to expand your network services beyond the standard network cable.

Manageability

One of the biggest problems with earlier versions of Windows on a network was how to manage the network's computers. Windows and Windows programs are far more complex than their DOS counterparts. DOS applications usually install to one directory; they couldn't care less what other applications you had installed. They include their own printer support and are relatively small. Windows programs are nothing like that.

Files for a Windows program can be scattered in many places throughout the hard disk. The program files go in one main directory. If the program requires specialized dynamic link libraries (DLLs), it could copy those to the C:\WINDOWS\SYSTEM directory. It probably needs to modify the WIN.INI or SYSTEM.INI files in the C:\WINDOWS directory and might maintain its own .INI file, either in the C:\WINDOWS directory or in it's own directory. Windows applications rely on Windows to provide the print drivers, so the communication between application and operating system must be foolproof. And Windows applications can be huge, taking megabytes and megabytes of disk space. All of this complexity can lead to nightmares for the network manager.

A Manageable Platform

Windows 95 provides the network manager with the tools needed to monitor, query, and configure Windows 95 PCs. The tools are the Registry, the SNMP agent, and the desktop management interface (DMI) agent. The Registry is a database on each Windows 95 system that contains the information needed to configure that machine. It contains information about the system hardware and the software that is running on the system. It also includes data about user preferences and user-specific application information. Since the Registry database already contains the crucial information about how a computer is configured, the network manager can use tools to query this database remotely and get valuable data about the computer.

The SNMP agent built into Windows 95 also will respond to queries generated by a remote SNMP management console. SNMP is a standard protocol used to transport management information and commands between the console and the managed device. The DMI specification has been created by the Desktop Management Task Force (DMTF) to aid in systems management. The DMI agent supports management information files (MIFs) that contain information about a specific hardware or software component. A management application called a management interface (MI) can query these files to get specific information about the components of the system. DMI agent will be released 60-90 days after launch of Windows 95.

Windows 95 as a Client

Most of the time when we talk about running Windows 95 on a network, we speak of it as a client of the LAN. So many improvements have been made over Windows 3.1 that Windows 95 is one of the best network clients around. The Windows 95 networking architecture is now fully 32-bit. It has 32-bit client software, 32-bit file and printer sharing software, 32-bit network protocols, and 32-bit NIC drivers. This design makes Windows 95 network support extremely fast.

But more than speed, Windows 95 is a robust client. It provides support for multiple protocols and operating system redirectors over one NIC. This means Windows 95 can be a client to many network operating systems (NOS) at once. You can run Windows 95 as a client to Novell NetWare (both 3.x and 4.x systems), Windows for Workgroups, Windows NT Workstation and Windows NT Advanced Server, LAN Manager, LANtastic, Banyan VINES, DEC Pathworks, and SunSelect. Windows 95 comes out of the box with support for Novell and Microsoft networks. Other NOS vendors will provide the necessary drivers and redirectors to run Windows 95 on their systems.

Your Network Neighborhood

Most of the browsing of network resources will start from an icon, called the Network Neighborhood, installed on your desktop. This folder is so easy to use because it is virtually identical to browsing files and directories on your own computer. Simply double-click the Network Neighborhood icon and a window will open showing several of the network servers. If the server you want to browse is not listed (only your most commonly used servers are), then click the Entire Network icon.

Windows 95 supports pass-through security so that if there are any servers you need to authenticate to, Windows 95 will prompt you for the user name and password information and pass that information along to the server. It does not matter if the server is running NetWare 3.12, Windows NT, or Banyan VINES.

Peer Services

Because Windows 95 provides peer networking services, you may find yourself running Windows 95 as the only NOS. It can act as a peer (client and server) to other machines running Windows 95, Windows for Workgroups, and Windows NT. The networking in Windows 95 is easy to set up and configure—sharing a local directory or printer is as easy as clicking on the object, then defining how you want to share it from the properties menu.

Summary

There are a number of reasons why users will want to run Windows 95 in a network environment. The first reason is because of its stability and reliability. Network administrators used to cringe five years ago when users insisted on running Windows 3.0 on their network because of the nightmarish support costs. But Windows 95 was designed to run on the network. The tools and utilities discussed in this chapter prove that.

Second, Windows 95 is easier to use than other operating systems. Through a refined user interface and support for the Plug and Play standard, network managers will need to spend less time helping users out with their software and hardware problems. Adding a new component to the system will be easy enough for most users to handle on their own.

Next, Windows 95 is a manageable platform. With built-in SNMP and DMTF support, network administrators have access to the information needed to manage a system remotely. Additionally, the Registry database created on each Windows 95 machine provides information about what hardware and software components the system is using and where potential problems might be found.

Finally, Windows 95 was designed to connect. The messaging and networking elements are built into the operating system. These components are 32-bit and therefore give you excellent performance while communication with others on the network or sharing information. The rest of this book will teach you the best ways to install, configure, and use Windows 95 on a network—no matter what type of network that may be.

Chapter Two

Networking Basics

"Information Wants To Be Free"
                    —Anon

The act of sharing and obtaining information, be it the outcome of Sunday's basketball game, a drawing, holiday plans, or an interesting rumor, comprises a familiar and constant aspect of modern society. To access such information, for example, you may commonly choose to communicate over the telephone. However, the telephone (and other similar mediums like television or the radio) presents fleeting and unreliable data because it does not convey information in a permanent format and, more often, does not contain desired information. Comparatively, a *computer network*, in its most basic definition as the connection of two or more computers, is a medium through which you can obtain information that is both enduring and reliable. (See Figure 2-1.)

Explaining Networks

Information about the basketball game mentioned above can arrive in the form of a database of player statistics; a drawing can appear as a graphic image; holiday plans can arrive as data maintained within a scheduling program; and rumors can surface as a word processing document. Of course, since most computer networks occur within the business, educational, and research environments, databases, graphics, schedules, and documents usually contain information appropriate for such atmospheres. For example, computer networks allow you to share and access a spreadsheet containing the afternoon's stock market information, a video file containing a lecture on anthropology, and a document containing satellite trajectories and schedules.

Keep in mind that as more and more Personal Computers (PCs) connect through networks (such as the Internet) and through online services (such as CompuServe and Delphi), the scope of shared information will continue to expand into all aspects of life, perhaps uniting the two worlds of personal and professional communication.

You can find excellent examples of the diversity of networks in just about every walk of life. A hospital, for example, may rely upon a wireless network of Personal Data Assistants (PDAs), with which doctors prescribe treatment and medicine while nurses keep track of the those prescriptions, the effected patients, and numerous hospital functions. Another network could encompass a vast number of DOS or Windows workstations spread across the globe, conducting international business. Or, a network could simply contain your notebook and desktop computers. The variants are endless, but do not think that because networks are complex, they are incomprehensible. Just like an elephant, they are made up of pieces: trunk, feet, body, head, and tail. By understanding what each part does and how each part relates to the other parts, you can reconstruct an elephant, even if you've never seen one.

As with the elephant, we will reconstruct a network from its pieces as a mental experiment in which you can create a network from the ground up, taking into

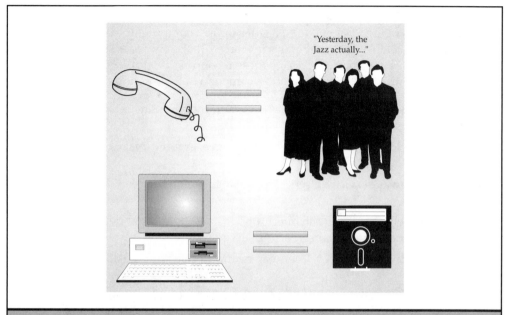

Figure 2-1. *Computer networks convey information much like a telephone conversation; however, the data passed is more lasting and predictable*

consideration each variable required to make a network work. The remainder of this chapter is dedicated to just such an experiment. We will start by defining the physical items that constitute a network. We will discuss the different network nomenclatures that have evolved around different network configurations, such as Local Area Networks (LANs) and Wide Area Networks (WANs). We will explore the uses of comparable network computing models like client/server and peer-to-peer. And finally, we will outline the actual, physical types of networks from the cabling system to network protocols.

Networks Are Resources

Networks are far more than a number of connected personal computers. The actual components can range in size and power from a digital pager to a mainframe computer. Between these two devices lie Intel and RISC-based workstations, multiprocessor servers, printers, PDAs, fax machines, dumb terminals, etc. What is important to remember is that any set of devices that enables individuals to access and share informational services comprises a network. However, regardless of the number or type of devices comprising a network, certain hardware and software features are elemental to all networks.

Network Operating System

The Network Operating System (NOS) resides upon a computer (be it mainframe or PC) and makes available that computer's resources. It also provides some sort of security capabilities that control access to those resources. The following services are either included with a network operating system or available as add-on programs:

- **File services**: Users can access files stored on the computer's hard disk, CD-ROM, etc.

- **E-mail services**: Users can exchange messages, graphic images, spreadsheets, text files, etc.

- **E-mail gateway services**: Users can exchange e-mail between different mail systems.

- **Database services**: Users can query, update, and administer databases like Novell's btrieve and Microsoft's SQL server.

- **Communications services**: Users can communicate with outside services and networks.

- **Archive services**: Users can manage NOS files by backing them up to tape, optical, or other media.

- **Print services**: Users can print documents to a large number of printers.

- **Fax services**: Users can send and receive fax information.

- **Telephony services**: Users can access voice mail through their workstations.

- **Video services**: Users can view, create, and participate in video conferencing.

Servers

Network operating systems and dependent services run on computer systems called servers. Peripherals like printers are often attached directly to the server. These platforms can range from an Intel single-processor 286 PC to a multiprocessor gigabyte-storage mainframe computer.

Client Workstations

In order to utilize a network operating system, individual PCs require software that enables them to communicate with the network via an internal Network Interface Card (NIC). The type of software utilized depends upon the type of network present. A UNIX network, for example, generally requires a TCP/IP protocol stack, while Novell NetWare utilizes IPX/SPX. Because network adapters are able to send and receive multiple protocol stacks, a workstation can contain software for both types of networks.

Cabling System

A network cabling system simply connects workstations with network operating system-based servers. Although cabling, as the name implies, usually involves physical cables, networks can be connected via satellite, broadband, and infrared wireless technologies. For the most part, though, networks are connected with coaxial, fiber, or telephone-like cable.

Peripherals

Although many peripherals are attached directly to a network server, many are connected either to workstations or directly to the network. Printers and fax machines, for example, can be attached in either fashion. These devices do not contain a network operating system, per se; however, they do contain software and hardware that enables them to advertise themselves as shareable network devices. By attaching these resources directly to the network cabling system, you can minimize the server resources required to run your network by reducing the load on your server.

Types of Networks

Networks, as mentioned above, are simply based upon connected devices, but the simplicity ends there. The scale of a network can range in size from two home computers to the millions of world-wide machines found upon the Internet. These two ends of the spectrum comprise two basic types of computer networks: WANs and LANs. Within this range lie a number of interrelated network types, each arising from a specific networking need, be it geographical, financial, or populace proportional. A network can span the globe, or it can span a single room. It can support hundreds of thousands of users, or it can support a solitary individual. As long as there are varying needs, there will be varying network types.

Generally, LANs are found in localized, geographically restricted areas such as in a single home or business building. WANs, in contrast, can connect machines between two buildings or two continents. LANs also contain a limited number of computers, while WANs contain as many as 2.17 million machines (as found on the Internet as of July, 1994). This dichotomy of size and distance does not mean that the two types of networks do not interrelate. Far from that, they often occur together since LANs are often a subset of a WAN. (See Figure 2-2.)

From a technological viewpoint, WANs and LANs differ in the way they are connected. A LAN, for example, is usually connected by privately owned cable in a privately owned building, while a WAN is usually connected by services that are not distance-dependent, such as public and private telecommunications facilities, microwaves, and satellites.

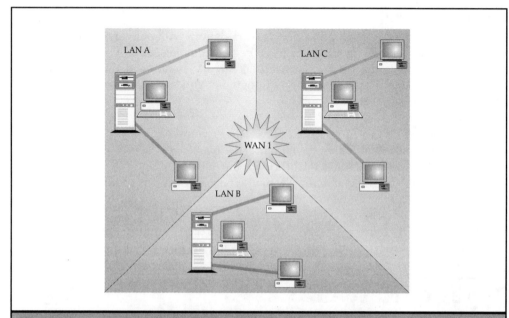

Figure 2-2.   *A WAN can contain a number of interconnected LANs*

Imagine a large bank with various branch offices. Within each office, people use their computers to communicate with one another, exchanging deposit and withdrawal information, sharing loan processing data, etc. That is a LAN. Now imagine that same bank sharing the same information with a number of other banks in other cities. That is a WAN. Between these two distinctions there are a number of interesting variants.

Network Segment (Subnetwork)

A network segment contains a limited number of devices (workstations, servers, peripherals) that all share a specific network address. Within an Ethernet network segment, for example, all computers are able to see each other's network broadcasts. Unless connected by a bridge or router, network segments do not share information. A LAN, therefore, can be made up of interconnected network segments. This is called an *internetwork*.

Campus Networks

These networks span buildings like WANs; however, unlike WANs, they do not have to rely upon outside cabling sources. Usually found on school campuses and large business facilities, these networks connect geographically separate buildings through a campus-wide, high-speed backbone such as fiber-optic cable or other high-speed media. Within each connected building, network segments or LANs exist.

Metropolitan Area Networks

A type of network that is often confused with a WAN is the Metropolitan Area Network (MAN). This type of computer network is actually a connection of computers regulated by local or state utility commissions. A local phone company or cable company may provide LAN services in your area. Companies needing to communicate within a metropolitan area that contains public rights-of-way can rely upon a set of standards as set forth in the IEEE 802.6 to obtain high-speed network connections between buildings. A MAN, therefore, is really a WAN that merely relies upon a specific set of networking standards.

Enterprise Networks

An *enterprise network* can include LANs, MANs, or WANs. This type of network, however, interconnects network resources regardless of the network operating system, geographical dispersion, cabling differences, protocol diversities, application differences, etc. In this way, these networks allow users transparent access to all resources. Three main connectivity strategies that enterprise networks rely upon are directory services, middleware, and e-mail switches. Directory services, often based upon CCITT X.500 standards, help network administrators organize the voluminous amounts of user and resource information found on an enterprise network. For example, Novell NetWare's NetWare Directory Services (NDS) is an X.500-like product that makes user and e-mail addresses available to every resource on the network. Middleware enables different protocols and applications to share information as though they were exactly the same. E-mail switches, which are usually based upon the ITU X.400 standard, allow different e-mail packages to transparently transfer electronic mail.

Network Strategies

Two important and closely related aspects of networking that can be found in any network type involve the manner in which users access and share information. These two strategies are called client/server and peer-to-peer. Both share a common ancestry in that they evolved from a move away from the old model of computing found within mainframe and minicomputer systems, in which a centralized computer containing many processor units and massive file storage space provided processing power for a number of simple keyboard/monitor workstations (dumb terminals). Users entered information via the dumb terminal and that information was processed and stored on the centralized computer.

As PCs moved into corporations, scholastic organizations, and research institutes, the centralized processing power of the mainframe was slowly succeeded by the processing power of individual workstations. Although mainframes and minicomputers like the IBM Corp. AS/400 are still used for their sheer processing power, the decentralization of this processing power allowed individual workstations to actively share processing, file storage, and printing services with other workstations.

Peer-to-Peer Communication

When two machines share the services previously mentioned, the arrangement is called *peer-to-peer* networking because both machines can act upon one another in identical ways. (See Figure 2-3.) Macintosh networks, until recently with the advent of workgroup file and print servers, are an excellent example of a peer-to-peer network. First, each Macintosh computer advertises its availability on the network; then, as needs dictate, a computer can log into another computer and access that computer's information. In essence, each workstation acts as a client. One client can be a client to another client.

Many NOSes offer peer-to-peer communication. Although many of these NOSes function as client/server platforms, they all exhibit features specific to peer-to-peer networking. Some peer-to-peer operating systems are described next.

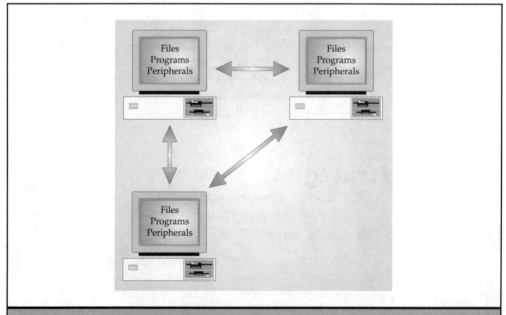

Figure 2-3. *Peer-to-peer networking lets users access resources on one another's computers in a relatively equal fashion*

Microsoft Windows for Workgroups

This operating system allows users to not only share files and peripherals (such as a printer), it also provides a platform for Microsoft's object technology, called Object Linking and Embedding (OLE). With this technology, you can maintain a spreadsheet, for example, on your machine, while allowing another user to store a linked copy of it on his/her own machine in a word processing document. When you update the spreadsheet, the user holding the copy sees the update automatically. OLE does not just appear on Windows for Workgroups, however; it can be found on Microsoft Windows NT as well as Microsoft Windows 95. Other useful peer-to-peer features of Windows for Workgroups include a schedule, e-mail, calendar, chat, and terminal emulation programs.

Microsoft Windows NT

This powerful 32-bit network operating system lets you take advantage of the same features available within Windows for Workgroups. However, it also contains additional security as well as the ability to act simultaneously as a peer-to-peer and client/server platform.

Microsoft Windows 95

By combining many of the security enhancements of Windows NT with the peer-to-peer capabilities of Windows for Workgroups, Windows 95 gains the best of both worlds through its 32-bit processing power, its integrated telephone, fax and e-mail package, and its ability to integrate closely with many network operating systems like Windows NT and Novell NetWare.

Artisoft LANtastic

LANtastic, although strictly a network operating system for peer-to-peer services, has recently enlisted the power of Novell NetWare to boost its file and peripheral-sharing capabilities.

IBM LAN Server

This 32-bit network operating system functions on top of IBM OS/2 as either a client/server or peer-to-peer operating system. It provides users with a distributed object technology much like OLE as found in the Microsoft family of operating systems. Called OpenDoc, IBM's object strategy (developed in conjunction with Novell, Inc. and Apple Computer Corp.) not only allows objects to be shared across applications and networks, it breaks them down into tasks. With OpenDoc, users will be able to create applications that are not monolithic like Microsoft Word or the WordPerfect Group's WordPerfect, but job-specific pieces that integrate to form new programs as needed.

Peer-to-peer networks offer many advantages. They are generally less expensive than client/server networks, they allow data and processing power to be distributed over a larger area, and they enable users to dynamically organize computing requirements. Information distributed across a peer-to-peer network can by broken down into related groups, such as an accounting group, a marketing group, etc., without necessitating the reorganization of the actual data.

There are some disadvantages to peer-to-peer networking, however. If you are a user, peer-to-peer services are functional and easy to use, but you may find it difficult to keep track of file locations as they are usually spread across many different machines. If you are a network administrator, peer-to-peer services can be difficult to govern because of this distributed data. For example, if files are continually changing from machine to machine, then how do you decide which machines, which directories, and which files to back up? Another problem occurs when too many people attempt to access a single workstation's resources. Because of the additional overhead of each client, that station's performance becomes degraded—sometimes beyond use.

Client/Server Communication

The client/server model of computing also grew out of the decentralization of mainframes and minicomputers. However, as a sort of hybrid, client/server retained a great number of the mainframe and minicomputer features while adding its own peer-to-peer-like capabilities. Instead of a workstation merely accessing data on a second workstation, both machines take an active role. In other words, intelligent workstations, called "front-end" systems, communicate not with another front-end as in peer-to-peer, but with a server (called a "back-end") that provides specific processor-dependent services. Your Windows 95 workstation can accommodate both peer-to-peer and client/server configurations.

An excellent example of a client/server configuration can be found in database applications. For instance, a Database Management System (DBMS) comprises two parts: the client that executes a series of instructional statements called Structured Query Language (SQL), and the server that houses the database. The client (front-end) initiates a directive, such as a search request, and the server (back-end) acts upon that request. At first this may not seem that much different than when a peer-to-peer workstation accesses a database file on another peer-to-peer machine. However, there are two fundamental differences that illustrate the power of client/server. First, the back-end database (called a database engine) takes care of a great deal of the processing duties. If you ask a client/server database to find a specific piece of information, it does not return with the results from each record as it passes through the database. It only reports the final results. Second, if your client workstation, which contains the database application, fails during a database transaction (like the addition of a record), the server will automatically "roll-back" the transaction in order to maintain database integrity. No peer-to-peer database system can offer such services.

This active interaction between the front-end database application and back-end database engine constitutes a client/server relationship. Another excellent example of a client/server relationship can be found within many network operating systems. These systems provide front-ends with many file and print-related services as well as DBMS support. Some of these powerful, PC-based network operating systems are described next.

Novell NetWare   In addition to file and print services, this network operating system offers a full range of features like an e-mail system, directory and name services (similar to the X.500 standard), and a method allowing third party developers the ability to create additional services called NetWare Loadable Modules (NLMs). With NLMs, users gain access to fax, backup, virus protection, and many other third party services.

Banyan VINES   With its well developed StreetTalk name and directory services, Banyan VINES is an excellent network operating system for WAN-based client/server computing. Users, regardless of their location, can gain access to file, print, mail, and other services quickly and easily.

UNIX   The various flavors of the UNIX network operating system, including SUN Solaris, SCO, and UnixWare, contain many powerful client/server features. The UNIX system was the first home, for example, to the powerful Distributed Computing Environment (DCE), in which multiple servers work in unison to provide a network service.

Windows NT   This powerful 32-bit operating system in many ways threatens the power and scaleability of Novell NetWare through its preemptive multitasking, symmetric multiprocessing (the capability of using multiple microprocessors to perform tasks at the same time), and gigabyte memory addressing capabilities. This operating environment will serve as the centerpiece in many Windows 95 networks.

IBM LAN Server   LAN Server also rivals Novell NetWare's scaleability and power through its newly acquired symmetrical multiprocessing. However, it is unable to dynamically acquire new network services as NetWare can through its NLM architecture.

There are many different faces of client/server computing since multiple network operating systems, like those mentioned above, can interoperate. For example, you can combine a NetWare server with a Windows NT to give users the additional benefits of both network operating systems. With such a combination, a user can use the NT server as a gateway to some of NetWare's services (like print services), thereby adding a second layer of network security. You can also combine servers to improve performance. (Refer to Figure 2-4.)

Regardless of the configuration, client/server networking provides many advantages over peer-to-peer networking. It can help companies downsize from mainframe and minicomputer configurations. Since in a client/server network the server handles the majority of the data processing duties, network traffic between the server and the client is minimized. By centralizing data, client/server architecture promotes tighter security and facilitates data protection and recovery. And data required by every system on the network is centralized in one memory pool, thereby reducing the amount of processing required on the workstations.

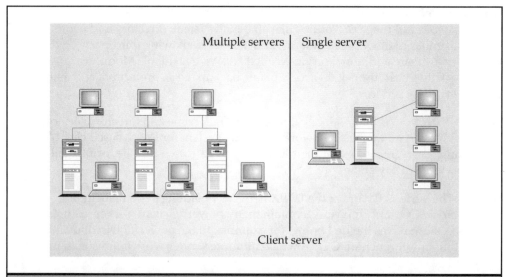

Figure 2-4. *Client/server computing can transparently provide single or multiple server and operating system support*

Combining the Two

Although client/server boasts many advantages over peer-to-peer networking, a combination of the two can provide excellent benefits for all members of a company or institution. For example, a network comprised of NetWare client/server operating systems could provide a centralized storage solution for Windows 95 workstations, which dynamically formed peer-to-peer workgroups could utilize. These workgroups would then be free to share scheduling, printing, and e-mail services without disturbing those organization-wide services provided by the NetWare server. (See Figure 2-5.)

How Network Devices Connect

Computer networks, regardless of constitution, type, or strategy, must allow network operating systems, servers, workstations, and peripherals to communicate. To accomplish this, you must first install a communications medium (cabling). Second, you must incorporate a cabling strategy (topology). Third, you must choose a corresponding network protocol. And lastly, you must select the appropriate hardware to connect these devices. There are no right or wrong methods to connect a network, only appropriate and inappropriate. For example, you can wire a wide area network with coaxial, twisted-pair, fiber-optic, or wireless technologies; however, depending upon the current situation, only one would be the most appropriate. If your wide area

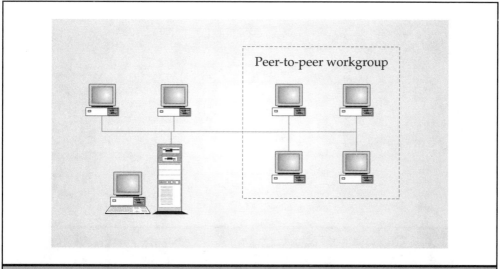

Figure 2-5. *The combination of client/server and peer-to-peer networks enables users to create workgroups within an organization*

link will transport time-sensitive video images, you may want to consider a T1 line running a high-speed network such as Asynchronous Transfer Mode (ATM). But if your wide area link will transport only e-mail, you may want to utilize either a dial-up router running TCP/IP, or an e-mail gateway based upon a standard telephone line.

The most important elements to keep in mind are that each cabling type has certain limits in speed and distance. All cabling types have one thing in common, however. Their speed and distance capabilities are directly proportional to their cost. Fiber-optic cable, for example, can transmit data at rates exceeding 155Mbps (megabits per second) over great distances. However, it exacts higher costs than a twisted pair cable, which can transmit data at speeds reaching 100Mbps over relatively short distances (100 meters or less).

Cabling Types

The first required connectivity component is cabling. It is the lowest common denominator to all networks, and there are four basic types: coaxial, twisted pair, fiber-optic, and wireless (no cable at all). Each type evolved out of specific network needs, and each solves a specific networking problem.

Coaxial

Coaxial cable consists of a solid copper core surrounded by an insulating layer and a shielding layer of finely woven wire, as shown in Figure 2-6. Thus it is highly resistant

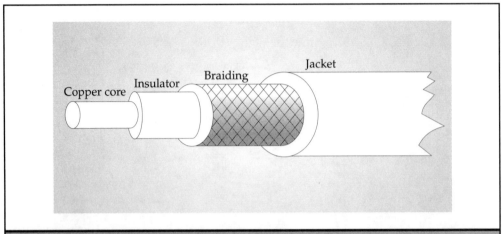

Figure 2-6.   *Coaxial cable is comprised of a solid core wrapped in an insulating layer and a shielding layer of braided wire in a jacket*

to external interference. If you have ever connected a television set to a video recording device, you have worked with coaxial cable. It can transmit data at rates reaching 100Mbps; however, it is usually found in 10Mbps Ethernet and 2.5Mbps ARCNET installations. In these environments, it functions as either a bus, ring, or star topology.

Coaxial cable has an advantage over twisted pair cable: it can transmit data over greater distances. When used in an ARCNET environment, it can transmit data up to 2,500 feet. In an Ethernet environment, it can transmit data 607 feet. Thus, with coaxial cable, as with many other cable types, to obtain greater distances, you must sacrifice transmission speed.

For small Ethernet installations, you may want to choose coaxial cable over the popular twisted pair cable for two simple reasons. First, you can spread up to 30 nodes (workstations) across 3,035 feet with only four inexpensive repeaters over Ethernet 10base-2. With a twisted pair 10base-T cabling system, you must utilize additional hardware (concentrators as well as repeaters). However, because this 10base-2 cabling scheme functions as a linear topology, a break in the cable could bring the entire network down. The 10base-T network, on the other hand, utilizes a star topology that is immune to such disasters because if one cable length breaks, only the directly attached workstation/server fails.

Twisted Pair

Twisted pair cabling is very popular in LAN environments because of its low cost, high speed, and reliability. (See Figure 2-7.) Twisted pair cabling comes in two basic formats: Unshielded Twisted Pair (UTP) and Shielded Twisted Pair (STP). Both consist

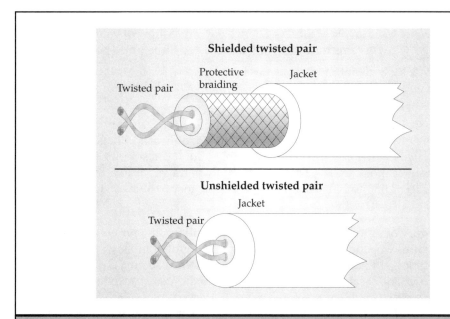

Figure 2-7. *Twisted pair cables are comprised of twisted pairs of wires housed in a protective coating. UTP cable and STP cable differ in the fact that STP cable contains a braided wire coating to prevent cable interference*

of a pair of twisted wires that form a circuit. They are twisted in order to prevent interference problems. More than one pair of wires can be bundled together within a twisted pair cable. The only difference between the two is that STP contains braided metal shielding much like coaxial cable. This helps to prevent external crosstalk. For example, if you are planning to wire a network in an area containing florescent lights, you may want to choose STP in order to prevent signal interference.

This cable type is quite prevalent in Ethernet and token ring networks as either a bus or star topology. Ethernet cable, in comparison with coaxial and fiber-optic cable, is very inexpensive. Moreover, it already exists in many buildings as telephone wiring. And yet Ethernet cabling can support transmission speeds as great as 100Mbps. This scaleability directly relates to the manner in which you wire your Ethernet network. There are five basic ways you can wire an Ethernet network, as described in the EIA/TIA 586 Commercial Building Wiring Standard:

- **Category 1**: If your telephone system was installed before 1983, this is the cable type you use every day when you place a telephone call. It is valid for voice transmissions but not for data.

- **Category 2**: Consisting of four twisted pairs, category 2 cable can transmit data at rates reaching 4Mbps. It is the least expensive data-quality twisted pair network cable.

■ **Category 3**: This twisted pair wiring scheme can transmit data at 10Mbps. It is very prevalent within older Ethernet networks and 4Mbps token ring networks. Category 3 wire contains four pairs of wires twisted three times per foot.

■ **Category 4**: By transmitting data at 16Mbps, category 4 cable can handle both Ethernet and 16Mbps token ring networks. This cable also contains four pairs of twisted wire.

■ **Category 5**: The most expensive and the most powerful, category 5 cable is ideal for many networking situations. For example, not only can it transmit all of the data handled by the preceding category cables, but it can support newer high-speed technologies like Fast Ethernet (which travels at 100Mbps) and ATM. Actually, according to AT&T Paradyne, UTP category 5 cable can transmit data at 950Mbps.

Which category of cabling you choose should depend upon your network's immediate and future needs in conjunction with the amount of money you are able to expend for cabling. In many instances, companies choose category 3 or 4 cable because of its price and its ability to transmit data at high rates of speed (10Mbps and 16Mbps respectively).

No matter which category you choose, twisted pair wiring is an excellent choice simply because it is so adaptable. Of course, category 5 is the most compatible in that its component parts (connectors, faceplates, hub connections, etc.) can support voice, ISDN, token ring, Ethernet 10base-T, Ethernet 100VG-Any LAN, and future ATM applications.

Fiber-Optic

An excellent choice for networks requiring reliable, high transmission speeds over great distances, fiber-optic cable can function effectively in many networking venues. Because of its high rate of speed (100Mbps), it is perfect as a backbone technology. In this way, it can connect many devices that require a consistent high transmission rate like video servers and video conferencing workstations. The manner in which fiber-optic cable relays information is not through electrical signals, but through photons (basically, flashes of light.). Since fiber-optic cable is made of glass, it is not subject to the following copper cabling problems: attenuation, capacitance, and crosstalk.

■ *Attenuation* is basically a loss of signal that occurs as data moves across large distances. This is why twisted pair and coaxial cable require repeaters, and why Ethernet requires both repeaters and concentrators.

■ *Capacitance* is simply a distortion of the signal traveling over a copper cable that increases with the length of the cable. Light is not subject to distortion (only interference from other sources of light).

■ *Crosstalk* occurs when the signal on one wire interferes with the signal on another wire. Since light does not produce an electrical field, it does not interfere with other fiber-optic cables.

Although Ethernet can transmit over fiber-optic cabling systems, you will most likely see Fiber-Distributed Data Interface (FDDI) as the medium of choice. (See Figure 2-8.) This is because with FDDI, there are not as many distance restrictions as with Ethernet. For example, a single Fast Ethernet packet traveling over a fiber-optic segment can only reach 450 meters. This is much further than the 100 meters with copper wire Ethernet 10base-T. However, it pales in comparison with the over 2 kilometers available to FDDI over fiber-optic cable.

In addition to these features, fiber-optic cable is the best alternative in many instances because of its ability to last. A laser for fiber-optic media (which is simply a high-powered transmission device) has a Mean Time Between Failures (MTBF) of 114 years. Also with the laser transmitter, you can obtain transmission distances of up to 160 kilometers.

Since fiber-optic cable transmissions are comprised solely of light, there is no radiation outside of the fiber-optic cable. This means that it is virtually impossible to "hack," or monitor, transmissions.

Wireless

An intriguing alternative to coaxial, twisted pair, and fiber-optic cabling systems does not involve a wiring system at all. Instead it revolves around either radio or infrared transmissions. This quickly evolving format allows you to connect networks without laying any cables. Called wireless communications, it comprises two distinct networking issues: mobile and wireless LAN networking. With LAN networking, machines are connected via transmitters and receivers. With

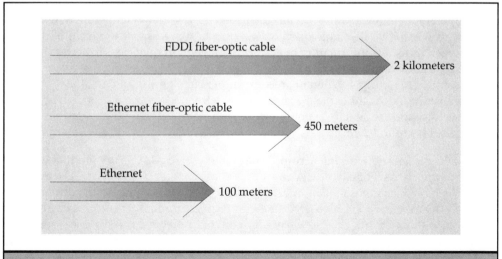

Figure 2-8. *FDDI over fiber-optic cable far outstretches the reach of standard and Fast Ethernet*

mobile networking, machines are connected via cellular communications provided by telecommunications providers.

The types of machines you can connect in this manner are varied, including PCs, PDAs, pagers, or notebook computers. Accordingly, wireless networking can solve a varied number of networking problems in situations forbidding standard wiring practices. For example, it can be used in a building of historic value, an electronically noisy area, closely situated buildings, or any situation requiring a non-intrusive network link, be it for disaster recovery or simply for backup measures.

For wireless LANs, there are mainly the following three different communication methods.

- **Infrared Light**: This technique offers the fastest transmission rates (up to 10Mbps) over the infrared spectrum of light. Although initially infrared was subject to line of sight transmissions, in which the transmitter and receiver must be able to "see" each other, newer, diffused infrared communication can work out of the line of site. Thus an infrared wireless network can function around corners, over cubicles, and across hallways. However, even diffused infrared cannot communicate in an environment filled with bright and changing light sources.

- **Narrowband radio**: This method does not require line of sight because like a radio station signal, you can receive it through walls. It is therefore ideal at sites where infrared cannot function. However, it, like the radio station signal, must be regulated by the FCC. This means that if you want to use narrowband radio networks, you must purchase a network with a specific frequency from either the FCC or the wireless network manufacturer. This type of network operates at speeds around 4,800Kbps (kilobits per second). (See Figure 2-9.)

- **Spread-spectrum radio**: To avoid the problems associated with obtaining a narrowband wireless network, you can turn to spread-spectrum technology, which transmits information over a wide range of frequencies. To accomplish this, a spread-spectrum receiver and transmitter utilize identical frequency jumping algorithms. When the receiver jumps to a new frequency, the transmitter does the same. Because its radio frequencies are not as high as narrowband radio, it does not interfere with standard radio transmissions. Its speed is around 250Kbps.

Mobile wireless networking accomplishes what wireless LANs do, but it does it over wide area links. For example, you can purchase a pager from a wireless company called SkyTel, which gives you an Internet address. With this address, you can receive e-mail from anyone who is connected to the Internet, regardless of your location. You can also use a modem attached to the modem of your notebook computer to remotely dial into your office as though you were directly connected to a telephone line.

Do not believe that wireless communications are a panacea of networking solutions. They are expensive, slower than standard cabling, poorly managed, subject

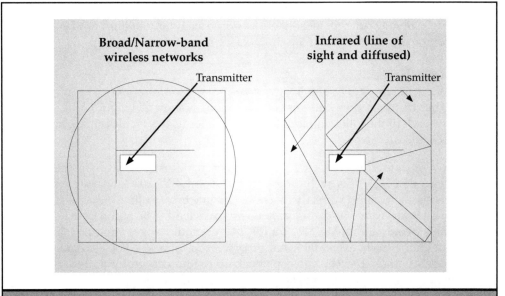

Broad/Narrow-band wireless networks

Infrared (line of sight and diffused)

Transmitter

Transmitter

Figure 2-9. *Infrared light networks must communicate within a line of site (direct or diffused), while spread-spectrum and narrowband networks can transmit through objects like walls and around corners*

to interference, and unsecured. However, as they increase in popularity, these issues will subside. There is an IEEE (Institute of Electrical and Electronic Engineers) committee hard at work on a communications standard for wireless computing, called 802.11. Transmission speeds are increasing over infrared links, and Data Encryption Standards (DES) security is available for some networks.

How Networks Connect

For workstations, printers, fax machines, servers, etc. to communicate effectively, they must be connected in a standardized fashion to accommodate future adds, moves, and changes, as well as possible connections with other networks. The standards used to connect devices in a network are called network topologies, and they revolve around the type of cable used in the network.

Network Topologies

The physical manner in which you cable a network defines its topology. This depends heavily upon the network's cabling, protocol system, and network type. To understand network topology, then, the place to begin is with either the subnetwork or connection of subnetworks, called an internetwork or LAN. You can cable each subnetwork in an internetwork as a different topology. However, each topology corresponds to the immediate wiring and protocol scheme. For example, a twisted pair Ethernet subnetwork will most likely be wired as a star topology, in which all workstations and peripherals radiate from one or more central locations.

LAN Topologies

Basically, there are four types of LAN topologies: star configuration, star-configured ring, star/bus configuration, and bus configuration, as shown in Figure 2-10. Notice how each of the following topologies corresponds to specific cabling and protocol schemes.

■ **Star Configuration**: This configuration is used almost exclusively by Ethernet twisted pair networks, including IEEE 802.2 and IEEE 802.3. Because each workstation connects directly to a hub, any line breaks effect only the attached workstation. Thus star configuration networks tend to be highly resistant to total network failure. Moreover, adds, moves, and changes are made simple through the easily expandable nature of the star topology. For each cable emanating from a server, you can attach up to four concentrators and/or repeater hubs. If you need to add another 10 to 12 people, simply pop on an additional hub. When one station transmits a signal, every other station attached to that segment (subnetwork) sees the packet; however, only the intended station acts upon that packet. This is called a Carrier Sensing Multiaccess with Collision Detection (CSMA/CD) cable access method. This type of broadcast method of communication is what allows you to install workstations, servers, and any other peripheral at any point upon a subnetwork.

■ **Star-Configured Ring**: This is used primarily by IEEE 802.5 token ring networks. Here, a token is passed around a cabling circle. Attached to this ring are all of the workstations, servers, and peripherals for a single subnetwork. An attached device can pick up the token and transmit a message. Compare this with the broadcast topology of Ethernet in which stations may attempt to simultaneously transmit. The benefits of this sort of configuration, until recently, were mainly related to speed since IEEE 802.5 token ring allowed 16Mbps transmission rates. Although this is only 6Mbps faster than standard Ethernet, because Ethernet's CSMA/CD carries a great deal of overhead (roughly 30 percent of the available bandwidth), the 16Mbps of token ring far outperforms Ethernet. With the advent of high-speed Ethernet, however, this advantage has been somewhat nullified. Another problem with this topology rests in its susceptibility to complete failure. For example, if a break occurs in a ring, every device attached to that ring will fail. There is a second protocol, however, that takes advantage of the star-configured ring topology, provides even faster transmission rates, and boasts cable failure protection. It is called FDDI. This protocol can transmit at speeds reaching 100Mbps, and if a ring is broken, the ring simply reroutes itself back through the unbroken portion of the cable to recreate the ring.

■ **Star/Bus Configuration**: A combination of the star and star-bus configuration topologies, this method connects groups of star wired devices via one or more linear bus trunks. By combining the two topologies, you can more easily configure and reconfigure network devices. As with star topologies, this method caters mostly to the twisted pair Ethernet subnetwork. A 10base-5 or 10base-2 linear bus can be used to connect 10base-T hubs, from which devices radiate in the star topology.

■ **Bus Configuration**: Ideal for smaller subnetworks, or subnetworks in which each device resides directly in line with the next, the bus topology attracts Ethernet 10base-5 and 10base-2 cabling schemes. The bus topology basically connects all devices to a central cable. However, if a break occurs anywhere along that cable, the entire subnetwork will fail. This is a drawback to the star/bus configuration as well.

Internetwork Topologies

The manner in which you connect subnetworks and groups of subnetworks (LANs) is called internetwork topologies. Where hubs, concentrators, and repeaters connect devices within a subnetwork, bridges and routers and superhubs connect subnetworks and LANs. For example, a bridge is used to connect two or more subnetworks, while a router is used to connect two or more LANs. Based upon these pieces of hardware, there are three different types of internetwork topologies: meshed network, backbone network, and interlink star network.

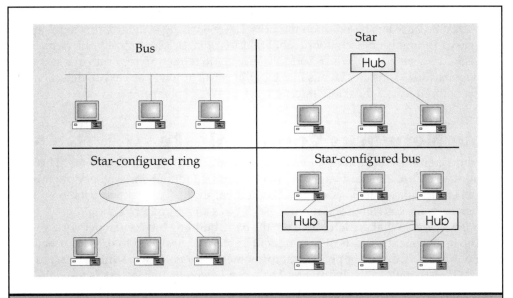

Figure 2-10. *The star, star-configured ring, star-configured bus, and bus subnetwork topologies*

Mesh Network   When large networks need to be connected over long distances via telecommunication links, this is by far the best topology. By connecting routers to routers, you enable the network to choose the fastest route for a given transmission. The way this occurs is quite ingenious. Since each router learns the addresses of all network devices to which it is attached, when a packet enters a given router, that router estimates the amount of time the packet will need to reach its destination along all possible paths. When it finds the quickest path, it sends the packet in that direction. This allows the network to automatically adjust both to changes in network utilization (percent of bandwidth occupied by traffic) as well as any router/cable failures. If a connection fails, all other routers automatically route packets around the failed line of communication.

Backbone Network   To connect campus and office networks, it is often prudent to utilize a single bus or ring topology to connect various subnetworks or LANs through bridges or routers. This backbone usually functions over a high-speed cabling system such as fiber-optic cable. The protocol of choice is usually FDDI, as it can span the distance required to connect the disparately located subnetworks and LANs while providing the bandwidth and fault tolerance necessary to handle a large organization's entire flow information.

Interlink Star Network   New to the scene of internetwork topology, interlink star networks take advantage of a new breed of superhubs to connect a structured wiring system as set forward by the EIA/TIA 568 wiring standard. These hubs act like a backbone network in miniature. They contain a very fast medium, called a backplane, to move the organization's data from the centralized hub out to distributed hubs and vice versa. Because it is based upon the EIA/TIA 568 wiring standard, this topology is very easy to administer. Each floor (subnetwork) contains a centralized hub (which could also be a superhub), which connects directly to the centralized hub in a star topology fashion. Thus any breaks in the cabling structure will be easy to detect and correct without fear of the entire internetwork or WAN collapsing.

How Networks Communicate

Networks communicate through two basic elements: hardware and software. This excludes, of course, the hardware not directly required for networking: peripherals such as printers, fax machines, etc., and computers such as servers, workstations, etc. Furthermore, the software used upon these devices and peripherals should be excluded as well. What are left, then, are the basic building blocks of a network.

The first element consists of a number of appliances designed to pass information from one network device or peripheral to another, such as Network Interface Cards (NICs). These comprise the hardware. The second element, in contrast, is the information passed between one network device or peripheral to another, such as networking protocols. These comprise the software.

Network Protocols

To understand how hardware and software combine to form a network, it is best to start with the protocols used by hardware to communicate. Protocols, like wild creatures, come in all shapes, sizes, and temperaments. Novell NetWare, Banyan VINES, UNIX, Apple, and LAN Manager, all utilize completely different protocols to connect their services to the outside world. Although you may wonder how these operating systems could ever coexist, do not worry. There is a template from which all protocols derive their individual traits. This template is a methodology developed by both industries and consortiums as an information standard. With a standard, different protocol animals are able to get along peacefully and even work together.

Created by the International Organization for Standardization (ISO), this template, called the Open Systems Interconnection (OSI) model (as shown in Figure 2-11), acts as a mold from which protocol development teams can create interoperable hardware. By creating a model of layers (OSI layers one through seven), ISO enables two devices to map corresponding device and application functions to an OSI layer, since each layer represents a different function. The layers are physical, data-link, network, transport, session, presentation, and application. As an example of how these layers work, consider that the physical layer carries coded electrical signals, while the data-link layer carries data that is hardware specific (such as NIC driver information). If you study the OSI model, you will understand all of the different protocols available under different network operating systems. For more information on these protocols, refer to Appendix A, "Networking Protocols."

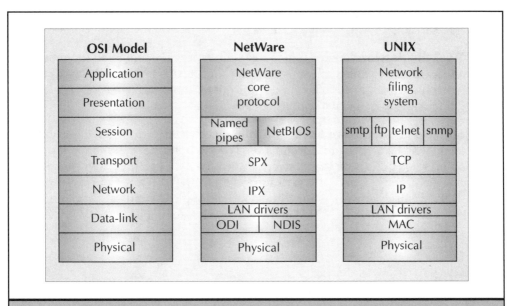

Figure 2-11. *The open systems interconnection model can be directly compared to the protocols used by NetWare and UNIX*

Layer One, the Physical Layer   Here, a workstation, for example, communicates the characteristics and settings of its NIC.

Layer Two, the Data-Link Layer   This layer creates a set of rules that the sending and receiving workstations must follow in order to communicate. It also provides error detection. This is also where bridges function. When a packet travels from one subnetwork to another, it must pass through a bridge. If the subnetwork address matches the current subnetwork address, the packet is forwarded to the appropriate network. The data-link layer also supports the software drivers used by the workstation's NIC.

Layer Three, the Network Layer   This layer defines protocols used by network operating systems for basic communication. It also defines device addressing information. This is why routers operate upon this level. When a packet arrives at a router and contains a network or device address not found in the current network, the packet is forwarded to the appropriate network. Some important protocols specific to this layer are the deeply entrenched Internet Protocol (IP), Novell's Internet Packet Exchange (IPX), Banyan VINES Internet Protocol (VIP) and the wide area connectivity protocol, X.25.

Layer Four, the Transport Layer   Providing improved error-handling capabilities and security features, the transport layer provides connection-oriented services between two network devices. Common packets found in this layer include Microsoft NetBIOS/NetBEUI, Banyan VINES Interprocess Communication Protocol (VIPC), Internet Transmission Control Protocol (TCP), Internet User Datagram Protocol (UDP), and Novell's Sequenced Packet Exchange (SPX).

Layer Five, the Session Layer   This layer simply provides a method for network applications to restart a failed transmission if a connection is temporarily lost. It also includes techniques designed to let these applications know when one set of data has finished transmission and when another set has begun.

Layer Six, the Presentation Layer   Within this layer, data is encoded for proper presentation when it arrives at its destination. For example, the presentation layer formats a print job differently than a screen dump, even though they both contain the same data. Here, you can find protocols such as NetWare' NetWare Core Protocol (NCP), UNIX-centric Network Filing System (NFS), Apple Computer's AppleTalk Filing Protocol (AFP), and LAN Manager's Server Messaging Blocks (SMBs).

Layer Seven, the Application Layer This layer handles file transfers, e-mail transports (X.400), transaction processing, and directory services (X.500). Applications talk directly to this layer to accomplish tasks. For example, to log into a NetWare file server, the application layer carries your request to and returns the response from the server.

Summary

The combination of the elements presented in this chapter should give you a good idea of the manner in which networks operate, how they are constructed, how they process information, and how they communicate. Your installation and use of Microsoft Windows 95 will involve most of these concepts. For example, you may want to connect your workstation to a Microsoft LAN Manager; you may want to connect to a separate subnetwork; you may even want to set your Windows 95 workstation up as a file and print server. Whatever the case, knowing the type of environment you and your Windows 95 workstation will encounter will make the installation far more pleasant and productive.

Chapter Three

Preparing to Install

"Why William, on that old grey stone,
Thus for the length of half a day,
Why, William, sit you thus alone,
And dream your time away?"
  —William Wordsworth,
    from "Expostulation and Reply"

Thought before action. In no situation is this maxim more important than in the installation of an operating system. Before beginning the installation of Windows 95, you should follow this chapter closely. Even though this operating system can automatically lead you through the installation process, the steps it executes to do this are not trivial. Windows 95 is not a Windows application; it does not "ride" upon DOS. It is its own operating system. After installation, when you boot up your computer, DOS will not load—only Windows 95 will load. Therefore, you should thoroughly prepare for your installation, because an operating system, unlike a simple program, can leave your workstation unusable if it is not installed correctly.

After reading this chapter, you should have a good understanding of the Windows 95 installation process from many different perspectives. You should be able to determine whether or not your current PC can support a successful installation. You should also have an understanding of the different options available to you during the installation process. For example, you should know what to do if you have OS/2 on your PC, what to do if you do not have Windows 3.1, what to do if you do not know your system's configuration, and what to do if you want to install Windows 95 on a given network.

Installation Procedures

Microsoft Windows 95 boasts a novel installation because it is modular. When you install Windows 95, you actually complete four different procedures, or modules, as depicted in Figure 3-1. Those procedures are hardware detection, configuration questions, copying Windows 95 component files, and final system configuration.

Hardware Detection

During the hardware detection phase, the setup program analyzes your computer's installed system components and detects any peripherals connected to your computer. This step actually detects your computer's Interrupt Requests (IRQs), Input/Output (I/O) addresses, and Direct Memory Access (DMA) addresses. With this information, the setup procedure builds what is called a hardware tree in the computer's registry. If the concept of a registry sounds a bit highbrow, do not worry. It is merely a centralized storage unit for the information formerly held within .INI files.

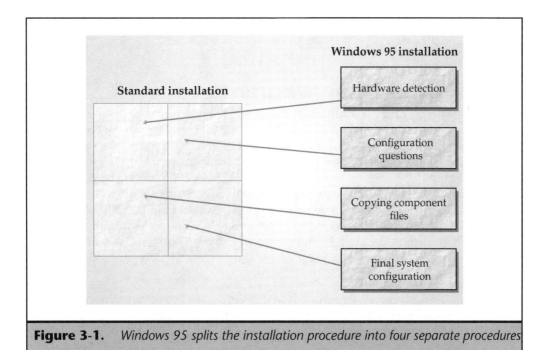

Figure 3-1. *Windows 95 splits the installation procedure into four separate procedures*

Configuration Questions

This phase allows you to see just what hardware items and peripherals Windows 95 found during the hardware detection phase. If need be, you can review these items, or you can even verify each item that was detected during the previous phase. After Windows 95 assesses and verifies your system's configuration, it presents you with a view of the components Windows 95 will install. You can then remove or add any of them.

Copying Windows 95 Component Files

This is the easiest phase of the Windows 95 installation because it does all of the work by copying files from the installation disks, CD-ROM, or network drive onto your PC.

Final System Configuration

During this step, the setup program actually upgrades your current version of MS-DOS or MS Windows to MS-DOS 6.22 and the new Windows 95 operating system.

Once this has finished, the setup program will help you configure any attached peripherals, like a printer or a modem.

Installation Improvements

This new installation approach affords Windows 95 many advantages over its predecessors, Microsoft Windows 3.1 and Windows 3.11. However, one of the largest advances over these versions appears in a rejection of the Windows 3.1 .INI files. Instead of packing the system, user, hardware, and software information into a number of flat-file ".INI" files, as with Windows 3.1, Windows 95 stores such information in a hierarchical database file (the registry). Centralizing information in a central location allows you to better manage your system. To better understand how this departure in operating system management improves Windows 95's installation process, and more importantly, how it increases Windows 95's overall functionality, you should consider some of the problems associated with Windows 3.1 .INI files listed below.

■ Widely dispersed system information that is stored in CONFIG.SYS, AUTOEXEC.BAT, PROTOCOL.INI, SYSTEM.INI, WIN.INI, and other private .INI files is subject to an increased chance for damage. Also, they make system maintenance (especially software removal) difficult if not impractical because often the information specific to an application is spread out over a number of .INI files in a format that is unrecognizable. Therefore, if you try to uninstall an application, you may not be able to remove all of the .INI information.

■ .INI files are text-based, cannot house more than 64K of data, and support only get/write functions through Microsoft's Application Programming Interface (API).

■ Information stored in .INI files is flat (nonhierarchical) and therefore can hold only two key names and section headings.

■ .INI files contain no support for user-specific information, which prevents multiple users from effectively sharing a computer.

■ There is no easy method for a network administrator to remotely administer .INI files. This makes it difficult to manage networks containing a number of Windows clients.

■ .INI files, by their very nature, are enigmatic through the multitude of switches required for most statements.

By avoiding these .INI drawbacks, Windows 95 is able to provide network administrators with some powerful management features, such as a simplified support scheme; centralized configuration information; storage for use, application, and computer-specific information; and local/remote access to that information. (See

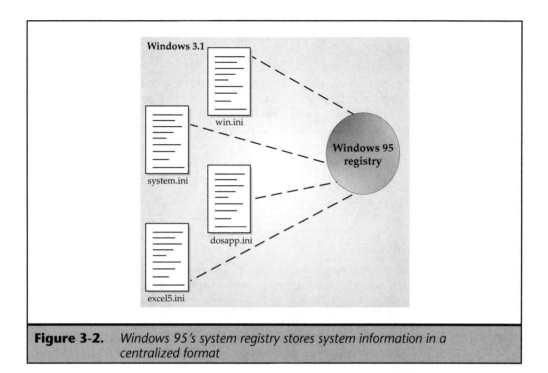

Figure 3-2. *Windows 95's system registry stores system information in a centralized format*

Figure 3-2.) However, .INI files are still used by Windows 95 in order to maintain compatibility with Windows applications requiring such conventions.

While this improvement is important, there are other features within Windows 95 that make its installation much easier than Windows 3.1 and 3.11. These are as follows.

- The entire installation process occurs within a Graphical User Interface (GUI). This will save you from having to run the SETUP.EXE file for installation modifications (such as video card definition mistakes) as you did with Windows 3.1 and Windows 3.11.

- The installation boasts advanced hardware device detection and configuration techniques. It will actually detect your monitor type and the device drivers needed to run it, for example.

- You have more control over installation components. If you do not want to set up a printer during installation, you don't have to. Similarly, if you do not want to create support for a modem during installation, you don't have to.

- There is an installation recovery system for a failed setup attempt. If, while the setup program is detecting your system's hardware, the installation fails, you can reboot the computer and pick up where you left off. Specifically, if your system fails, the setup program sets a flag within the installation code that tells the setup program to skip the process that initially failed. In this way, you can manually navigate the troubled spot the next time you run the installation program.

■ If important system files are deleted or corrupted during installation (or anytime thereafter), Windows 95 can verify those files and either correct them or prompt for replacements. This acts a bit like booting insurance. With it, you will not have to worry about having to reinstall Windows 95 because of a single file's corruption. The worst case scenario, barring complete hard-drive failure, would require the restoration of files from the Windows 95 installation disks.

■ A number of network configurations are automatically included within the installation process. During installation, if the hardware detection phase discovers a Network Interface Card (NIC), it automatically configures the system with the appropriate drivers and copies the associated files from the installation diskettes.

■ Through batch files, you can automate multiple installations. If you are a network administrator, you can define a single installation configuration that defines which network users can install Windows 95. The users won't need to answer many installation questions.

■ Value Added Resellers (VARs), PC installers, and Information Systems (IS) organizations can incorporate custom software into the Windows 95 installation. If you have created a piece of software that operates within Windows 95, like a program that dials CompuServe from within the mail client, you can incorporate its installation into that of the Windows 95 installation.

Installation Considerations

Although these features make Windows 95 seem like it could install itself, you must ensure that the appropriate environment exists for the operating system to not only install correctly but operate correctly as well. First, you must determine whether or not you have a workstation that can support the operating system. This includes items like hard-disk space, memory size, and Central Processing Unit (CPU) type.

Once you have authenticated these variables, you must take a close look at your current operating system. Do you have MS-DOS? Do you have Windows 3.1? Or, do you even have an operating system? If you do have an operating system, what do you want to do with it after Windows 95 is installed? Do you want to maintain it, or would it be better to discard it?

The third and perhaps the most important area you should survey is the network upon which you intend to install Windows 95. First, you should find out if your network is supported by Windows 95. Then you should assess how you want to install the Windows 95 workstation upon that network. For example, you must ask yourself: Do I have to modify my workstation configuration in order to communicate with the network after installation? Do I need to have a network client installed before I install

Windows 95? And what steps will I need to take to ensure security for my workstation and my network?

Workstation Considerations

The best place to start in considering whether to install Windows 95 is your workstation. If your workstation's hardware and software cannot support Windows 95, there is no sense in mulling over network support for Windows 95 until you can accommodate the necessary requirements.

Hardware Requirements

The hardware required to install Windows 95 should be your first consideration. Only install Windows 95 if your workstation meets the following criteria.

40MB of Free Disk Space on Your Hard Drive

Although you may not choose to install all of Windows 95's features, you should reserve this amount of disk space in case you choose to add features during the final system configuration portion of the installation. If this seems too demanding, just compare Windows 95 with its competition, IBM Corp.'s OS/2 platform, which requires roughly the same amount of disk space. The same is true for the Santa Cruz Operation, Inc.'s SCO Open Desktop. Although many developers would disagree with this current operating system trend toward mammoth disk space requirements, such prerequisites are brought on by the enormous demands made upon operating systems. For example, preemptive multitasking, built-in network support, mini application suites, etc., are common items in today's 32-bit desktop operating system, all of which require disk space.

A 386 or Higher Central Processing Unit (CPU)

The 32-bit file and processing system of Windows 95 requires a 32-bit machine architecture. The inability to run Windows 95 on a lesser system, like an AT 286 machine, stems not from the lack of speed or processing power, but rather from the inability to process the Windows 95 code.

4MB of Random Access Memory (RAM)

Since most Microsoft Windows 3.1 and 3.11 machines already contain 4 megabytes of memory, you will most likely not be burdened by this prerequisite. If you find it too costly, think of IBM Corp.'s OS/2 operating system, which until quite recently required at least 8MB of RAM to adequately function. Many OS/2 users, however, did not balk at such requirements for the simple reason that OS/2 could preemptively multitask applications. In other words, it could simultaneously run more than one program, which is no small task. Now, if you consider that Windows 95 also preemptively multitasks within 4MB of RAM with no noticeable performance degradation, the required 4MB of RAM may not seem as costly.

However, do not install Windows 95 if you have partitioned your hard drive with any third-party partitioning tools. If you have partitioned your hard drive, for example, with anything other than the FDISK.EXE utility, which is included with MS-DOS, please refer to Chapter 4, "Installation Overview," before you install Windows 95. Also, if you intend to install Windows 95 on a diskless workstation, one that utilizes a network drive as its boot disk, you should refer to the aforementioned chapter as well.

Plug and Play Hardware

Despite your ability to meet the minimum requirements for a Windows 95 installation, your current hardware may not be compatible, which can consequently prevent you from installing Windows 95. Unless terms like Direct Memory Access (DMA) addresses, Interrupt Request (IRQ) numbers, and Input/Output (I/O) addresses hold special meaning to you, installing a new operating system over your current hardware can be a very daunting and frustrating task. Conversely, installing new hardware components such as hard drives, serial devices, and network adapters can elicit the same problems. For example, when you install IBM Corp.'s OS/2 operating system, unless your hard drive can utilize an interrupt 13 driver, you had better have a compatible driver. If not, your installation will certainly be short-lived.

The problem here is that on a PC the operating system and applications cannot tell what hardware components are installed. When you buy a communications package like Symantec Inc.'s PC Anywhere, for example, you cannot simply install the software and use your modem. You must install the software and then tell it what type of modem you have, and what type of initialization string it has. This can be quite frustrating if you do not know the make and model of your modem, or if the installation program does not have a driver for your type of modem.

Windows 95 Plug and Play Strategy

With the introduction of Windows 95, Microsoft hopes to lessen these headaches through their Plug and Play technology, as depicted in Figure 3-3. During the hardware detection phase of the installation, Windows 95 actually identifies the components of your PC: its hard drive, its expansion cards, its Personal Computer Memory Card International Association (PCMCIA) cards, etc. When it detects a NIC expansion card, for example, it queries the card, asking it about its make and model, its DMA and I/O address, its interrupt number, and its network type (token ring, Ethernet, etc.). The installation process then installs the required network driver with the appropriate configuration information. You do not need to do anything.

Plug and Play technology reaches beyond the installation process by providing you the ability to dynamically add and remove these types of devices as well. You can add a PCMCIA memory card and immediately use it. You can install a CD-ROM drive and immediately use it. Don't think, however, that Microsoft's Plug and Play technology is a cornucopia of interoperability. Because it requires an agreement on

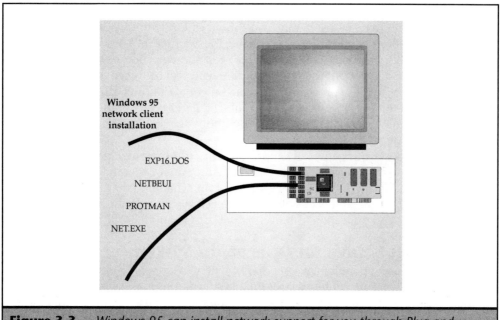

**Windows 95
network client
installation**

EXP16.DOS

NETBEUI

PROTMAN

NET.EXE

Figure 3-3. *Windows 95 can install network support for you through Plug and
Play technology*

both Microsoft's and the device developers' behalf, not all devices can be installed and
configured in this manner. Currently, there are many vendors providing Plug and Play
cooperation. Some of their products follow:

3COM Corporation's Etherlink III parallel tasking adapter
Adaptec's SCSI "Plug and Play" host adapter
Sundisk Corporation's DP Series PCMCIA FlashDisk
Intel Corporation Ether Express 16 ISA adapters
Sundisk SDI Series IDE FlashDisk

Your Current Workstation

There are no definitive operating system software requirements for installing
Windows 95. You can have MS-DOS 2.x, IBM Corp.'s OS/2, or Windows for
Workgroups 3.11 installed on your system. Windows 95 will either work with
or replace whatever operating system you possess. However, there are some
repercussions depending upon the method you choose in dealing with any
existing operating systems.

Since your current workstation most likely contains an operating system, data, and programs you use from day to day, you should carefully think out your plan of action when installing Windows 95. If you have, for example, a Windows 3.1 operating system and a number of communications packages, and you choose to install Windows 95 alongside the Windows 3.1 program, you will be forced to manually create all references to these programs and data on your computer. Conversely, if you choose to install Windows 95 over your current installation of Windows 3.1, you forfeit all chances of running standard Windows 3.1 without deinstalling Windows 95 and reinstalling Windows 3.1.

Therefore, choose your course of action carefully. Think through your current and future needs. For example, ask yourself: "Do I need to run an operating system like Windows NT in addition to Windows 95? And if I do, what hard disk storage space requirements will I incur, and how will I boot to each system?" In this regard, you should consider each application's ability to dual boot to another operating system.

If You Do Not Have an Operating System

If you do not have an operating system, do not worry. Windows 95 does not require MS-DOS or the Microsoft Windows operating system in order to install, boot up, or run the Windows 95 workstation. During its installation, if the setup program detects no operating system, it automatically creates a mini-Windows system and installs Windows 95 over the top of it.

If You Have MS-DOS

If you have MS-DOS and no other operating system, you also need not worry. Although Windows 95 requires the Windows operating system in order to be installed, it has the ability to creatively sidestep an absence of Windows. During installation, if the Windows 95 SETUP.EXE file is executed from MS-DOS, it automatically attempts to find an installed copy of Windows. If it cannot find one, it will ask you if you want it to install a miniature version of Windows from which it will automatically install Windows 95, as shown in Figure 3-4.

Of course, keep in mind that if you have only MS-DOS and you want to maintain its inherent capabilities, Windows 95 lets you dual boot to a limited MS-DOS 6.22 configuration or to Windows 95. During the bootup process, you can simply press F4 and you will be left at an MS-DOS prompt. For specific instructions on this subject, please refer to Chapter 4, "Installation Overview."

If You Have Windows 3.1

If you have Windows 3.1, you have basically two choices. First, you can install Windows 95 over your current Windows 3.1 operating system. This is recommended because in upgrading Windows 3.1 to Windows 95, all of your program and program group icons will be automatically migrated to the Windows 95 interface. Of course, if things go sour during the installation you may have to scrub the Windows 3.1

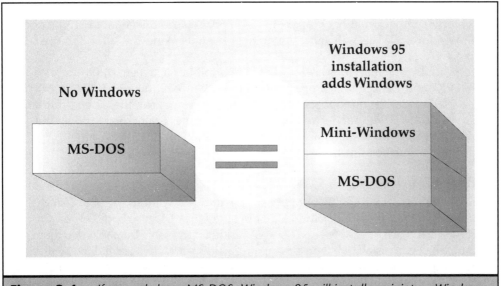

Figure 3-4. *If you only have MS-DOS, Windows 95 will install a miniature Windows operating system*

operating system anyway, which is yet another good reason to fully back up your entire hard disk before installing Windows 95.

The second installation alternative if you have Windows 3.1 is to install Windows 95 in a separate directory. With this choice you can dual boot to MS-DOS 6.22 and then run Windows 3.1. As mentioned earlier, if you want to do this, you need only press F4 during the booting process.

If You Have Windows 3.11

If you have Windows 3.11, you have the same choices as you would with Windows 3.1. You can install Windows 95 directly over Windows 3.11 or you can install them side by side. If you rely upon the peer-to-peer networking capabilities of Windows 3.11, you may want to perform the latter of the two choices. In that way, any incompatibilities between Windows 95 and Windows 3.11 will not preclude you from working effectively in both environments.

If You Have Windows NT

If you have Windows NT, either advanced server or standard edition, you can boot between it and Windows 95, but only if you have installed Windows NT on a FAT volume. If you have installed Windows NT on a high-performance Windows NT File System (NTFS) volume, Windows 95 will not run under multiboot mode. To take advantage of Windows NT and Windows 95, you must first install Windows NT (on a FAT volume) with its dual-boot capability enabled. You can then boot to MS-DOS and install Windows 95. This will allow you to boot to either Windows NT, Windows 95, or MS-DOS 6.22.

You should note that there are some incompatibilities between Windows NT's LABEL.EXE and CHKDSK.EXE programs and those of Windows 95. If you install Windows 95 under the multiboot configuration, you cannot run these two programs under Windows 95 without destroying all long file names (names longer than the standard MS-DOS 13 characters). For more information on this, please refer to Chapter 4, "Installation Overview."

If You Have OS/2

If you have IBM Corp.'s OS/2 operating system and you want to use both it and Windows 95 from the same partition, you are out of luck because both OS/2 and Windows 95 replace MS-DOS—both cannot reside on the same bootable partition. You can, however, install OS/2 on a primary partition, boot to a secondary MS-DOS partition, and then install Windows 95. In this way you can take advantage of OS/2's powerful boot manager program to set different partitions as the active, boot partition. (See Figure 3-5.) This will allow you to make either the OS/2 partition or the Windows 95 partition the active, boot partition. The main directive here is to install OS/2's boot manager and OS/2 first, and then install Windows 95.

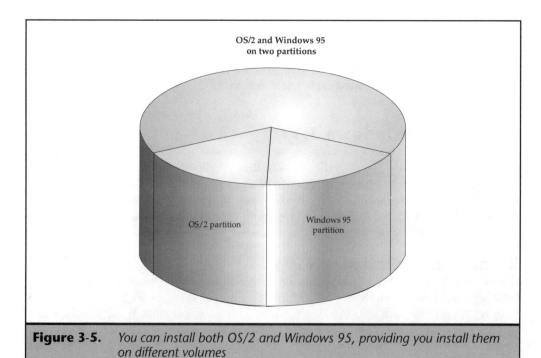

Figure 3-5.   *You can install both OS/2 and Windows 95, providing you install them on different volumes*

If You Have Windows 95

If you have Windows 95 already installed, you can reinstall Windows 95 with a dual-boot configuration even if you did not initially install such a feature. However, there are many steps you must follow to do this. For more information on this procedure, please refer to Chapter 4, "Installation Overview."

Network Considerations

Since one of Windows 95's strongest capabilities is its networking feature set, you will most likely not need to spend an excessive amount of time preparing for this portion of your installation. However, there are some salient points you should consider for your Windows 95 installation within a network environment that are specific to each type of network (for example, within Microsoft networks or third-party networks). Third-party networks are those belonging to vendors other than Microsoft. However, because Novell NetWare integrates well with Windows 95, you should consider it as you would a Microsoft network.

With a third-party installation, you must take into account whether your network is supported by Windows 95, you must consider whether your network's protocol stack is supported by Windows 95, and you must assess these two areas in conjunction with the chance that you will be utilizing more than one type of network.

With Microsoft networks, you will not be presented with many network integration problems because Windows 95 can seamlessly work with Windows NT, Windows for Workgroups 3.11, and Windows 95 networks. Within this environment, the only items of importance encompass security decisions. With the addition of user-level security to Windows 95, you must decide how to best implement both file-level and user-level security measures before you install your Windows 95 workstation.

Security, however, does not apply to Microsoft networks alone. With all network configurations, the question of how best to control and defend your data should be the final (and most important) decision you make prior to installation. Without security, not only is the data on your workstation at stake, but the data of your entire company is at stake.

Networking Improvements over Windows 3.1 and Windows 3.11

Before continuing on to the network-specific installation considerations, it will be helpful to understand some of the general improvements Microsoft Windows 95 has made regarding network installation, management, and use. In many ways these improvements will make your task of selecting and utilizing a network service (both third-party and Microsoft networks) quite simple. Some of the improvements Windows 95 has made over its predecessors are as follows:

■ A 32-bit networking architecture, which includes a 32-bit network client, 32-bit file and printer sharing software, 32-bit network protocols, and 32-bit network card drivers. Of course, to take advantage of these powerful networking features you must have a computer that will support 32-bit network access through either an extended industry standard architecture (EISA) or a Peripheral Component Interconnection (PCI) compatible computer and NIC. The most noticeable differences between a 32-bit architecture and a 16-bit architecture is speed, since data can pass between your network adapter card and the Windows 95 operating system at twice the speed as 16-bit architectures.

■ Support for multiple redirectors, multiple protocols, and network card drivers. Through either Open Data-link Interface (ODI) or Network Driver Interface Specification (NDIS) drivers, you can load multiple protocols simultaneously. You do not need to supply anything to take advantage of this feature if you are going to utilize Transmission Control Protocol/Internet Protocol (TCP/IP), Internet Packet Exchange (IPX), or NetBIOS Extended User Interface (NetBEUI). Basically, if your network supports one of these three protocols, you can immediately begin networking with your Windows 95 workstation.

■ Extended workstation management features through Simple Network Management Protocol (SNMP) and Desktop Management Interface (DMI). With these two standards, you can manage your Windows 95 workstation from a network interface such as Hewlett Packard Corp.'s OpenView.

■ Extended support for Novell Inc.'s NetWare through a 32-bit Windows 95 client capable of attaching to both NetWare 3.x and NetWare 4.x (in either bindery emulation or NetWare Directory Services (NDS) mode) and peer-to-peer resource sharing under NetWare peer-to-peer networking (Personal NetWare).

■ Built-in systems management utilities that let you administer Windows 95 workstations, including your own. Powerful auditing tools and a user security monitoring interface lets you control how others use your workstation.

■ Improved remote network access, in which you can connect to remote Microsoft network servers, Novell NetWare servers, and UNIX servers through the remote access protocols: Point-to-Point Protocol (PPP) and Serial Line Internet Protocol (SLIP). (Refer to Figure 3-6.) If your company has direct access to the Internet, you can use these two protocols to access over 2.17 million networked computers.

■ Improved network printing. This improvement enables you to select a printer through a common syntax. In this way you can select a printer just as you would any other network service, such as a network drive or program.

The Windows 95 Network Client

The built-in 32-bit client software and Microsoft's Plug and Play architecture solve a number of network installation problems. The type of NIC and protocol to use are

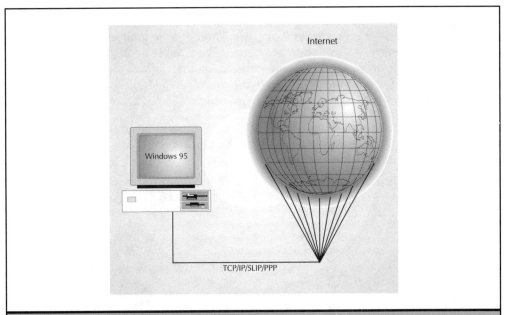

Figure 3-6.   *Your Windows 95 workstation is ready to connect to the Internet via TCP/IP, SLIP, or PPP*

resolved during the installation process. This built-in client will make the network portion of your Windows 95 installation relatively painless because, although planning for network integration under Windows 95 requires you to know what type of network you are going to connect with, the built-in client does not in most situations require you to obtain networking software for that network. The usefulness of the network client software within Windows 95 becomes apparent when you consider the following network installation scenario in which a Windows 95 client is being installed upon a Novell NetWare 4.1 network.

First, assume that the workstation already has client software installed (IPX ODI drivers). When you install Windows 95, you can choose whether you load the ODI drivers already on your workstation or the NDIS drivers shipped with Windows 95. If you choose to use your ODI drivers, you will not have to perform any additional configuration tasks. When you reboot the workstation, it will simply use the ODI drivers. Similarly, if you choose the NDIS drivers, Windows 95 will automatically load and configure the appropriate drivers for your network adapter.

Second, assume that the workstation does not have any client software installed. When you install Windows 95, it will detect your NIC and load the appropriate NDIS drivers for your network. You need only reboot the workstation to take advantage of the network. No configuration is required on your part. It all occurs automatically during installation.

Windows 95 Client Capabilities

In addition to the ease with which you can install and use the built-in Windows 95 network client, there are many features that make it a viable option when you consider how to connect your workstation to a network. If you install Windows 95 on a Novell NetWare network, for example, and you choose to utilize the built-in 32-bit client, you will be able to take advantage of the following features:

- *High performance:* The Windows 95 client is 200 percent faster than a Windows 3.1 operating system running a NetWare Virtual Loadable Module (VLM) client in certain circumstances.

- *No conventional memory footprint:* Since the Windows 95 client replaces NetWare's real-mode 16-bit drivers with protected-mode 32-bit drivers, you can save tremendous amounts of memory for MS-DOS programs.

- *Auto-reconnect feature:* When a connection is lost, the Windows 95 client will not lockup your workstation. It will simply tell your applications to wait a moment until the connection is reestablished. If it is not reestablished, the client will simply notify the affected applications.

- *Packet burst protocol support:* This is also supported in the standard NetWare client. It basically allows you to transmit data at a higher rate by transmitting multiple packets at one time. Normal protocol communications requires a response for each packet.

- *Client-side cashing:* Requests can be cashed within the client before being sent across the wire. This is an important feature when you enter the world of preemptive multitasking applications in which vast amounts of data can be sent to the Network Interface Card (NIC) at one time.

- *Plug and Play aware:* As mentioned previously, during installation the Windows 95 client can automatically interrogate your hardware and configure its drivers to comply with that hardware.

- *Fully integrated with the Windows 95 interface:* This simply means that you do not have to load your network drivers outside of Windows 95. Loading, unloading, and configuring drivers takes place within the Windows 95 Graphical User Interface (GUI).

- *Graphical logon/logoff capability:* With the Windows 95 client, you can logon or logoff a NetWare 3.x and 4.x server without having to exit Windows 95 and type in the applicable commands from an MS-DOS prompt.

- *User-level security using "pass-through" bindery or NDS:* This means that in order to share information with other Windows 95 workstations, NetWare's security system must be used to authenticate identification.

- *Point and Print support:* After you enable a printer, you can simply point to a file and print it with a click of the mouse.

Although some of these are specific to Novell NetWare networks, many are present on all computer networks, such as the no-memory footprint, auto-reconnect, client-side caching, Plug and Play, Windows 95 integration, protocol independence, and Point and Print services. Additionally, the Windows 95 client provides protection against aberrant Windows programs by running at Ring 0. In this way, a crashed program cannot affect your network connection within other programs.

Multiprotocol Support

A second advantage, aside from excellent network operating system integration, is that the Windows 95 network client has the ability to simultaneously load multiple drivers. (See Figure 3-7.) This is a trait common to many network clients. However, with the Windows 95 client such a task is made easy. If you want to switch between ODI and NDIS drivers, or if you want to load TCP/IP instead of IPX protocol, you can simply specify such through a Windows 95 Control Panel. Through the same panel, you can even choose to load them simultaneously. To activate these changes, you then reboot the computer. That's it. You will not have to modify the PROTOCOL.INI or NET.CFG files again.

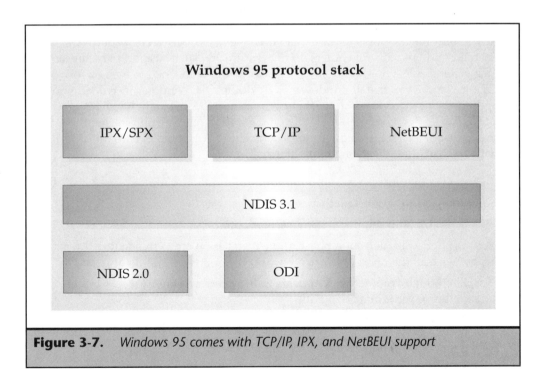

Figure 3-7. *Windows 95 comes with TCP/IP, IPX, and NetBEUI support*

Network Operating System Considerations

There are many network operating systems supported by Windows 95. The networks supported by Windows 95 include:

- 3Com 3+Open, 3+share
- Artisoft LANtastic
- Banyan VINES
- Beame and Whiteside: B&W-NFS
- DEC PATHWORKS
- IBM: LAN Server and LAN program and C LAN program
- Microsoft LAN Manager, MS Net
- Novell NetWare
- SunSelect PC-NFS
- TCS 10net

Because Windows 95 attempts to automatically install support for these networks, certain limitations within each network will affect the manner in which you install Windows 95. Some networks require that you have network drivers loaded at the time you install Windows 95, while others do not require any such support to be present.

As a general rule, you should have your workstation attached to the network of your choice before you install Windows 95. By doing this, Windows 95 will attempt to configure your new workstation for that network and the installation will progress smoothly. If after installing Windows 95 you want to utilize the built-in client, you can use the Control Panel to do so quite simply. Installing Windows 95 with third-party network support should go something like this:

1. Install network support.

2. Start Windows 95 installation.

3. Choose Custom setup and then Network options.

4. If the hardware detection phase of the installation correctly identified your network adapter and network software, your network should appear.

5. Even though your network appears in the window, you must select Add and then Client from the menu.

6. The remainder of the installation should continue normally.

For explicit information on this methodology, please refer to Chapter 4, "Installation Overview."

Network Capabilities

Although you can connect to all of the previously mentioned networks with third-party network clients, some networks provide more capabilities through the Windows 95 client. This is not to say that some networks are better than others, however. It simply means that the union between Windows 95's built-in client and certain networks yields better opportunities. For example, if you intend to install Windows 95 on a Banyan VINES network, you will be able to access and utilize VINES print services from your workstation. But if you install Windows 95 on a Novell NetWare network, not only can you use network print services, you can provide such services as well.

Novell Networks

As mentioned previously, if you install the Windows 95 client for your Novell NetWare network, you can obtain many benefits. Some additional features available to you will require some pre-installation thought. For example, if you desire, you can take advantage of NetWare's printing services. By installing Windows 95's "PSERVER" program on your workstation, you can spool network print jobs to a printer attached to your workstation. Because these services tie directly into NetWare print services, they can be administered from within NetWare. (See Figure 3-8.)

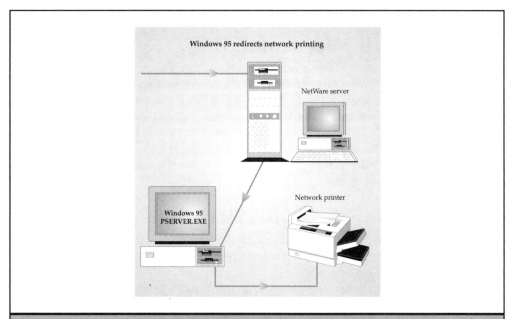

Figure 3-8. *The Windows 95 client can accept Novell print jobs*

You can also take full advantage of NetWare login scripts. When you log in to a NetWare network with the Microsoft Windows client, all of your drive mappings, printer port redirections, and even search drive mappings will be automatically implemented.

Microsoft Network Operating Systems

The second group of network operating systems containing the most integrated elements with Windows 95 belongs to Microsoft, which includes Windows NT Workstation, Windows NT Advanced Server, Windows for Workgroups 3.11, LAN Manager, Windows 95 clients, and any other Microsoft LAN Manager compatible network. Connecting your workstation to any of these networks will give you printer and file-sharing capabilities. You can both share your own services or access another shared service on the Microsoft network. If your installation is only going to involve these networks, it would be best to install only the Windows 95 32-bit client.

Advanced Network Considerations

Microsoft and Novell networks provide special facilities in that through the built-in client alone you can obtain both client/server and peer-to-peer networking capabilities. Most other networks will require you to first install the third-party client for client/server networking; then, if you want peer-to-peer networking, you will have to also load the Windows 95 client after the installation has finished.

Networking with Microsoft

In this configuration, you should obtain information from your network administrator concerning domain and workgroup names. Additionally, you will have to decide whether you want user-level or file-level security on your workstation. Having this information available during installation will make things run much smoother.

The easiest way to install Windows 95 on a Microsoft network is to utilize a domain controller (either Windows NT or LAN Manager) for user-level security and access configuration. This will free you from assigning user accounts to your machine by making the domain controller's user database available to the Windows 95 client.

Microsoft Networking with NetWare

You can utilize NetWare services for your Windows 95 network in much the same manner as you do with a network that is uniquely Microsoft. Here, instead of a Windows NT acting as a reference point for security issues (domains, user-ids, and file and print sharing privileges), a NetWare 3.x or 4.x server acts as a reference point for these items. Using what is called "pass-through security," you will not need to create user accounts for each person you wish to have access to your PC. Instead, you must create user security specifications for users possessing a NetWare account.

General Security Issues

As you can see, there are many security elements that must be taken into consideration before you install Windows 95. One important area that applies to all types of networks involves a concept called master key services. Just as a master key unlocks all doors within an organization, the master key of Windows 95 can unlock all or as many doors as you want on your computer, as shown in Figure 3-9. You can basically set Windows 95 up to ask you for just one login name and password, which will simultaneously unlock file servers, peer-to-peer machines, e-mail systems, even files. For example, you could, through a single logon name and password, open your Windows 95 client, your NetWare file servers, your Microsoft Mail client, and a locked spreadsheet.

This does have one drawback, in that it provides a single point of failure for your network security system. If you compromise the master key password, all protected network services will be open to intruder incursions. Furthermore, Windows 95, because it utilizes a File Allocation Table (FAT) file system, can be broken into through a boot disk. By booting from a floppy disk, an individual could gain access to all files on your hard disk. However, the intruder would not be able to access the network.

Figure 3-9.   *Windows 95 allows you to unlock numerous password-protected resources*

Summary

Before installing Windows 95, you should consider many requirements and variables that can affect both your ability to install and the ease with which you can use Windows 95. The process of installation is broken down into four separate phases. Through this segmentation, the installation of Windows 95 can better respond to failures. For example, if the hardware detection phase encounters a problem, you can reboot the computer and bypass the troubled area.

Before installing Windows 95 you should find out if your workstation's hardware can support the Windows 95 operating system. However, because the installation routine utilizes Plug and Play technologies, your workstation's hardware should not pose many compatibility or support problems if your are using Plug and Play components.

Secondly, you should consider what to do with your current operating system. If you have Windows (3.1 and 3.11), you may want to install Windows 95 in a separate directory, thereby preserving these operating systems for future use. Conversely, if you have Windows NT or OS/2 and want to preserve their operability, you will have to perform some special tasks.

Thirdly, you should look at the network configuration upon which you wish to install Windows 95. Microsoft Windows 95 comes with a very powerful 32-bit client that in many ways can surpass the abilities of third-party network client software, especially with NetWare. With this in mind, you will want to consider whether or not to use the Windows 95 client for your third-party network. Also, there are other network-dependent installation issues such as printer support, file sharing options, and security.

By analyzing these necessities and concerns before you install Windows 95, the entire process will run smoothly and you will be able to take full advantage of Windows 95's powerful operating system and network client features.

Chapter Four

Installation Overview

*"The man who said 'The harder the
toil, the sweeter the rest,' never was
profoundly tired."*
—*John Muir, "An Adventure with
a Dog and a Glacier"*

Now that you have analyzed the general requirements and considerations involved in the installation of Windows 95, the next step is the actual installation. In most situations, the process should progress quite smoothly. The automatic hardware detection and configuration will free you from most compatibility questions. The fail-safe installation will even make corrective procedures much easier—it will also make it easier to return to your initial system should an unrecoverable error occur. However, although these and many other features place the intricacies of installation entirely upon Windows 95, there are some duties and preparations you should perform before running the installation program. Then, you will be able to install your new operating system easily and assuredly.

Installing Windows 95

This chapter will address the preparations and tasks involved in properly installing Windows 95 on your workstation and your network. We will begin by discussing the steps you should take before you install Windows 95, such as the proper configuration of your workstation, the creation of a safety disk, etc. We will then attack the many stumbling blocks you may encounter with different configurations, such as Personal Computer Memory Card International Association (PCMCIA) cards and disk partition configurations. Following this, we will walk through the installation of Windows 95 from a number of different perspectives, like installation from CD-ROM, floppy disk, and a network. We will address the installation of network support under Windows 95 and, finally, we will talk about the steps required to finalize and clean up the installation process.

Pre-Installation Preparations

Before you run SETUP.EXE and install Windows 95, there are some necessary steps you should take. By following these guidelines you should be able to configure your system for a smooth installation and avoid any installation tragedies.

Safety Procedures

The first task involves the procurement of an insurance policy that will allow you to restore your original system configuration should things go wrong during the installation process. By protecting the single most tangible element of your computer system, namely the installed software, you can quickly recover from any sort of mishap, such as a driver failure or file corruption. This involves two important steps: system backup and the creation of a backup diskette, as depicted in Figure 4-1.

System Backup

Any time you make changes to your computer, you should back up the data stored on its hard disk. There are many methods available to do this. You may already utilize an automated backup program such as 5th Generation's FastBack or Microsoft's backup utility, which is included with MS-DOS 6.0 and higher. Since your workstation is most likely connected to a network, your network administrator may even have a backup program installed, like Palindrome's The Network Archivist, that will let you backup your hard drive to the network.

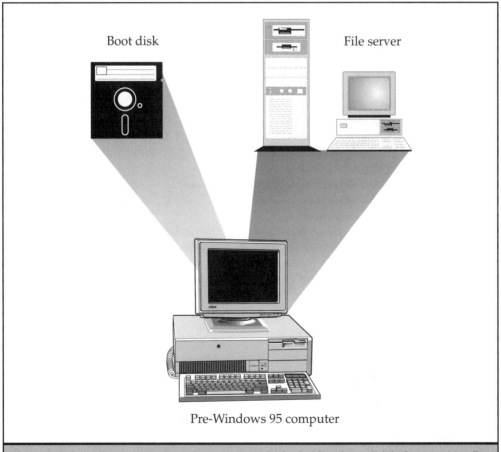

Boot disk

File server

Pre-Windows 95 computer

Figure 4-1. *Create a backup of your system and a backup boot disk before you install Windows 95*

If you have an automated backup program, you should immediately follow the necessary steps to completely back up your hard drive. Make sure in doing so, however, that your backup program copies all of the hidden and system files that may be on your system. For example, your Windows 3.1/3.11 swap disk file, which is marked both hidden and system, must be restored to your hard drive along with the rest of the Windows files. If this file is not restored, you will receive a recoverable, albeit unfriendly, error message the first time you start Windows.

Alternative Backup Procedure   In case you do not own an automated backup program, do not worry. There are other methods available for you to back up your data. The first, and easiest method is to obtain a file compression program that can both compress your data and back it up to a safe place. An excellent shareware compression/backup program called PKWare can be obtained from many Bulletin Board Services (BBSs), from the Internet, and very likely from your network administrator. The best versions of this program are 2.04 or higher. Although there are many older versions available, the newer versions allow you to back up data across many floppy disks. This will be most helpful if you do not have a larger media such as a network drive, tape drive, or read/write optical disk available for data storage.

For example, a PKWare backup routine utilizing a hard drive labeled C: and a floppy disk labeled A: should be followed like this: Make ready sufficient floppy disks to backup your entire hard drive. An easy way to assess your needs is to run CHKDSK.EXE on your hard drive and divide the total amount of used disk space by the capacity of your floppy disk drive. Of course, through compression, the number of disks needed will be far fewer than the number required to contain all of your data; however, because not all files compress with the same efficiency, you should ready a number of disks nearing the entire size of your hard disk.

Next, run the PKWare program. Your command line should look like this:

```
PKZIP -&sc a:\backup.zip
```

The "-&" means to back up your entire disk, "sc" indicates that you want to back up your disk labeled C:, and "a:\backup.zip" represents your target drive and the file name you want to store your data in.

Backup "Boot" Diskette

After you have secured all of your data, you should create a backup diskette. This disk, which should contain your system's precious configuration information, can be used to restore your workstation to its original state from a complete system failure. The way it works is quite simple. By duplicating the information your computer uses to boot up from your hard disk and a floppy disk, you should be able to boot from either medium. This diskette should be used not just for the installation of an operating system like Windows 95, but for any situation in which your hard drive may become unbootable. You may accidentally delete your COMMAND.COM file; you may overwrite your AUTOEXEC.BAT file; you may even format your hard drive. In all of these situations, a backup diskette can save the day.

This diskette should contain a number of files. First, it should be able to boot up your system. To accomplish this, you need to format a disk with the "/S" option. This will copy the system and COMMAND.COM files to the diskette. You should copy your AUTOEXEC.BAT and CONFIG.SYS files to your floppy diskette. Once you have done this, you may need to edit those files to do away with any device drivers (lines beginning with "DEVICE=" in your CONFIG.SYS file) that are not pertinent to the functionality of your computer. Also, within your AUTOEXEC.BAT file, you may need to remove any commands that load programs such as Windows or a network client. Of course, you will have to copy the files referenced by your CONFIG.SYS and AUTOEXEC.BAT to the A: drive, so be spartan about your choices.

Other files you should place on this floppy disk, if you are currently using either Windows 3.1 or Windows For Workgroups 3.11, include these important .INI files:

```
C:\WINDOWS\WIN.INI
C:\WINDOWS\SYSTEM.INI
C:\WINDOWS\PROTOCOL.INI (for Windows For WorkGroups)
```

Optionally, you can include the following files on the floppy diskette:

```
C:\WINDOWS\*.GRP
C:\WINDOWS\CONNECT.DAT
C:\WINDOWS\*.PWL
C:\WINDOWS\*.INI
```

If you do not or cannot copy these files to your floppy diskette, make sure that they are at least backed up.

Drastic Measures

Usually, you do not need to take such drastic measures for the installation of most software products, such as a spreadsheet, a word processor, or even Microsoft Windows 3.1. However, because Windows 95, as a true replacement for an operating system like MS-DOS, changes the way your hard disk boots, all of the data on that hard disk is subject to corruption.

Machine Preparation

The second most important step you can take in preparing to install Windows 95 is to prepare your machine for installation. This includes making sure that you have enough disk space, analyzing your current system configuration, and removing any devices that may cause incompatibility problems.

Machine Requirements and Required Information

As mentioned previously in Chapter 3, "Preparing to Install," you will need at least 4MB of RAM, 35 to 40MB of disk space, and an Intel 386 or 486 machine to install Windows 95.

Before you install, you should gather as much information about your system as possible. Although Windows 95, through its hardware detection capabilities, should be able to take you through the installation without requiring any information on your behalf, it is a good idea to maintain system information in the unlikely event that there are compatibility problems between devices or support problems between a device and Windows 95. For example, you should obtain the name and type of video card your computer has. If you are using a Simple Computer Systems Interface (SCSI) hard drive, you should obtain its interrupt number, Direct Memory Access (DMA) channel, and Input/Output (I/O) address.

Similarly, you should obtain this information for your Network Interface Card (NIC). If you are unsure about its configuration (for example, if it uses a soft-set configuration capability in which you cannot see its jumper settings), simply look either in the PROTOCOL.INI (for NDIS drivers) file or NET.CFG (for ODI drivers) file. They should contain all of the information you will need in a readable format. It would be a good idea to print these files for later reference.

System Configuration Considerations

There are some changes to your system's configuration that may be necessary before you begin to install Windows 95. These changes will not only make your installation smoother, they will ensure that it is successful.

Multiple Drives   If you want to install Windows 95 on a drive other than your primary, active disk (or partition), you will need to ensure that the primary device has at least 6MB of disk space available. You can then install Windows 95 to any device you want. But remember, when you run the installation process, it will not ask you to ensure the availability of the disk space because you will enter a target drive letter other than the primary device.

Compressed Drives   If you wish to install Windows 95 on a compressed volume (through products like MS-DOS's DoubleSpace utility, or Stacker) you must ensure that there is at least 10MB of disk space available outside of your compressed volume, as shown in Figure 4-2. In other words, the physical disk upon which your compressed drive resides must have 10MB of free disk space. To make any changes necessary, you should be able to resize the compressed drive through a configuration utility available within the compression program. For example, on a computer utilizing MS-DOS's DoubleSpace program, you can type **DBLSPACE** at a command prompt and then select the Change Size option.

After you install Windows 95 on top of a compressed drive, you will have to dual boot to MS-DOS in order to run the DBLSPACE.EXE for any sizing or defragmentation

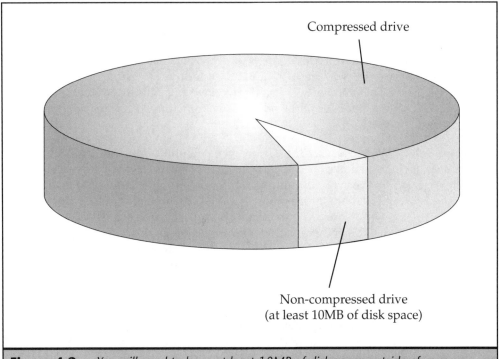

Compressed drive

Non-compressed drive
(at least 10MB of disk space)

Figure 4-2.   *You will need to have at least 10MB of disk space outside of your compressed drive to install Windows 95*

routines. Be aware that in doing this, DoubleSpace will destroy all of the long file names you have created in Windows 95. You can avoid this problem and save your long file names by downloading a utility called LFNBK from the Windows 95 support forum on CompuServe and running it prior to DoubleSpace. Then, after running DoubleSpace, you can simply restore the long file names through the same utility.

Multiple Configurations Within CONFIG.SYS   With MS-DOS 6.0 and above, you can create different boot-up sections within your CONFIG.SYS file, called Multiconfig sections, which give you a menu of system configuration options when you boot. However, when you install Windows 95, it takes each multiple configuration and changes it into a Windows 95 section. Specifically, it adds the device driver references and environmental settings necessary for the proper functioning of Windows 95 to each section, regardless of that section's purpose. To counter this problem, you can either completely remove the Multiconfig sections from your CONFIG.SYS file, or you can review the changes Windows 95 makes to the file after you install the operating system. If you choose the latter of these two methods, be careful not to reboot Windows 95 before reviewing the CONFIG.SYS file.

Single or No Operating System Installation   If you have only one operating system, such as MS-DOS, or if you do not have an operating system (your hard drive cannot be booted), you will find the Windows 95 installation quite easy. With an MS-DOS operating system, you will not need to make any pre-installation decisions. When you install Windows 95, it will set up a miniature Windows operating system through which it will install itself. Similarly, if you do not have an operating system , Windows 95 will make your disk bootable and load the same miniature Windows program prior to installation.

Windows 3.1 or Windows 3.11   If, however, you utilize the Windows operating system, you will have to make special allowances in response to your decision either to install Windows 95 over your existing Windows operating system, or to install it in a separate directory. For more information about the consequences of each decision, please refer to Chapter 3, "Preparing to Install." If you choose to install Windows 95 in a different directory, remember to allow for the additional disk space required to maintain both operating systems. Also, if you do this you will have to reinstall your MS-Windows applications since you will not be able to adequately import them into Windows 95's system information repository. You cannot simply copy the .GRP and .INI files from your Windows directory to that of Windows 95.

Windows NT   If you have Windows NT installed on your computer upon a FAT volume, the only task you need to perform occurs during the installation. When you reach the screen that allows you to choose between normal and custom installation methods, choose custom and ensure that Windows 95 installs within a directory separate from your Windows NT directory.

OS/2   To install Windows 95 in conjunction with OS/2, you will need to maintain at least two hard disk partitions. For more information on this, please refer to Chapter 3, "Preparing to Install." Before running the installation program for Windows 95, you should boot to the partition not containing OS/2. From that moment on, you can proceed with the installation normally.

Hardware-Specific Preparations

Although Windows 95 allows for many disparate hardware devices to work together, there are some problems that demand your immediate attention prior to your installation of Windows 95.

PCMCIA Preparations

Windows 95 comes equipped with protected-mode drivers for Databook and Intel compatibility as a part of its Plug and Play architecture. They will allow you to dynamically insert, configure, and remove PCMCIA cards from your machine. During installation, Windows 95, upon detecting a PCMCIA slot, checks for the presence of current drivers. If it finds these drivers, it incorporates them into Windows 95 and continues. Therefore, if you currently utilize real-mode PCMCIA drivers, you can choose to either use them or abandon them for the Windows 95 drivers. To maintain your own drivers, all you need to do is ensure that they are installed and running when you install Windows 95.

If, however, you choose to install the Windows 95 PCMCIA drivers, you will need to edit your CONFIG.SYS file and remove (or "remark out") any references to them. You should then reboot your computer before continuing with the installation.

PCMCIA network adapters, on the other hand, require some special considerations. Regardless of whether or not your PCMCIA network adapter is Intel or Databook compatible, you should use your own PCMCIA drivers if your Windows 95 does not have a protected-mode driver for your card. If so, ensure that the drivers and the PCMCIA card are working at the time you install Windows 95.

After you install Windows 95, you can go back and enable/disable PCMCIA support. Furthermore, if you insert a PCMCIA card after installation, Windows 95 will automatically attempt to utilize that card. If it does not belong to the list of cards natively supported, it will ask you if you want to install drivers for the card. The cards, by manufacturer and type, automatically supported within Windows 95 are

- Xircom
- Socket EA, EA+
- Fujitsu

Pen Computers

Although Windows 95 supports pen computing, you will have to take some pre-installation steps to ensure that your pen computer will continue to function under Windows 95. If you currently utilize Windows 3.1 with pen support, you should not install Windows 95 over your Windows 3.1 operating system without first removing the pen support. If you do not, your system will most likely crash during installation. To remove pen support from your Windows 3.1 operating system, you only need to edit your SYSTEM.INI file and remove the line that reads

```
PENWINDOWS=<path to penwin.dll>
```

It is located under the "[boot]" heading within this file.

Last Minute Tasks

There are basically two things you need to do before you install Windows 95. First, you should check your hard disk for any errors. If you are using MS-DOS 6.0 or later, execute either CHKDSK.EXE or SCANDISK.EXE. These programs will prompt you to fix any problems that may exist, such as cross-linked files or bad sectors.

The second task involves ensuring that your network client software and hardware are installed and operating properly. To ensure the functionality of your workstation, simply log into an available server. At a less obvious level, you should ensure that within your AUTOEXEC.BAT file's PATH statement is contained a reference to the directory in which you have installed your network client.

If you are using Novell ODI drivers, ensure that the NET.CFG configuration file resides in the same directory that your LSL.COM and network device driver files are located in.

If you are utilizing the older IPX.COM network driver configuration, in which you generate the IPX.COM from the Novell utility WSGEN.EXE, you should replace it with either ODI or NDIS drivers. Windows 95 will provide support for the IPX.COM drivers; however, because they are not extremely reliable, it would be worthwhile to adopt the newer drivers.

Pre-Installation Checklist

The following list is a quick reminder of the primary tasks you should perform before you install Windows 95:

- Back up your system.
- Create a boot disk.
- Gather system hardware information.
- Decide whether or not to install Windows 95 over your existing Windows operating system.
- Ensure that your compressed drive has enough space outside of the compressed volume.
- Correct any problems with multiple configurations within your CONFIG.SYS.
- Check for incompatibilities between your PCMCIA interface and Windows 95.
- Remove any pen driver support from your Windows 3.1 operating system.
- Check your hard disk for any errors.
- Ensure that your NIC is properly installed and functioning.

Installation Walkthrough

The remainder of this chapter will focus on the actual steps involved in the installation of Windows 95. If you like, you can follow this section while installing your new operating system. When variations occur, such as with the installation from floppy disk or CD-ROM, those variations will be followed until they rejoin the main installation line.

Getting Started

To install Windows 95, you will need to run SETUP.EXE. This program will first see if you have Windows (3.1 or 3.11) installed. Of course, if you have Windows installed, you should execute the SETUP.EXE program from within Windows. If you do not have it installed, you will see a message indicating that Windows 95 is copying the necessary files to your hard disk. It then creates a miniature Windows program, from which it will execute the remainder of the installation as though you had Windows installed on your system.

Installing from Floppy Disk

The SETUP.EXE program is located on the first of your Windows 95 installation disks. To execute the program, simply place the floppy diskette in either your A: or B: drive, change to that drive, and type **setup**.

Installing from a Network Drive

Make sure that your network card and drivers are installed and functioning normally, as mentioned previously. Log in to your network and change to the drive containing Windows 95. Of course, the methodology you use to reach the installation directory will be different for each network operating system; consult your network administrator before you begin searching for Windows 95. The administrator can tell you the exact directory the SETUP.EXE program will be in and how to get to that file. On a Novell NetWare network, for example, you should follow these steps:

1. Log in to the file server containing Windows 95. If you are on a NetWare 4.x network, you may need to issue a change of context command with the CX utility.

2. Map a drive, if necessary, to the volume containing the Windows 95 installation files. For example: MAP X:=KRITEN/SYS:.

3. Change to the appropriate drive and find the Windows 95 directory (or the directory created by your network administrator). You should then see a directory structure that looks something like Figure 4-3.

4. Change directories to the installation subdirectory and execute the program labeled SETUP.EXE.

Installing from a CD-ROM Drive

Since your system administrator most likely copied the Windows 95 installation CD-ROM directly to the network for the previous installation routine (installing from a network drive), you should execute the SETUP.EXE file from the installation subdirectory. However, instead of mapping a network drive before you execute the installation program, you need only access the CD-ROM drive, which is usually D: or E:.

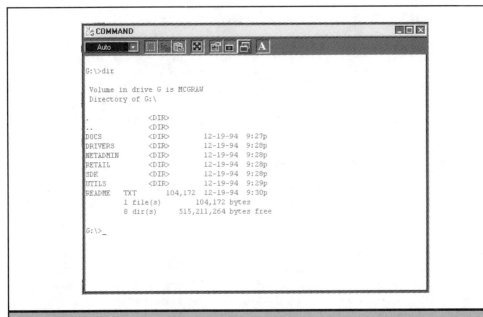

Figure 4-3.   *A typical directory structure for Windows 95*

Step One: Hardware Detection

After you have executed the SETUP.EXE program, you will be asked to insert the
second installation disk. If your system contains any OS/2 system files, the installation
routine will give you the option to exit. If you have simply forgotten to remove the
hidden and system files from a previous OS/2 installation, don't worry. Just select
Continue. Only do this, however, if you are sure that you do not have OS/2 installed
on the active partition. Since both operating systems boot directly at startup, both
cannot coexist. If you install Windows 95 on the same active partition as OS/2, your
OS/2 operating system will not boot.

If you are running any other Windows or DOS programs from a current version of
Windows (3.1 or 3.11), you will be given the option of either quitting the installation or
closing the active application. By failing to close any open applications, you will most
likely cause the Windows 95 installation process to fail. Therefore, if you have an
application open, simply use the ALT-TAB key sequence to change to each open
application, which you can safely close, and then return to the installation program.

If you are installing Windows 95 from floppy diskettes, you will be presented with
a screen like the one shown in Figure 4-4. This screen will be present during much of
the installation routine. If you want to exit from the installation process at any time,
simply click the box labeled Cancel in the upper right-hand corner. However, be aware
that after you begin copying files, you may need to reboot your system with the

Figure 4-4.   *Windows 95 main installation screen*

backup boot disk you created previously and re-create the MS-DOS system files on your hard drive.

During the hardware phase of the installation Windows 95 will interrogate your computer regarding its hardware configuration. Do not become alarmed if this process takes an extraordinary amount of time. Just watch the magnifying glass in the lower-left portion of the screen. As long as it keeps spinning, the installation process is progressing normally. If, however, it stops for an inordinate amount of time—longer than ten minutes—please refer to Appendix B, " Troubleshooting Windows 95."

Because Windows 95 comes with a fail-safe installation program that detects a previous installation attempt, if you exit from the Windows 95 installation prematurely, you will be presented with a screen asking whether or not you want to verify and update files or run a full setup routine. Select the "verify and update files" selection regardless of the situation because it will give you the opportunity to correct any system problems *during* the installation instead of *afterward*.

Configuration Questions

After Windows 95 scans your computer's hardware, it will present you with a welcome screen. At this point, you will be asked to either begin the actual installation process or to customize it. (See Figure 4-5.) Most people will choose to begin the installation as Windows 95 automatically installs the components necessary for full operating system functionality. However, if you have hard disk space concerns, or you think you may

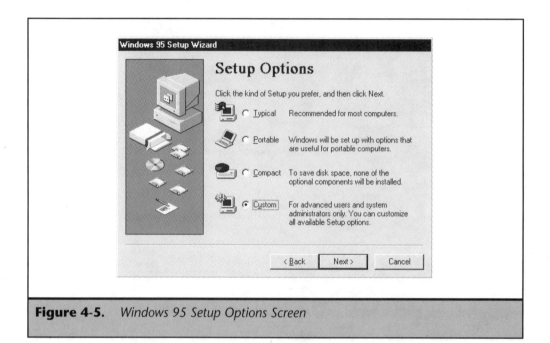

Figure 4-5. *Windows 95 Setup Options Screen*

not need to install all of the available components, you can remove certain components from the custom installation options area by using the Select Components screen after selecting Custom Installation from the Setup Options screen. (See Figure 4-5.). If you want to change the way Windows 95 functions as a network client, you can select the Network Options menu item. Likewise, if you want to verify or change the hardware devices Windows 95 detected during the hardware detection phase of the installation, you can select the Change Computer Settings button.

If you want to install Windows 95 in a different directory, you can specify the directory and drive. As discussed previously, this should only be done if you want both Windows 95 and a second operating system (3.1, 3.11, or Windows NT) to coexist on the same machine. To change the directory and drive, simply click the folder icon and enter the appropriate information. If you would like to have Windows 95 present Windows 3.1 program manager, you can select it here.

Before selecting your custom components, you will be asked to install support for a number of Microsoft communication programs, including Microsoft Mail, Fax, and the Microsoft Network. (See Figure 4-6.) If you forget to select any of these components, you will be able to either select them during the Select Components phase or after installation through the Windows 95 Control Panel.

Custom Installation Options
You can feel comfortable changing these settings because they can be modified later if you find that an option is needed after you complete the installation process.

Furthermore, Windows 95 will not let you remove any of the components necessary for the operation of the operating system. However, it is a good idea to follow the instructions outlined in this section. The different options you will be presented with are select components, network options, and change computer settings.

Select Components Click the button labeled Select Components if you want to either add or remove any of the Windows 95 elements. (See Figure 4-7.) In most instances, the only reason you will have for choosing not to install a certain component will be because you do not have enough disk space available. Of course, you may also choose to not install a component if you don't need it. A checkmark in the box to the left of the component's name indicates it will be installed. Click the box with the mouse to choose not to install the component. The selections you will see are: Communications, Disk Tools, MS Exchange, MS Fax, Multimedia, and MS Network. These selections include the following applications:

Applets You can install Windows 95's built-in calculator, paint program, WordPad, phone dialer, calendar, notepad, etc.

Desktop Bitmaps You can install bitmapped images that display as your Windows 95 desktop's background. You can, if you are short on disk space, choose not to install these images and instead utilize a solid color as your background.

File Synchronization With File Synchronization, you create what is called a *briefcase*, from which you can transfer files from your desktop computer to your

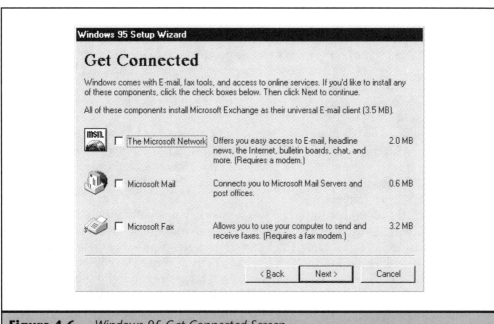

Figure 4-6. *Windows 95 Get Connected Screen*

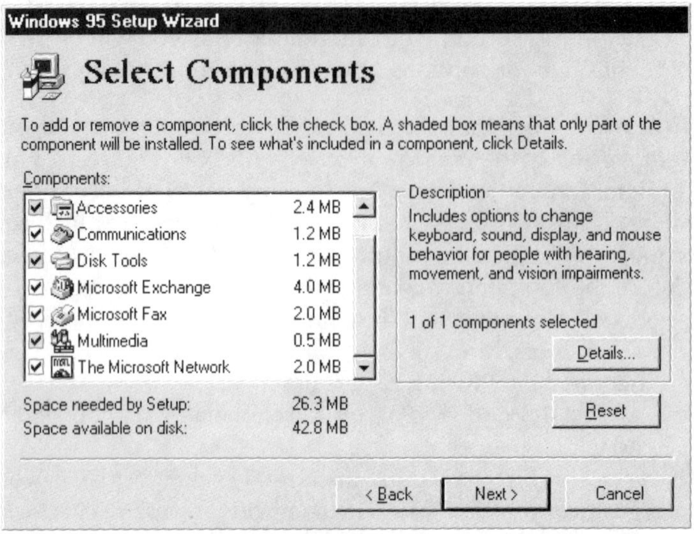

Figure 4-7. *Select Components*

notebook computer and back again. With this tool, you can be assured that you will always have the most current version of a selected file regardless of your current computer. If you do not have a notebook computer, you should not select this feature.

File Viewers By installing File Viewers you will be able to look at the contents of files through a quick-look document viewer. Only deselect this component if you are short on disk space.

Games If you have the time, install these old favorites (GO, Hearts, etc.).

Image Color Matching Unless you have a color printer, you will not need this component as it works solely to make your color documents look the same on your printer as they do on your screen. You may want to enable it if you will be formatting documents for service bureaus.

Exchange Client If you are attached to a network, you should install this item. It will allow you to not only send and receive messages, but also send and receive images, sounds, and even folders (which can contain any number of these items). Moreover, when Microsoft Information Exchange server ships, this component will act as its mail client. This mail client will be Messaging Application Programming Interface (MAPI) compliant; therefore, the Windows 95 info center will be able to send and receive messages from any MAPI-compliant messaging system such as Microsoft Mail, Davinci eMail, Lotus cc:Mail, etc.

Multimedia Sound and Video Clips   To fully enjoy this component, you need a sound card or a high-resolution color monitor. It will work without these two items; however, the clarity and resolution will not be extremely enjoyable.

Network Admin Tools   Install this item if you are attached to a network. It will help you monitor your system resources when they are accessed by other network users.

Remote Access   This highly beneficial component should be installed if you have a modem attached to your Windows 95 workstation. With it you will be able to dial into the Windows 95 computer and gain access to both your Microsoft or third-party network resources.

Screen Savers   Much like your desktop background images, deselecting this component will save disk space.

WinPad System   It is a good idea to install this enhanced document editor, as it contains many powerful word processing features similar to those of WordPad.

Network Options

After you have finished selecting Custom Components, you will be asked to install and configure networking software, shown in Figure 4-8. This is the most important element in the Windows 95 installation process, and the most confusing. Within this section you can change the network client software, the adapter definition, the network protocols, and the types of services you can use on your Windows 95 network client. Change them with care. If you select the wrong network interface card

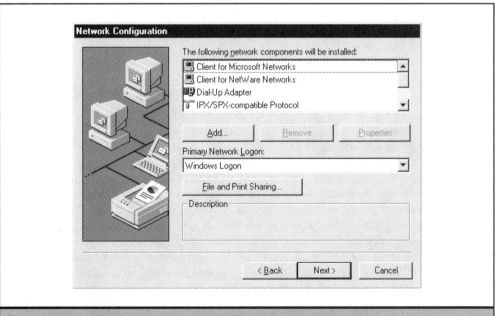

Figure 4-8.   *Windows 95 Network Configuration screen*

driver, your workstation will be unable to connect with your network. Likewise, if you change your network protocol to one not supported by your network operating system, you will not be able to utilize any network services.

Most of these items will not need further configuration. Windows 95, through its Plug and Play technology, will accurately determine your network interface card, network operating system, and predominant protocol.

You can also change your workstation's identification information. Here you can select your computer's name, the workgroup to which you belong, and give your workstation a brief description. For a more thorough explanation of these features, please refer to Chapter 5, "Windows 95's Networking Tools."

Client Configuration   To modify this setting, click the Client button. It will present you with a configuration screen containing all installed network client software. If you had network client software functioning before you began to install Windows 95, you will most likely see both a Microsoft network client and a third-party network client. From this option you can set one client as the default client. This will not prevent you from using any other network clients. It simply means that the default client loads and processes first.

You may want to select the button labeled Properties at this point to review its configuration. If you are using a Microsoft client, you will be able to choose the domain name of a primary Windows NT server and even choose to have Windows 95 use that server's password as your primary password. You can also have the client verify that your network resources are available when you first log on to Windows 95. Remember, any changes you make here can be undone or changed very easily after installation. By choosing the Properties button for a third-party network client (such as the Microsoft client for NetWare), you will be able to change your machine's context or preferred tree for NetWare 4.x using NetWare Directory Services (NDS). You can also enter the preferred server for NetWare 3.x networks as well as specify the first network drive letter you will have access to. Of course, if you are using a different network operating system client, your configuration options will vary according to that network operating system. For more information on networking on these different operating systems, please refer to Chapters 8, 9, and 10.

If you would like to add an entry, simply click the Add button and click the type of network you are interested in. Be aware that even though most cards support multiple protocols, and hence multiple network drivers, you cannot add two competing protocols for the same network operating system. For example, you cannot install both the LAN Server 2.0 client and the LAN Server 1.3 client. When you're done, click the OK button, and then click the Close button. This will save your configuration.

Adapter Configuration   Configuring your network adapter is not an easy task. If Windows 95 has detected your network interface card correctly, do not change any of these settings. You should merely verify that the detected configuration matches your actual configuration. If you jotted down the I/O base address, IRQ number, and DMA channel, click on the Properties button, highlight the adapter you wish to verify, and then select the tab labeled Resources, as shown in Figure 4-9. This screen displays the hardware configuration of your adapter card. Unless the network adapter was created

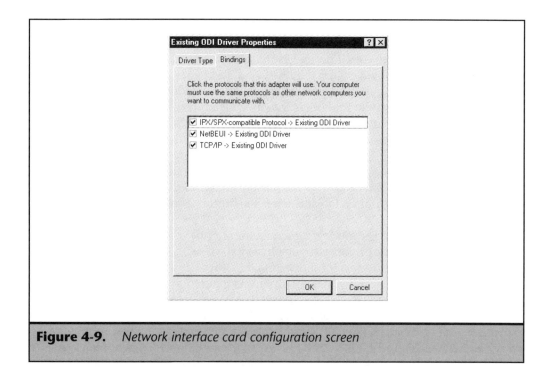

Figure 4-9. *Network interface card configuration screen*

specifically to be Plug and Play compliant, you may need to adjust these settings. The I/O base address and IRQ will most likely represent your card's default configuration (the one it is shipped with), so if you do not know your card's information, and if you have not modified that card's settings, you can just leave these numbers intact. On the other hand, if the card's settings do not match those listed on the Resource tab, make sure that you adjust them accordingly.

The Advanced tab contains information relating to Extended Industry Standard Architecture (EISA) machines, in which your network card's configuration information is held in your computer's memory and referenced through its slot number. If you have an EISA machine, ensure that this number corresponds to the actual slot in which your card is installed. If you are not sure, simply look at the back of your machine and count slots from the power supply (usually) until you reach the network adapter card.

By selecting the tab labeled Bindings, you can view and change the protocol stack(s) your network adapter will utilize. Usually, you will not need to change this setting; however, if it is incorrect, you must change the protocol configuration (discussed in the following section) and then return to this menu and change the default protocol by making a checkmark in the appropriate box. Remember, you can bind your card to multiple stacks, so don't worry if you see more than one protocol here.

The Driver Type tab lets you select the type of network driver you want to use. If you have a 32-bit network interface card, by all means select the Enhanced mode (32-bit and 16-bit) NDIS driver. If not, select the same driver type your workstation currently possesses. This will ensure that the installation goes more smoothly. If you are not sure about which type of driver you have (NDIS or ODI), ask your network administrator. An easy way to find out is to note which type of configuration file your machine uses to connect to the network. If it is called PROTOCOL.INI, then you have NDIS drivers. Conversely, if you have a configuration file called NET.CFG, then you have ODI drivers.

Protocol Configuration   This section is very easy to understand and configure, but if configured incorrectly it can cause you the most trouble. Select the button labeled Protocol from the Configuration tab and select the button labeled Properties for the default protocol.

The NetBIOS tab enables you to choose whether or not you want NetBIOS support running over your current protocol. If you already have NetBIOS installed as a full protocol, do not include support for it here. On the other hand, if you do not have another NetBIOS protocol, and you have programs that require such support, make sure that you select to install NetBIOS support. If you are not sure about the types of applications that may require this protocol, it will not hurt to install it anyway.

Selecting the Advanced tab will reveal a number of foreign-sounding entries for you to modify (see Figure 4-10), but do not worry, you will most likely not have to change any of these settings. The only one you should worry about during the

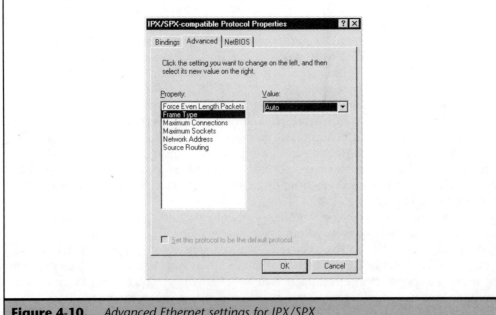

Figure 4-10.   *Advanced Ethernet settings for IPX/SPX*

installation process, if you connect to an Ethernet network, is the frame type field. To change this setting, click the properly labeled Frame Type and then select the down arrow on the drop-down box to the right labeled Value. The most important thing here is to ensure that the frame type selected matches that used by your network. If you are not sure, ask your network administrator. Or, you can check the contents of your PROTOCOL.INI or NET.CFG file for a line defining one of these frame types. Chances are if you are connected to a NetWare 4.x network, you will be running Ethernet 802.2. If you are running a NetWare 3.x network, on the other hand, you will most likely be running Ethernet 802.3.

The Bindings tab simply contains the components that will take advantage of this protocol. Do not install every listing, however, because different protocols may be used by different clients. For example, if you utilize a Microsoft network, such as a Windows for Workgroups 3.11 network, in addition to a Novell NetWare network, you may want to reserve the Microsoft Network Client component for the NetBEUI protocol. You would, therefore, only select the Microsoft Client for NetWare to run with your IPX/SPX protocol stack.

Service Configuration   This section covers the services, usually file and printer sharing, available to you on your network. This section will most likely be blank, so if you want to allow others to access your workstation's files or use a printer attached to your workstation, you will have to add network services support. If you have a Microsoft and NetWare network installed, you should click the Add button and then highlight the Microsoft item under the heading labeled Manufacturers. Here, you can either select to use just Microsoft file and print sharing or you can select Microsoft's NetWare client file and print sharing services. By selecting the NetWare model, you will only need to load the Microsoft NetWare client. You will not have to install a second Microsoft client. Both methods will accomplish the same tasks, so the choice is yours.

Identification Configuration

Before you leave the Network configuration portion of the custom installation routine, you may want to give your computer a name. Select the Identification tab under the window labeled Network and enter a computer name. You can name your machine anything you want. However, your network administrator may have a machine naming scheme, so inquire about this before completing this step. Second, you should tell Windows 95 to which workgroup it belongs. This is only necessary for Microsoft Windows networks; therefore, you can leave this blank if you do not have a Microsoft network. Also, if you are unsure about which workgroup your machine belongs to, you can just leave this blank and fill it in after the installation process has been completed. The description field is just a longhand identifier for your computer. It can be anything that will help you and others recognize your workstation within a Microsoft network.

Change Computer Settings   This section should not need any configuration. It contains all of the information Windows 95 detected during installation, as shown in Figure 4-11. You should carefully review these items, however, because if any are

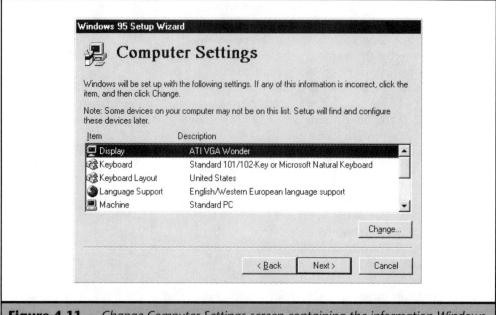

Figure 4-11. *Change Computer Settings screen containing the information Windows 95 gathered during the hardware detection phase of the installation*

incorrect, you may not be able to boot up Windows 95 after the installation process is complete. If any heading looks incorrect, click it and select the correct definition from the available options.

Do not worry if not all entries are defined. Some may appear as unknown devices. For example, the Monitor item may appear as (Unknown Monitor). If your Display item is correct, the Monitor item will have no impact upon the functionality of your installation. If you cannot find the appropriate definition for your installed hardware, you should contact Microsoft directly and ascertain from them the most compatible definition available under Windows 95.

As a special note, certain machines will not be automatically detected by the Windows 95 installation program. These machines are

- Zenith: Data Systems: all machines
- NCR: all 80386- and 80486-based machines
- AST Premium 386/25 and 386/33 (CPUID)
- Everex Step 386/25 (or compatible)
- IBM PS/2 Model L40sx
- NEC Powermate SX Plus
- Toshiba 5200
- Standard PC

If you have one of these machines, highlight the entry labeled Machine from the Item list and click the button labeled Change. Then simply select the appropriate machine.

Copying Windows 95 Component Files

Windows 95 will now ask you, as shown in Figure 4-12, if you want to create a Windows 95 boot disk. You should obtain a floppy diskette, insert it, and select to make the diskette as it will enable you to start and configure Windows 95 should anything go wrong during the installation. This disk will even help after Windows 95 is installed. For example, if you change your video driver to a drive that is not supported by your monitor, you will be able to boot up with the floppy diskette and change the settings back to normal. After you have gone over your configuration options, the rest of the installation will progress quickly. (See Figure 4-13.) First, Windows 95 will determine which files to copy to your hard disk. This could take some time. You should only worry if the Drum icon in the lower-left portion of the screen stops drumming for an inordinate amount of time—longer than five minutes.

If you are installing from a floppy diskette, you will now be asked to reinsert diskette number 1, following which you will be prompted to insert each diskette as needed. If you place the wrong diskette in the floppy drive, you will receive a small

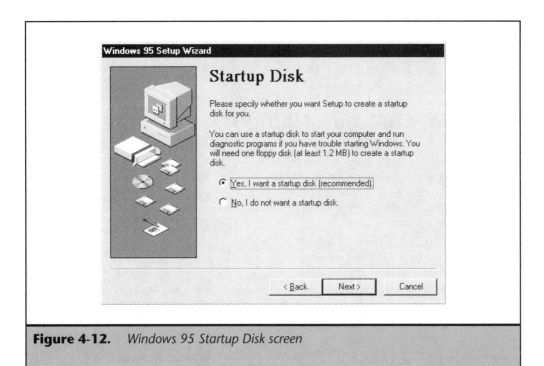

Figure 4-12. *Windows 95 Startup Disk screen*

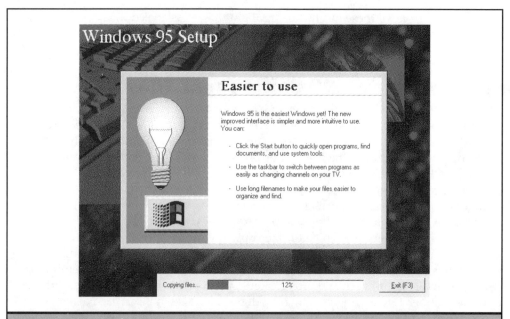

Figure 4-13.   *The third phase of the Windows installation process includes copying necessary files to your hard disk*

screen stating that the Windows 95 installation routine cannot find the desired file. In this situation, simply remove the diskette, replace it with the correct diskette, and click the OK button.

Final System Configuration

When all files have been copied to your hard disk, you will be prompted to remove all floppy diskettes, after which Windows 95 will reboot your machine under the Windows 95 operating system. Do not be alarmed if it takes a few moments to load. Windows 95 merely needs some extra time to configure your computer. The next time you boot up your machine, things will go much quicker.

Login to Windows 95

Once you see the background image for Windows 95, you will be prompted to enter a login name and a password. Since this is the first time you will have logged onto Windows 95, you can specify any name and password you choose. However, if you are utilizing pass-through security from either your NetWare or Windows NT server, you should enter the appropriate name and password just as though you were logging directly into either of those network operating systems. If the password is new, you will be asked to retype it for verification.

Configure a Modem

One of the last configuration chores for you to accomplish is to allow Windows 95 to detect and configure a modem. If you do not have a modem attached, but you want to install support for one you'll install later, select the button labeled Select. If you do not want to install a modem now, simply choose the button labeled Cancel. This will take you directly into Windows 95. This will not preclude you, however, from installing a modem at a later date.

After clicking Select, you should then highlight the modem that matches your own and choose the appropriate model. If your modem is not listed and you have a configuration disk for your modem, insert that disk into your computer and click the Have Disk button. After Windows 95 reads the configuration files for your modem, it will ask you to enter the communications port your modem will be using.

Installing a Printer

Before you can use Windows 95, you must install a printer. After your modem configuration is complete, you will be presented with a device installation Wizard. This program will walk you through the steps necessary to install and configure a printer. First it will ask you whether you want to install a network or a local printer. If you have both, don't worry. You can run the device driver installation Wizard from the Control Panel, which is under the Settings menu options of the Start button. (See Figure 4-14.) If you make a mistake along the way, you can click the Back button to return to the previous menu.

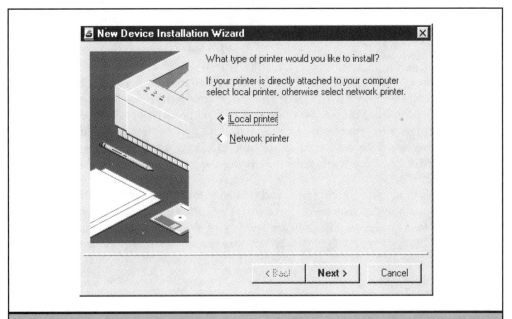

Figure 4-14. *Windows 95 printer installation Wizard*

After selecting which type of printer you want (network or local), you will be asked in a fashion similar to the modem installation procedure to name the manufacturer and the model of your printer. If your printer is not listed and you have the configuration disk for your printer, insert it, and click the Have Disk button. Finally, you will be asked to select the printer port you want your printer to utilize. If you are using a network printer, you will still see the LPT1, LPT2, etc., listings, but don't worry. Through the network client's redirector, these print jobs will traverse the network. When you are finished, Windows 95 will ask you to insert two to three disks from which it will install your printer. And that is all there is to it. You can even print a test page if you like.

Finally, Windows 95 will convert your old Windows program groups and program items into Windows 95 format and give you a welcome screen. To begin utilizing your operating system, all you need to do is click the button labeled Start at the lower-left corner of the screen.

Summary

Because Windows 95 is a true operating system that does not need to run on top of MS-DOS, you should fully prepare for its installation if you are installing on an existing system. First, you should create a complete backup of the machine upon which you will install Windows 95. You should then create a boot disk that contains all of the environment information and device drivers needed to run your computer should the hard drive fail during installation.

After you have secured your data, you should assess your computer's ability to run Windows 95 by checking its installed memory, hard disk space, and processor type. If all of these items are in order, you should write down your computer's hardware configuration, especially for your network adapter card (its I/O address, DMA channel, and interrupt number). Finally, before you install your new operating system, you should make sure that there are no known hardware compatibility problems (such as with PCMCIA cards) and check your hard drive for any errors.

The installation itself progresses quite easily through four phases: hardware detection, configuration questions, copying files, and final system configuration. The most important step involves the configuration questions. There, you will be able to verify the hardware Windows 95 detected during the previous phase and make any necessary changes.

The final two phases, copying files and final system configuration, will not require very much interaction if you have correctly configured your system during the configuration questions. The only questions you will have to answer regard the installation of a modem and a printer. You should not have any trouble with these configuration questions, as you will be walked through all aspects of their installation.

Chapter Five

Windows 95's Networking Tools

"He who is not liberal with what he has, does but deceive
himself when he thinks he would be liberal if he had more."
—W.S. Palmer

Now that you have Windows 95 installed and configured, you are ready to dive into connecting your system with others. If you didn't already do so during the installation procedure, the first thing you will want to do is to install the networking software that comes with Windows 95. This chapter will discuss all the important aspects of installing the network software and accessing other Windows 95 machines on the network.

Windows 95 includes, out of the box, support for other Microsoft networks. A Microsoft network may include a setup that is running LAN Manager, Windows NT workstation, Windows NT Server, and Windows for Workgroups. Windows 95 can be a client to each of these platforms, but it can also be a server. When you set up Windows 95 as a client and a server to other peer platforms, you have a peer-to-peer network.

Windows 95 also includes support for NetWare networks. You can use the Microsoft Client for NetWare, as included with Windows 95, or you can use the same real-mode IPXODI drivers you used with DOS and Windows 3.1. Because these drivers only provide 16-bit network support, you will probably want to load the Enhanced-Mode NDIS drivers from Windows 95. Either way, you will be able to access all the network resources you need. You will be able to browse the network, access network files, print to network printers, etc. By using the Network Neighborhood icon and command line utilities discussed later in this chapter, you will be able to do all of the things you did when you were a DOS and Windows 3.1 client, and more. For more information about accessing NetWare networks, see Chapter 10, "Networking with NetWare."

Support for networks other than those made by Microsoft and Novell is available, but the client software is not included in Windows 95. For access to these networks, you will need to get the appropriate drivers from that network operating system (NOS) vendor. But, with their software you will be able to browse the network, access files, and print to network printers just like you can with Microsoft and Novell networks.

Preparing to Connect

Before you can access any of the network resources on the network, you must first install the networking software. This chapter assumes you have already installed the networking hardware you need to connect to your LAN, including the network interface card (NIC) and whatever cable you need. Before you install the networking software of Windows 95, however, you should know the settings of the card you installed, including interrupt, port address, memory address, and direct memory access (DMA) channel. (Some cards do not require you to set memory addresses or DMA channels, so these may not be available for your configuration.) Of course, if you have a Plug and Play compliant system, Windows 95 will already be aware of these values and you will not need to provide them. If not, however, get ready to do some configuring.

Configuring Network Components

To install the networking software of Windows 95, you need to access the Network applet from the Control Panel. The Control Panel is shown in Figure 5-1. You can access the Control Panel a number of different ways. If you double-click the My Computer icon on your desktop, you will see a window with a number of different icons representing the resources of your computer. The Control Panel is one of those. To launch it, simply double-click the icon.

You can also get to the Control Panel by clicking your mouse on the Start button on the leftmost side of the Taskbar. Click on Start, then Settings, then finally on Control Panel. Another way to open the Control Panel is to type **control** at a command prompt. This is possible because Windows 95 supports launching Windows programs from a DOS prompt.

Once you have started Control Panel, double-click the Network icon. This will open up a box that will allow you to install or configure any of the software-based networking components of Windows 95. The box has three tabs across the top, which represent different configuration screens. Right now, leave the screen where it was when you opened it, with the first tab highlighted. This tab (Configuration) is shown in Figure 5-2.

The Configuration window contains four types of information, each representing an important networking component. The first element represents the client software

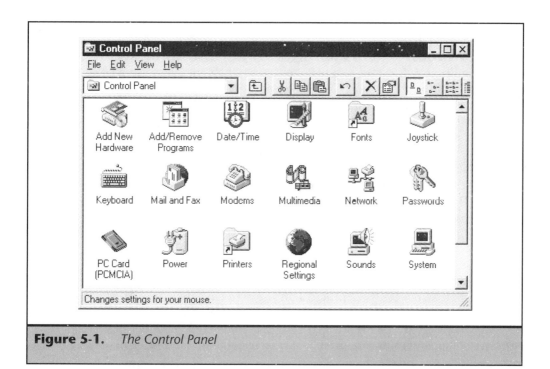

Figure 5-1.   *The Control Panel*

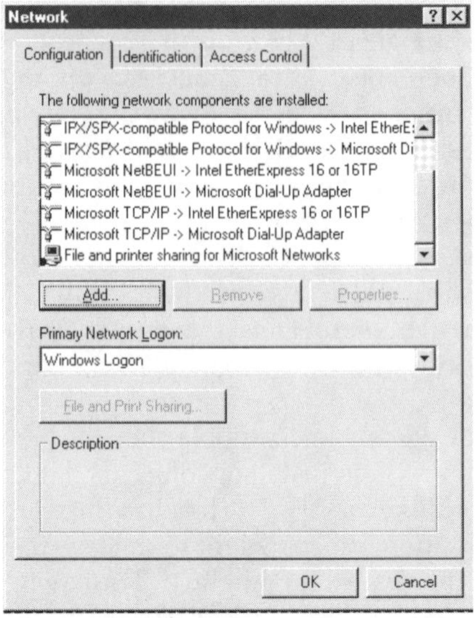

Figure 5-2. *The Network Configuration window*

you will be using. If you are running Windows 95 as a client to NetWare, Banyan VINES, or Windows NT, this is where you install that capability. Because Windows 95 supports multiple redirectors, you may have more than one client listed here. This means you could simultaneously access Windows NT and NetWare servers from the same machine without having to reset the client software.

The next element represents the kind of network adapter you have installed in the system. From this item, you can configure the interrupt, port settings, etc., so they match the properties of the card you installed. Of course, it's possible to have more than one NIC in your machine. If you need or want to install several protocols and clients on your machine, you may want to separate them between two or more network adapters. This will give you the best performance if you plan on accessing several network resources quite heavily.

Speaking of protocols, the next section of this Configuration screen is where you define which protocols you want to load. Protocols, as you learned from Chapter 2, "Networking Basics," is the language the network traffic speaks as it makes its way from one machine to another. As with the other network components, it is possible to load more than one network protocol on your system at one time. You have several protocols to choose from, but the two most popular protocols in use right now are IPX/SPX and TCP/IP. IPX/SPX is generally used in Novell networks; however, it can be used in other environments as well. TCP/IP is great for large-scale networks that require a lot of routing between different LANs. However, it is often used in smaller networks that require no routing because of its open architecture and manageable properties.

The final section of the Configuration screen is entitled Services and applies to Windows 95 as a peer server on the network. In this section you decide what services you want your machine to provide on the network. You will learn more about this section in the next chapter, "Windows 95 As a Network Server." For now, you will learn the things you need to configure to make Windows 95 an efficient and reliable client on the network.

Client Software

In the Configuration window, you can see the network clients installed on your computer (see Figure 5-3). If you installed network support when you first set up Windows 95, you will already have one or two entries in the list. You can delete one or more of the clients by highlighting the entry and clicking the Remove button.

Highlight the client selection, and click the Add button to see what other options there are for client support in Windows 95. Another window appears titled Select Network Client, shown in Figure 5-4. The window is divided into two sections: the different network vendors on the left, and different network clients on the right. As you highlight a NOS vendor, different client options appear. Some of the options are for the 32-bit protected-mode drivers of Windows 95. Others provide support for

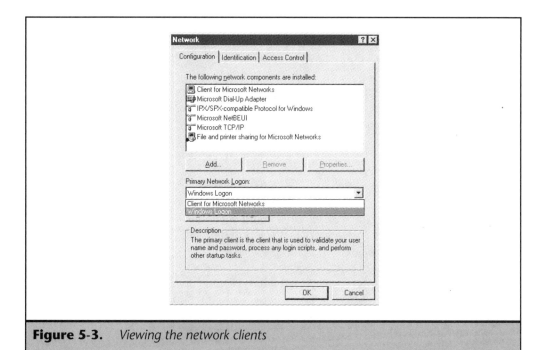

Figure 5-3. *Viewing the network clients*

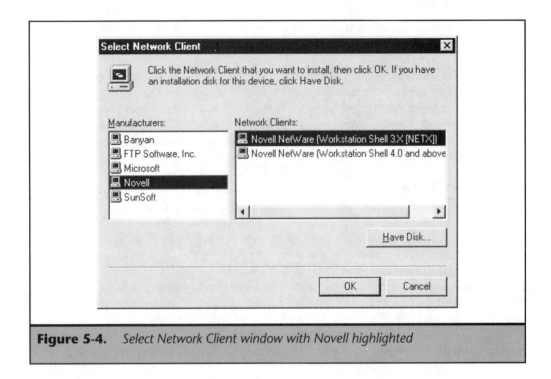

Figure 5-4.   *Select Network Client window with Novell highlighted*

16-bit real-mode drivers you may have used with DOS and Windows 3.1. What is the difference?

These protected-mode drivers will give you 32-bit network driver support, which means better performance. Additionally, these drivers run as Windows virtual device drivers (VXDs) and therefore take up no conventional memory. And since the operating system and the drivers are running in protected mode rather than real mode, there is no overhead associated with switching between real and protected-mode operation. Again, this means better performance.

So unless you have a specific application that requires use of 16-bit real-mode drivers, you are much better off using the drivers included with Windows 95. This backwards compatibility, however, ensures that if your system was a successful network client under DOS and Windows 3.1, it will be a successful client in Windows 95 as well.

Most of these NOSes will be covered in other chapters within this book, but take some time to look at a couple. First, click the Novell entry in the Manufacturers list. If you have elected to use real-mode ODI drivers in conjunction with either the NetWare shells, these are the clients you want to select. Windows 95 supports both the NETX shell popular with NetWare 3.12 and the VLM shell used in NetWare 4.x.

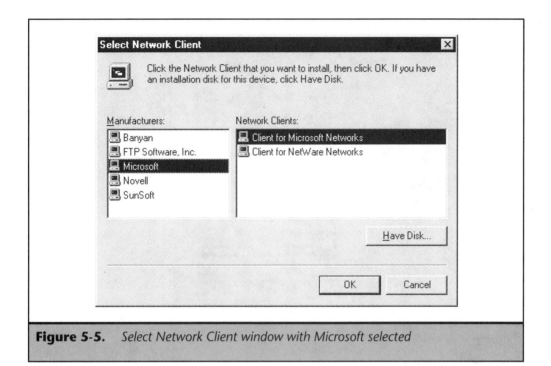

Figure 5-5. *Select Network Client window with Microsoft selected*

Next, look at the options listed under the Microsoft entry, as shown in Figure 5-5. Since NetWare is currently such a popular network operating system to support, Microsoft included a 32-bit protected-mode driver needed to access NetWare networks.

Another item in the model list is the client for Microsoft Networks. This is the piece of client software that you will most likely use to connect to all the Windows NT, Windows for Workgroups, and Windows 95 machines on the network. It is a 32-bit protected-mode driver, and therefore will give you better performance and all the other benefits just mentioned. However, in case you have some software that requires you to use a real-mode driver to connect to other Microsoft servers, select the Real mode MS-Net Compatible option. Most software in existence today will work fine with the enhanced-mode drivers.

If you click the other entries in the left-hand window, you will see client software options for several other networks. For now, concentrate on connecting your machine on a peer level with other Windows 95 or Windows for Workgroups computers.

With the Client for Microsoft Networks entry highlighted in the Network window, click the Properties button. What you see in the Properties window, shown in Figure 5-6, depends on which client you want to configure, but the Microsoft Network client has just two entries that you need to make decisions about. The first one is whether or not you want to log onto a Windows NT Server domain. If you will be running Windows 95 in your office and you are using an NT server with all of its security

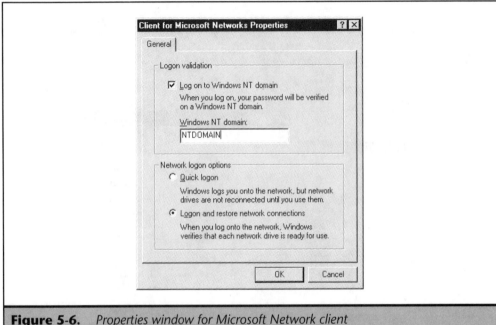

Figure 5-6. *Properties window for Microsoft Network client*

features, you will want to click on the box that forces Windows 95 to log onto the domain. You will then need to fill in the name of the domain in the field below. If you want a list of domains on the network, click the down arrow next to the field and a drop-down box will appear with domains listed.

Just because you have Windows NT servers on the network, it does not mean that you have to log onto their domain. It is still possible to access files on an NT server without doing so. However, the network manager might want to control things like user accounts and access rights to certain network resources. If this is the case, you should log onto the domain.

The other configurable option in this window defines whether or not Windows 95 will quick connect to the network. With the Quick Connect option selected (the default), Windows 95 will automatically try to log you on to every resource you have specified. With Verify Connect selected, Windows 95 will first try to confirm that the resource is available before it attempts to log you on to a connection. Generally, unless you are never sure which resources will be available when you start Windows 95, you will want to leave the selection on Quick Connect. You're done configuring the client software—now press OK, then Close until you return to the Network window. If you changed any of the Client software settings, you may be prompted to insert the appropriate diskettes so Windows 95 can copy the necessary files. Windows 95 will also probably warn you that any changes you made will not take effect until you restart the computer. If you want to, you can do that now, or you can continue on and configure the network adapter.

Configuring Your Network Adapter

If you haven't already installed your NIC, you should do so now. If it is a Plug and Play compliant card, all you need to do is shut down Windows 95, turn your machine off, put the card in, and turn the computer back on. If it is not a Plug and Play card, the process is a little more complicated. The easiest way to work it out is to use the New Device Wizard in the Control Panel. This will take you through all the steps of setting up the card to work with Windows 95.

If you already have the card installed, and we'll assume by now that you do, you can set it up by highlighting the adapter selection from the Network dialog box, shown in Figure 5-7. If the card was installed prior to setting up Windows 95, you may have an entry here already. To add a card, click the Add button, highlight the adapter selection, and click on the Add button again.

Like the Select Network Client window, this window is divided into two sections. On the left side is a list of NIC manufacturers. Next to it on the right is a list of cards that the highlighted company makes. Click on the manufacturer in the list labeled 3Com. The Network Adapters box will fill with entries showing the cards 3Com makes that currently work with Windows 95. (See Figure 5-8.) If you want to install a card driver right now, go ahead and select it and click on the OK button with your mouse. If your adapter was already installed, just click the Cancel button twice.

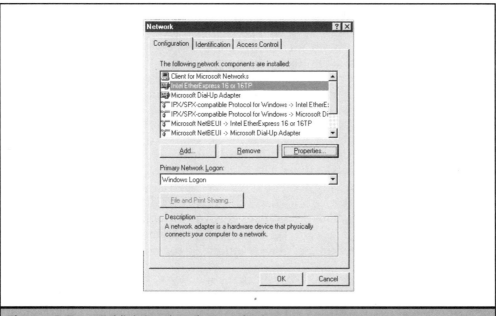

Figure 5-7.   *Highlighting the adapter selection*

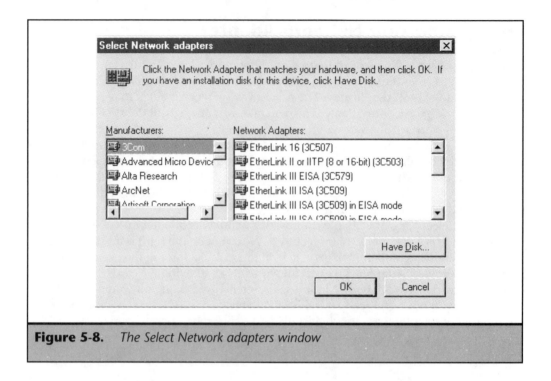

Figure 5-8.   *The Select Network adapters window*

Make sure the card is highlighted, then click the Properties button. You will be faced with another window, called Properties for Intel Ether Express 16 or 16TP, or whatever name matches your card. This window, shown in Figure 5-9, has four tabs across the top—Driver Type, Bindings, Advanced, and Resources. To connect to a network, you really need two pieces of software. You need the client software that was described in the last section. And you need an adapter driver.

Driver Type   When you set the driver type for the NIC, you have three options—Enhanced mode NDIS driver, Real mode NDIS driver, and Real mode ODI driver. The real mode drivers are 16-bit and need only be used if you have software that requires use of a real mode driver. The NDIS drivers are most commonly used in Microsoft or IBM LAN Server networks. You may have used NDIS drivers with Windows for Workgroups or a LAN Manager client. The ODI drivers are most commonly used in NetWare networks. Both driver types give you the opportunity to load multiple protocols on the same card. Where possible, you should select Enhanced mode NDIS driver for connecting to other Windows 95 computers.

Bindings   In order for the network driver to be functional, it has to be bound to a protocol. By default, Windows 95 installs two protocols—IPX/SPX-compatible Protocol for Windows and Microsoft NetBEUI, as shown in the Bindings tab in Figure 5-10. If you have installed just one network card, it will have to be bound to both

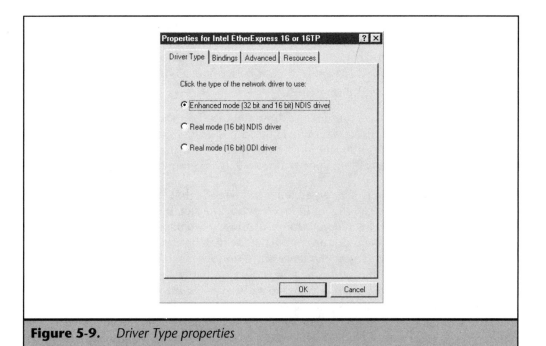

Figure 5-9.   *Driver Type properties*

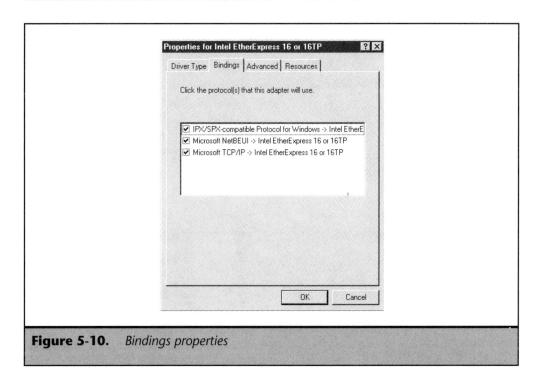

Figure 5-10.   *Bindings properties*

protocols. If you install any other protocols, they too should be bound to the network adapter. You may, if you wish, install two network adapters in your computer and bind one protocol to each. This will give you better performance if both protocols are very active on your network. However, if your network use is average, one card bound to both protocols is probably sufficient.

Advanced Some adapters present an additional Configuration tab labeled Advanced. This tab lets you set parameters that are specific to the selection adapter. With the EtherExpress 16, for example, you can specify how the I/O channel should be used and what type of cabling your Windows 95 workstation uses (see Figure 5-11).

Resources This section is where you tell Windows 95 what settings your card is configured for. If you have a Plug and Play network adapter, these settings will be automatically set for you. Even if you don't, Windows 95 will attempt to determine these settings during the network driver part of the installation. However, detecting the settings of a NIC is not an exact science and Windows 95 may not be able to determine the correct configuration, so you should probably check the Resources section of the Adapter Properties window to make sure the information is listed correctly. The Resources card is shown in Figure 5-12.

What settings you have to enter are determined by the type of NIC you have. Almost all adapters require an I/O Base Address (or Port Address) and an Interrupt

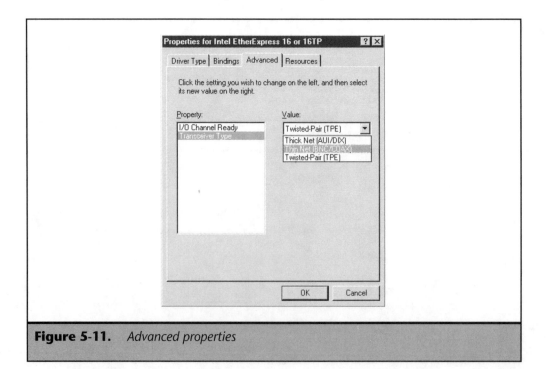

Figure 5-11. *Advanced properties*

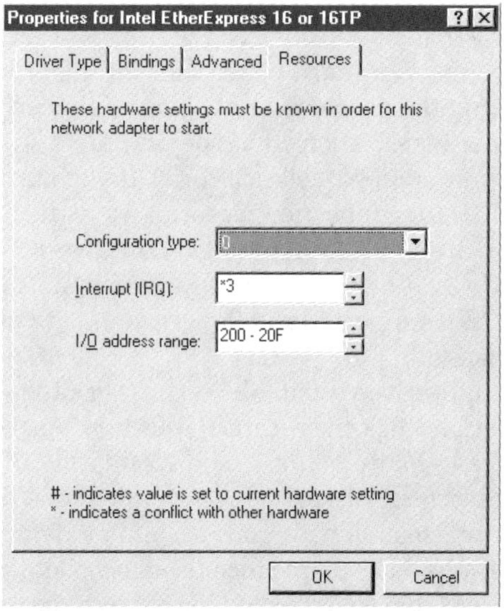

Figure 5-12. *Resources properties*

(or IRQ). Depending on the card you installed, you may also need to enter a value for a DMA Channel or a memory address.

If the field next to Configuration type is set to 0, then the values will be grayed out indicating that you cannot change them. This makes sense. You can't change the current configuration because if you changed it, it wouldn't be current any more. So, before you can enter new values you must change the configuration type. To do this, click the down arrow next to the field. Some cards have preset types—type 5 might be interrupt 5, port 360. But not all cards do. If the configuration type your card is set for is not listed, click on the 0 and define it yourself.

Pay attention to the numbers you enter in the fields. A pound sign (#) next to the number indicates that the value you entered matches what Windows 95 thinks the current setting is. If there is an asterisk (*) next to the value you entered, Windows 95 is telling you that value is used by another hardware device on the system, and if you choose it, you will probably experience problems due to a conflict. Bear in mind, however, that Windows 95 is not perfect in its detection of hardware settings.

That does it for the Adapter settings. Click the OK button and you will find yourself back at the Network window. As before, if you made some driver changes, Windows 95 may prompt you to insert a diskette or two so it can copy the necessary files to the system. Then it may ask you to reboot the machine. If you want to do that now, go ahead.

Protocols

Windows 95 automatically installs support for the IPX/SPX, TCP/IP and NetBEUI protocols. In the past, Microsoft primarily used the NetBEUI (which is a form of NetBIOS) protocol for network communication. However, because of the fact that it cannot be routed across networks, Microsoft is beginning to show more support for the IPX/SPX protocol, common in Novell networks. If you currently have Microsoft clients that rely on NetBEUI for connection, you can leave the NetBEUI protocol installed. However, if you are connecting to other Windows 95 machines, Windows for Workgroups server, Windows NT servers, or Novell NetWare servers, choose IPX/SPX. All of these NOSes support it, and it gives your network the ability to expand with the least amount of hassle.

To see what protocol options are available to you, click the Add button in the Network window and double-click the protocol selection. As before, the window is divided between two boxes—Manufacturers and Network Protocols. Click on the Microsoft entry in the Manufacturers list and look at your options. (See Figure 5-13.) In addition to the two protocols installed on your system by default, there is a third entry—Microsoft TCP/IP. The TCP/IP protocol is an excellent protocol to use in very large networks because it is highly routable and highly manageable. It is also the protocol most widely used in UNIX-based systems, so if you plan on connecting to one of those systems, you will probably need to install this protocol.

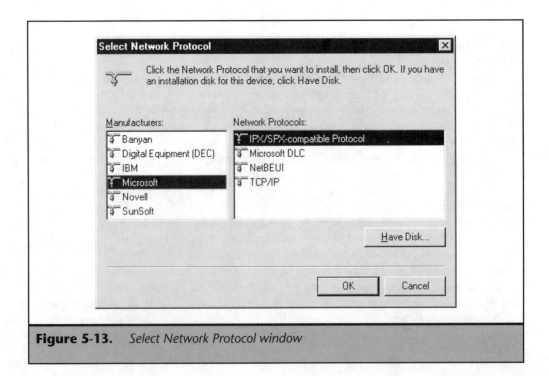

Figure 5-13. *Select Network Protocol window*

Click the Cancel button twice to return to the Network window. Since a protocol defines the rules that two computers use to communicate, how the computers are configured is very important. Highlight a Microsoft NetBEUI protocol and click the Properties button with your mouse. The screen that opens should look familiar. (See Figure 5-14.) Just as a protocol needs to be bound to the network driver, it needs to be bound to the client and server software as well. If Microsoft Network client is the only piece of client software you installed, then you should see it in this window.

Depending upon your configuration, you may also have an entry entitled Microsoft Network file and print sharing. This means that you plan on using this protocol to not just connect to other network resources, but to share your file and print resources with others on the network. If you found the need to do so, you could use one protocol for your client software and another for your server utilities; however, most people will use the same for both.

Click the Advanced tab at the top of the window and you will be able to set the values for some key NetBEUI properties. (See Figure 5-15.) The first is Maximum Sessions, the second is NCBS. Unless you come across a piece of software that requires you to change these settings, you can just leave them at their default values.

Click the OK button to return to the Network window. Use your mouse to highlight the IPX/SPX-compatible protocol for Windows and click the Properties button. Check out the three tabs across the top—Bindings, Advanced, and NetBIOS. The first one you will see is NetBIOS, shown in Figure 5-16. Windows 95 has the

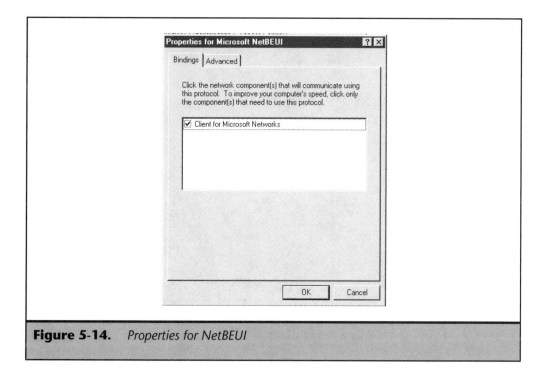

Figure 5-14.   *Properties for NetBEUI*

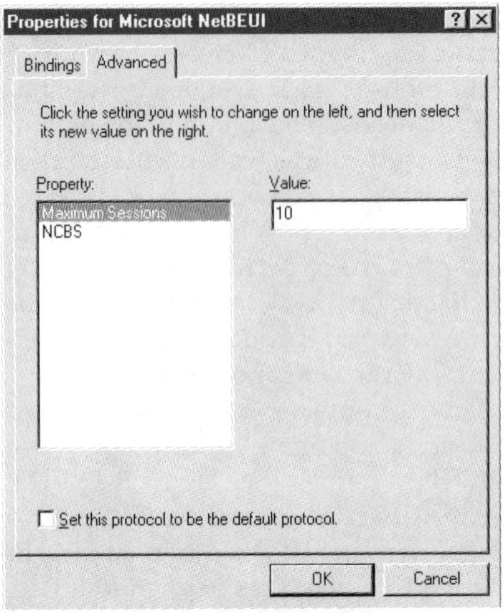

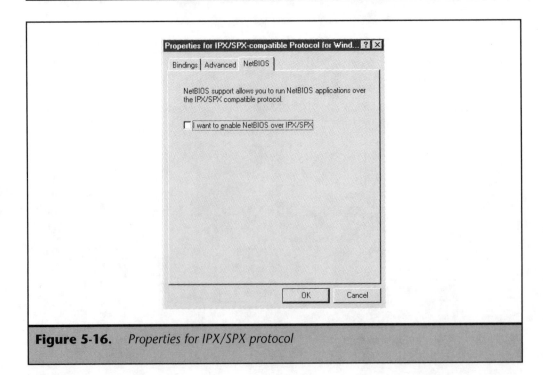

Figure 5-15. *Advanced properties for NetBEUI*

Figure 5-16. *Properties for IPX/SPX protocol*

capability to run the NetBIOS protocol over the IPX/SPX transport layer. That way, if you want to use IPX/SPX for the majority of your network connectivity, but you have an application or two that requires NetBIOS, you can effectively combine the two.

The Bindings tab is similar to the one you saw under NetBEUI. The Advanced settings (Figure 5-17) option has a few more values to configure. As mentioned above, you can probably leave these at their default values unless you install an application that requires a change. You will, however, want to check the value for Frame Type. If the protocol is the language that computers speak as they communicate, the frame is the vehicle that carries the message. It is essential that the frame type be identical among all machines that need to communicate.

The default frame type for IPX/SPX when installed by Windows 95 is 802.2. This is also the default frame type for all new NetWare networks. However, many networks are still using 802.3, so if you are having trouble seeing some servers, this could be the problem. Change the frame type and you will be set. Incidentally, if you are wondering what frame type most of your network traffic is using, check with your network administrator. To learn more about setting up your Windows 95 machine as a server, see the next chapter, "Windows 95 as a Network Server."

Identifying Your System on the Network

Back at the Network dialog box, you have setup options to consider other than those found in the Configuration window. Click the Identification tab on the top of the window

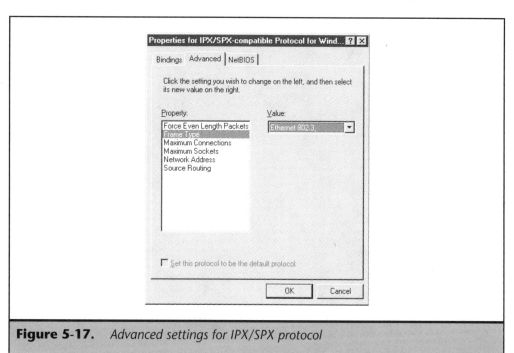

Figure 5-17.   *Advanced settings for IPX/SPX protocol*

and see what there is for you to set there. (See Figure 5-18.) These items were probably filled in while you were installing Windows 95. However, you may need to change them from time to time. The first item is Computer name. This can be whatever you want. This is how your system is identified to others on the network. The other field is where you enter your workgroup name. The default value for this field is simply WORKGROUP, so you will probably want to change this, if for no other reason than to come up with a more exciting name. Kind of like naming your dog "Dog." Workgroups are simply a way to portion a group of users on a network. You will probably want to make different workgroups for each of the departments in your office, for example. Just because some users are in another workgroup, that doesn't mean that you can't access their network resources. You can enter any type of name in the Computer Description field, but it should be meaningful to you and others who may access your workstation over the network.

Securing Your Machine

Windows 95 has a couple of different methods it uses to control access to shared resources on the network. If you click the Access Control tab from the Network window, the dialog box you will see shows two levels of security. (See Figure 5-19.) The first one, Share-level access control, is selected by default and allows you to define a password for each shared resource on the network. That means that if you want to share your \DOCS directory, you can use a password to control who will have access

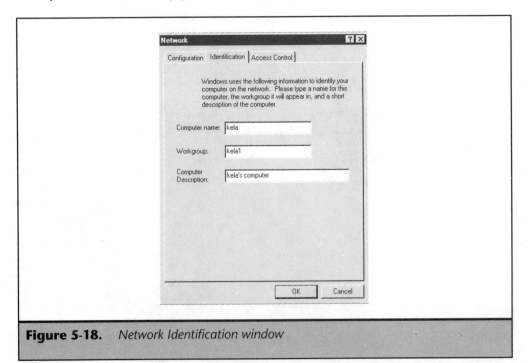

Figure 5-18. *Network Identification window*

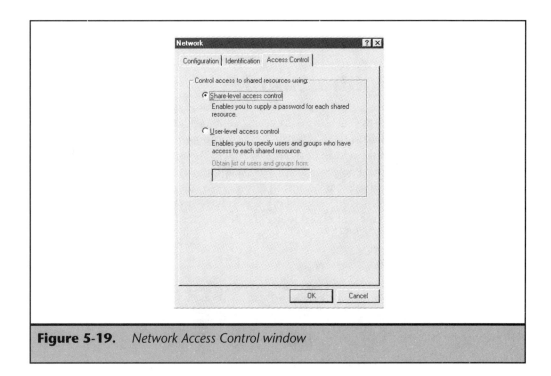

Figure 5-19.   *Network Access Control window*

to that directory and what kind of access they will have. If you want to grant some users full access, you can assign a full access password. If you want to provide other users with read-only access, you can assign a different password for read-only rights.

These are the same access controls used in Windows for Workgroups and they have their benefits and drawbacks. On the plus side, you can control who has access to the resource by only giving the passwords to certain people. But this can be a nightmare to manage. If you change your mind about one user, you have to change the password, then inform the remaining users of the change.

The other method, User-level access control, is more popular in large networks. With this method, you grant access to shared resources on a user-by-user basis. Windows 95 is not secure enough to keep its own user list effectively, so you must use the user and group lists from another source, usually a Windows NT server. Those users that wish to share a directory can specify which users or groups shall have access. The user name and password you use when you log onto the Microsoft Network is used when you request access to a network resource. If your name is not on the list, you won't be able to connect to that directory.

Although User-level access control may seem more orderly than Share-level access control, you must keep in mind that neither makes your network very secure. Windows 95 was not designed to handle highly restrictive security requirements. Anyone interested in getting to your computer's files is not going to be stopped by the security features of Windows 95. Remember, all anyone needs to do to access your computer's files is put a boot disk in the floppy drive and reset the machine.

Network Neighborhood

Now that you have all your network parameters configured, you can begin checking out all the resources Windows 95 has given you access to. The first place you will probably want to begin is with the Network Neighborhood window, shown below. Double-click that icon to take a look at what's available. You will see a few different types of icons. The Network Neighborhood only displays servers that are in your current workgroup. If you have connected to other types of networks, like NetWare, you may see other servers as well—especially if you have mapped to those servers in the past. For more information about using the Network Neighborhood in other network environments, see Chapter 9, "Networking with Windows NT," and Chapter 10, "Networking with NetWare."

Even though not all servers on your network may be listed initially in the Network Neighborhood, you still have access to them. The first icon in the window is the Entire Network. If you click this icon, you will see other domains and workgroups on your network, of which you may not be a member. So, if you don't see a server in the initial Network Neighborhood window, chances are you will find it by looking at the Entire Network window, shown here:

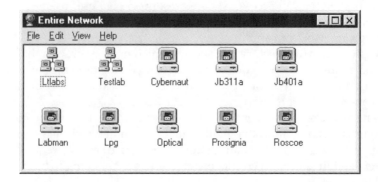

Another icon you will probably see in the Network Neighborhood window is the Remote Access icon. This is for the remote access services (RAS) of Windows 95. RAS is a feature of Microsoft networks that allows users to access the LAN from isolated sites. RAS has a number of uses, and you will probably want to familiarize yourself with this tool. You can use RAS to access the files or programs you need while you are on the road. You can use it to set up a wide area network (WAN) link between two networks. Or you can use RAS to hook two machines together with a null modem cable attached to their serial ports. It is a flexible and worthwhile way to expand your network services beyond the standard network cable.

Browsing the Network

So, if you can see the other servers on the network, what do you do with them? You can access any of the directories or printers the owners of those machines have shared for your use. To do this, simply use your mouse to double-click the Server icon and you will see the names of all the shared directories and printers that computer has configured.

A Windows 95 server on the network may have a shared directory called DOCS. If you double-click on that directory folder, you will see all the files on that machine that are in the DOCS folder. Additionally, you will see any directories under the DOCS directory as well. The important thing to consider here is that browsing through the files and directories on a shared network drive is just like browsing through the files on your own machine. Of course, you will only be able to see the resources you have security rights to. Windows 95 may prompt you for a password as you browse around, but other than that it will seem the same as looking through your own directories.

Creating Shortcuts to Other Servers

If you access the files on a certain server regularly, you may want to create a shortcut to that directory on your own desktop. The procedure for doing this is simple. Click that directory with the right button of your mouse. Then, with the button held down, drag the directory to your desktop. When the icon is where you want it, release the right mouse button. Windows 95 will immediately display a menu, shown below. Using the left mouse button, click on the words, "Create Shortcut(s) Here." This will provide you with an active link to the shared directory.

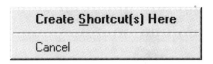

Mapping Drives to Other Servers

Creating a shortcut to a shared directory works great for documents, but if there is an application you need to access on a network server, you may need to map a drive to

that resource. Mapping a drive means that you assign the shared directory a letter of
the alphabet so you can see it just like you would your C: drive. Some applications,
in fact, require you to map a network drive for them to run properly. The process is
painless, and is in fact built in to the interface of Windows 95.

To map a network drive to a shared directory, first click the directory's icon with
your right mouse button. You will see a menu appear with a number of options. One
of the options should be Map Network Drive. Click this option with your left mouse
button and the Connect Network Drive dialog box shown here will open up with a
couple of options:

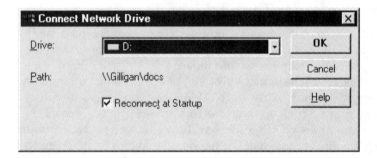

The first decision you must make is what drive letter to use to access this resource.
Windows 95 will default to the next available drive letter, but by clicking the down
arrow next to the Drive field, you will be able to choose almost any letter you wish.
The next option lets you configure whether or not you want to connect to this directory
every time you enter Windows 95. If this is a resource you will be connecting to often,
go ahead and click the box by Reconnect at Startup and Windows 95 will automatically
map the drive for you next time you boot your machine.

Connecting to Network Printers

Connecting to printers on your Windows 95 network is as easy as connecting to
directories. There are a couple different ways to do it—the standard way and the
shortcut. First, the standard way. Open the My Computer icon, then double-click the
Printers Folder. You will see the dialog box shown here:

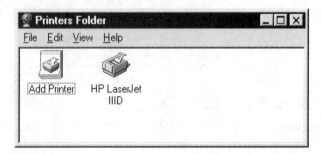

The first icon in that folder says Add Printer. Double-click it to start the Add Printers Wizard. Click the Next button at the bottom of the window. The Wizard asks you if you are installing a new local printer or a new network printer. In this case, you are installing a new network printer, so click the Network Printer button and click the Next button again.

The next thing the Wizard wants to know is how to get to this printer. In other words, the network path. Windows 95 uses the universal naming convention (UNC) format for accessing network devices:

*server**resource*

That's two backslashes, the server name, another backslash, and the resource name. So, in this case you would type two backslashes, then whatever server is sharing the printer, another backslash, then the share name of the printer that the user on that server defined.

Then the Wizard asks you to give this connected printer a name. You can usually leave the name at the default value, but if that name is taken in your printers folder, you will have to enter something different. Click the Finish button at the bottom of the window and you are done. Windows 95 automatically begins copying the necessary printer drivers from the machine where the printer is connected. This saves you a lot of hassle from having to insert a number of installation disks.

After the installation is complete, you will see a dialog box recommending that you test the printer driver and connection. It is probably a good idea to do this so that you know whether or not the printer is working. Incidentally, if you are having some problems, Windows 95 will launch a troubleshooting tool that will take you through a number of steps to try to determine what the problem might be. It will prompt you to do things like check your connections, check to make sure the printer has paper, and reinstall the driver. Somewhere along the way you should be able to find the problem. But if you are sure there is no problem and want to skip the printer test, click the Skip Test button.

You will then be returned to the Printers Folder, where the printer you just installed will appear. If you have a number of printers installed and want to make this new one the default printer for all your applications, click the Printer icon with your right mouse button. A few lines down the list is the option titled Set As Default. Click this entry with your left mouse button and all your applications will be configured to print to this printer, unless you instruct otherwise.

Here is another way to add a network printer that skips a couple of the steps above.

1. First you need to open the Network Neighborhood folder. Double-click the server that is attached to the printer you want to connect. You should see the printer in the window along with the shared directories.

2. Double-click the printer and the Wizard will pop up and ask you what you want to name this printer for your system.

3. Leave the default name or select a new one, then click the Finish button at the bottom of the window. Windows 95 will automatically copy the drivers from the server as before and prompt you to perform the printer test.

4. When you are done, you can open your Printers Folder and the printer you added will be there. Just a hint—you will always be able to tell network printers from locally attached printers in the Printers Folder by the icon. The network printers have an icon with a cable going through it to indicate that it's only available through the network.

Exploring the Network with the Command Line

By now you should be a pro at connecting to network servers, browsing through network directories, mapping network drivers, and connecting to network printers. All of what you have learned so far in this chapter has made use of Windows 95's graphical user interface (GUI). Whereas this is an extremely easy and effective way to explore your network—especially for new users—Windows 95 has another way to explore. It's not quite as sexy, but it can come in handy. Using the command line, you can do almost everything you did with the GUI, plus a few other things.

NET Commands

The command line utilities you can use to access network resources are all a subset of the NET utility. To execute command line functions, you need to first open a command prompt box. This is most easily done by selecting the MS-DOS Prompt icon from the Programs folder. With the command prompt available, you are ready to execute all of the NET commands.

NET HELP

This may be the most important NET command you learn, so it is listed here first and shown in Figure 5-20. If you ever forget how to do something with the NET commands, remember that help is not far away. By typing **NET HELP** at a command prompt, you get a list of all the available NET commands along with a brief description of what each can do. The list is too long for most screens to display at one time, so you should type **NET HELP ¦ MORE**, which will display the commands one screen at a time.

You can also use NET HELP in conjunction with any of the other NET commands to get a more detailed listing of what the command's function is. For example, if you want to learn more about NET USE, simply type **NET HELP USE** at the prompt and you will receive detailed instructions on using that function. Go ahead, give it a try. Because of this feature, this book need not cover everything about every command, nor will it attempt to. Get used to using NET HELP and you will have access to all the information you need.

Figure 5-20. *NET HELP screen*

NET START

This command is automatically entered for you in the AUTOEXEC.BAT if you have set up Windows 95 for networking. This is the command that starts loading the networking features. You can use it to start individual networking tools such as a certain protocol or piece of client software. However, you will probably not need this command very often because Windows 95 takes care of loading everything when it boots.

NET STOP

Not surprisingly, this is the opposite of NET START. You can use this function from a command prompt within Windows 95 to stop certain network functions from running. This can be useful if you decide you don't need a certain protocol anymore and you feel that stopping that service on your system will help performance.

NET VIEW

Use this function to check out what resources on the network are available to you. This is similar to using Network Neighborhood to browse the network servers for shared directories and printers. This command is also useful if you are not sure of a shared resource's name, which you need to complete some other task.

NET LOGON

This function is also started automatically by Windows 95 when it boots. It is the function that logs you onto the network by providing your name and password. It is useful from the command line if you want to log on as a different user or if you want to log onto a domain other than your default domain.

NET LOGOFF

Opposite of NET LOGON, this function logs you off the network and disconnects you from all of the network resources to which you may have been attached. You will not be able to access those resources again until you execute the NET LOGON function.

NET CONFIG

This function gives you a brief description of your machine's network configuration. It will tell you what the computer name is, what the user name is, the workgroup you are currently attached to, and what versions of the client software you are running.

NET DIAG

NET DIAG is short for network diagnostics. This function can be used to get information about the health of the connection between machines on the network. It really has two components. The first one uses the **/NAME** switch to check the connection between machines. The first machine that runs **NET DIAG /NAME** becomes the diagnostic server for the network, and specifies a name by which it may identify with other machines. It doesn't matter what that name is, but any other machine that runs **NET DIAG /NAME** will try to communicate with the DIAG server. It will send a query to the server and wait for a reply. If the reply is correct, you can assume the connection between the machines is healthy.

The other component is **NET DIAG /STATUS**. When you execute this function, you will be prompted for the name of another computer on the network. Once you enter that name, Windows 95 will give you some information about that machine's connection. If you press ENTER without naming another system, Windows 95 displays information about your own adapter's status.

NET INIT

This function is used to initialize a driver without binding it to the protocol manager. Some networks require you to initialize the driver, then bind it later using **NET START NETBIND**.

NET USE

This is probably the most commonly used NET command. This is the function that connects your machine with others on the network. You can use it to connect to shared directories and printers. The only catch to it is that you must use the UNC names for the resources. For example, typing **NET USE D: \\SKIPPER\DOCS** would map the D drive to the directory called DOCS on server SKIPPER. You can also use this function to delete network connections you have made.

NET PRINT

This function lets you send a file directly to the network printer. You can also use it to get information about the print queues on the shared printers on your network.

NET VER

This command simply displays the version number of the client software you are using.

NET PASSWORD

Use this command to change your password on the Microsoft network. You can also use it to change the password as listed in the user file on a LAN Manager or Windows NT domain. Of course, you must specify the old password before Windows 95 will let you enter a new one. This is to keep people from coming up to your desk and changing your password while you are away.

NET TIME

With this function, you can synchronize the clock on your computer with that of a time server found elsewhere on the network. Some shared applications require that the time stamps on all the running systems be identical or they won't run properly. This is the command that provides that functionality.

Batch Files

One of the biggest benefits of having command line utilities is that you can save your most common tasks to a batch file. For example, if you need to access a certain server in order to run one application, you can create a batch file that maps a drive to that server, runs the application, then deletes the mapping when you are done. You can also use it to set access to a certain printer you may need for one application. You may, for example, need to connect to a network plotter, but only when you run your CAD application. When that application is over, you might as well disconnect from the plotter. Since Windows 95 supports launching Windows applications from a batch file, all of this can be saved so you don't have to manually type it all in every time.

Summary

One of the most powerful new features of Windows 95 is it's built-in abilities as a client on a network. In this chapter we have just scratched the surface of Windows 95's client capabilities by talking about it only as a client to other Windows 95 or Windows for Workgroup computers. Other chapters in this book go into more detail about Windows 95 as a client in other specific network operating systems. However, before you go that far, read the next chapter, which explains how to set your Windows 95 system up as a server to other clients on the network.

Chapter Six

Windows 95 as a Network Server

"Beauty through my senses stole,
I yielded myself to the perfect whole."
—Ralph Waldo Emerson, "Each and All"

By default, whenever you install the networking services of Windows 95, it assumes you want to install the software necessary to make your machine a server on the network. However, don't think your machine will operate as a full-blown server that is accessible by hundreds of users. It wasn't designed with that goal in mind. That type of service is best provided by operating systems like Novell's NetWare and Microsoft's Windows NT Server.

However, in a workgroup environment, Windows 95 does very well. Others in the workgroup can see the files you are working on, or you can share a printer in a common work area. Dedicated file servers serve the large company, while Windows 95 servers work well in departments or small companies.

There are, however, a few caveats that you should be aware of before you start using your Windows 95 system as a server on the network. First of all, Windows 95 has limited security features. If security is important to you—either protecting your files against those with malicious intent or even those accidental mishaps that happen too often—then consider NetWare or Windows NT.

Second of all, since Windows 95 is not a dedicated file or application server, performance will not be as great as Windows NT or Novell NetWare. Users accessing the resources on another Windows 95 computer may notice the information traversing the network very slowly. Additionally, the people sitting at machines that share resources with others will notice their local processes—using local applications and files—may be slowed down by network use.

Beyond these drawbacks, however, two important issues remain that make Windows 95 an excellent machine on the network. First, the network services are closely integrated with the operating system. So, even though performance may be slower than a Windows NT or NetWare system, it will be better than most other peer systems. Second, the ability to share files on a local basis means that users are not dependent on larger systems that are difficult and expensive to maintain. There are tradeoffs for everything in computing, and this is no exception.

This chapter will teach you how to enable your system to share its resources, how to set some security elements that should help you avoid most unpleasant accidents, and how to manage a Windows 95 server so you know if it's time to dedicate a machine or possibly upgrade your system.

Enable Sharing

By default, the Windows 95 setup will enable your system for sharing. It provides the background means to do so, but it doesn't actually make your system's resources immediately available to other users. You must do this manually. This is a good thing, because you wouldn't want Windows 95 to automatically start sharing resources on your system before you were ready.

To install the sharing components on your system, if they aren't already there, you need to open the Control Panel, then double-click the Network icon. When you do this, you will see a screen that has three tabs across the top with a list of installed network components (see Figure 6-1). You are probably very familiar with this screen by now. Scroll through the list. If you see File and printer sharing for Microsoft Networks installed, the components are already there. If not, you will need to add them, so click the Add button.

Network Services

In the Select Network Component Type dialog box, you can choose from four different types of network components (see Figure 6-2).

Click the Service item to open the Network Services window (see Figure 6-3). As mentioned above, when you install the networking components of Windows 95, it

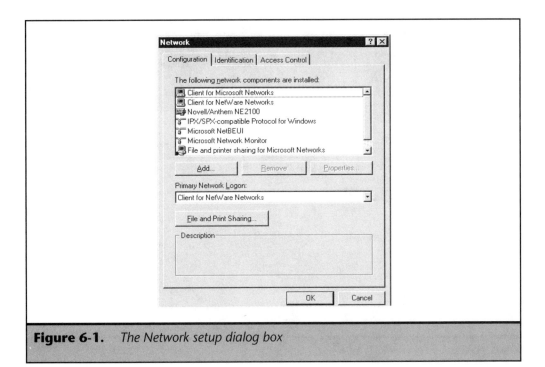

Figure 6-1.   *The Network setup dialog box*

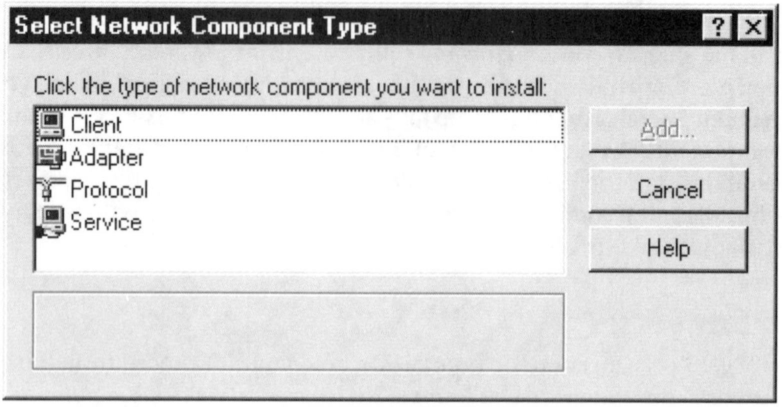

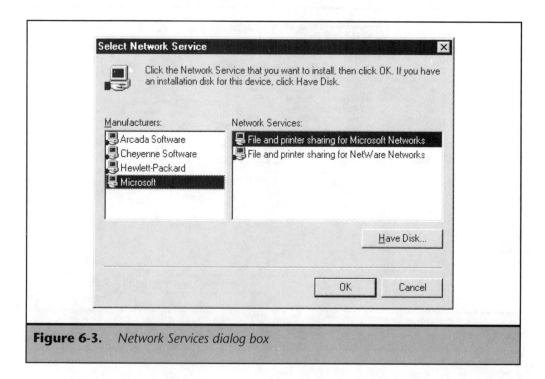

Figure 6-2. *Configurable network components*

Figure 6-3. *Network Services dialog box*

enables Microsoft Network file and print sharing by default. Click on the Microsoft entry in the Manufacturers list to see what options are available to you.

File and Printer Sharing for Microsoft Networks

This is what you would normally use for a Microsoft network. This option gives you the ability to share printers and directories with others on the network. You still control how these items get shared and who will have access to them.

File and Printer Sharing for NetWare Networks

The main difference between this option and the regular Microsoft Network file and print sharing component described above is that this alternative is useful if your Windows 95 network is going to interoperate with a NetWare network. What this option gives you the ability to do is to use one of your NetWare server's user databases for security and access. This option can be selected in place of the regular Windows 95 server services but not in conjunction with it. In other words, you can select one or the other, but not both.

If you select the File and Print sharing for NetWare option, you need to specify a NetWare server on your network that your machine will use to get access to the user information. When you specify a server, Windows 95 uses that system as a pass-through security model to grant access to your resources.

An example will help explain. When you use File and printer sharing for NetWare networks and define a NetWare server on the network to use for security, you will be able to use the user accounts on that NetWare server to grant access to local resources. See the Access Control section later in this chapter for more information.

Identification

The first thing you will need to do as you begin to share your system's resources on the network is to provide a way of identifying yourself to other users. Most likely this was done during the installation process, but it can be completed (or edited) later. To get to the identification screen in Windows 95, open the Network program from the Control Panel, and click the Identification tab at the top of the window. (See Figure 6-4.)

Computer Name

In order for other computers on the network to recognize your system as a server, it has to have a name. This name is used for identification purposes only and can be just about anything you want as long as it's under 15 characters. It should be a name that gives other users on the network some kind of indication as to which computer it is. For example, if your name is John, you may want to call your system "John's PC."

Sometimes it's helpful to pick a geographical description. For example, if the system sits in the conference room for anybody to use, you will probably want to call it "Conference Room." The key is to use a meaningful name that anybody else on the network will recognize as they browse their network neighborhood.

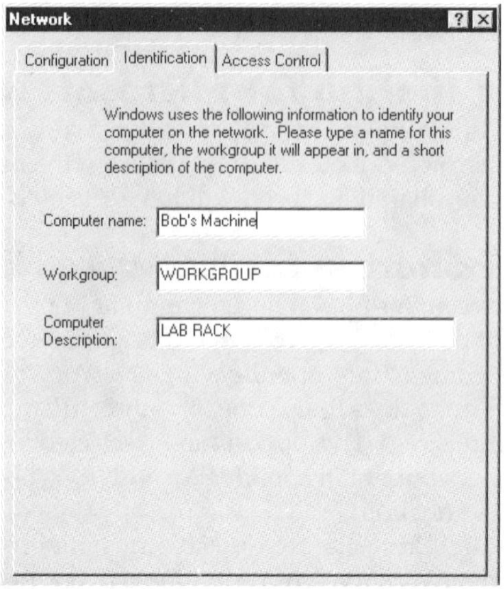

Figure 6-4. *Network Identification dialog box*

Workgroup

The next field you will have to enter data in is the Workgroup field. Microsoft introduced the idea of workgroups in their (aptly named) version of Windows called Windows for Workgroups. A workgroup is a natural collection of users on a LAN. Depending on your organization, you might divide each floor of your building into workgroups. Or you might want to put everyone in the same department in the same workgroup. Or perhaps you have a smaller company that can put everyone in the same workgroup. However you decide to make the workgroups is up to you.

Two things you should keep in mind are that (1) it's fairly easy to change to a different workgroup if you ever need to and (2) workgroups are more of an administrative designation to keep the list of machines you normally access small. Remember, you can still share and use the resources of other users that aren't in your workgroup. So, set up workgroups in a way that makes sense in your office. That may mean putting everyone in the same workgroup or defining a new workgroup for every few people. Whatever works for you.

Computer Description

The final field in this window is where you enter a description of your PC. This tells a user what the name doesn't. Since most people won't notice this information unless they have their Network Neighborhood window configured to show Details, you should put the most useful information in the name. For example, in Figure 6-4, the Workgroup name is "WORKGROUP" while the Computer Description is "LAB RACK."

Access Control

Once you start sharing your system's resources on the network, you will probably want to consider protecting parts of your system from unwanted access. Even if you are setting up your Windows 95 network in a small office or in your home, security is something you will want to consider. What you need to decide is not whether to implement security, but the level of security that is appropriate for your situation.

When most people think about securing their system, they imagine thieves sneaking into their offices in the middle of the night, trying to sabotage their business or steal precious secrets. But security means more than this. A secure system also keeps novice users in your office from accidentally deleting all the customer files from your database. A secure system will not fall prey to the careless fingers of a coworker who thought she was erasing her documents, not yours. At home, it can keep your curious three-year-old from changing numbers in your checking account. So, thinking you don't need to secure your system is like sticking your head in the sand (and while it's there, you might just get run over).

You have two security options when configuring your Windows 95 system as a server—Share level and User level (see Figure 6-5). The next two sections describe these options so you can decide which model works best for you. But keep this in mind: If you change from Share-level to User-level or vise versa, Windows 95 will delete all the shares you have defined and you will need to create them again. For reference, NTDOMAIN in the figure refers to a Windows NT domain controller from which you can derive user access rights.

Share-Level Access Control

This is the default option when you first install Windows 95's networking services. When you select Share-level security, this means that you can assign a password for each shared resource. If you want to restrict access to a printer attached to your system, you can assign a password to that shared resource. Then, when someone wants to print to your printer, they will have to enter that password or they won't be able to access it. The same holds true for shared directories. If you want to share a directory on your hard drive, you can assign a password and when anyone on the network wants access to the files in that directory, they will have to enter the password.

When you share a directory on your system, you will have the option of granting full rights to that directory or read-only rights. If users have read-only rights, they will be able to see the documents and files, read the contents of them, but not edit or write to them in any way; nor will they be able to delete them. If you like, you can use a combination of full access and read-only access. You can, for example, create one password for read-only rights, and a different password for full rights.

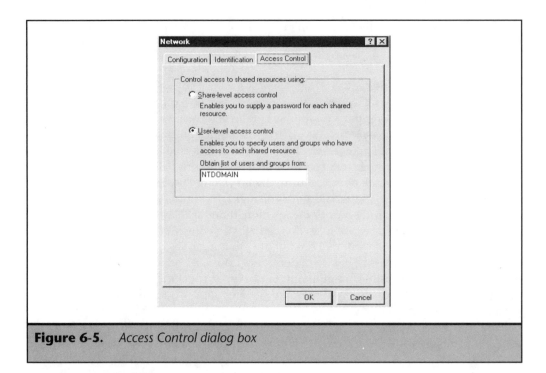

Figure 6-5. *Access Control dialog box*

Remember, anyone who logs onto your system with the password for full rights cannot only edit and add to the files in your shared directory, but they can also delete those files. As a general rule, you should grant read-only rights to a shared directory unless you know for sure that others need full access to your files.

Password Rules   When selecting the passwords you will use to grant access, keep in mind some simple rules (incidentally, these rules apply to any passwords you create, including a login password). Choosing the right password is probably the most important aspect of setting up a secure computer system. Picking the right password is the difference between a would-be thief succeeding in stealing your data and getting stuck in the process. Most people do not realize what makes a good password, so if you don't know, it's time to learn.

Because people want to make sure that they choose a password they will never forget, they make choices that are obvious to computer data thieves. Often, users pick the names of their children or spouses. Less thoughtful users may use their login names to avoid having to remember a password at all. Others choose common nouns like "horse" or "computer."

All of these are obvious passwords to those trying to break into your system. Most computer hackers with malicious intent are able to figure out passwords like these. It doesn't take much effort to do a little research on you or other computer users, find out your interests, learn the names of your children, and subsequently guess your passwords. And it may take no research at all if the person trying to break in works with you in your office.

There are even software programs that are designed to figure out users' passwords. These programs have a built-in dictionary of words, phrases, and names, and they just keep trying until they find the right match. That is why it is so important to have a good password.

Now that you know what constitutes a "bad" password, you need to know what makes a "good" one. The best passwords are words not found in any name book or dictionary. A series of random letters and numbers makes the best password, but such a password is also hard to remember. The next best thing is to take a couple of syllables and put them together in a way that does not make a sensible word. For example, take the letters P-E-R-F from the word *perform*. Add to them the letters P-L-A-S from the word *plastic*. When you put them all together, you have *perfplas*. It sounds silly, but it is a lot easier than trying to remember a series of random letters. If you want to improve on it, add a number to it, so you might have *perfplas96*. Of course, because this word has appeared in this book it is no longer a good password. Get creative and have some fun. Just remember, the more unusual and silly the word, the better.

Another word of advice about passwords is to change them often. It's probably not a bad idea to change them weekly or even daily. And once you change a password, don't go back to an old one. Many people change passwords for a day or two, but soon go back to an old password because it is easier to remember. Do not fall into this habit. Keep your passwords complex and keep them fresh. And by all means, don't write your password down and keep it in your desk.

One drawback of share-level security is keeping the group you want to give access to current. You have to verbally (or via e-mail) distribute passwords to the people who need access. When you change those passwords, you have to distribute them all over again. And if you change your mind about one user, you have to change the password, then tell the others about the change. By distributing passwords this way, you let others define the security of your system. There is nothing to stop someone else from distributing your password to whomever they please, thus making your system anything but secure.

And remember, if you don't have login passwords defined for your machine, anyone can sit down at your computer while you are not around and unsecure your system in a real hurry. So if security is important to you, log out of Windows 95 whenever you leave your machine for even a few minutes.

User-Level Access Control

User-level access is the control method used by most popular networks. With this method, you define on a user-by-user basis who you want to access your system's resources. To enable this method, you need to do two simple things. First, select the checkbox next to User-level access control in the Network dialog box. Second, enter the name of a server or domain that Windows 95 can use to verify user accounts.

If you have File and printer sharing for NetWare Networks installed, you will need to enter the name of a NetWare server. If you have File and printer sharing for

Microsoft Networks installed, you will need to enter the name of a domain on your system. Windows 95 will then use the user account lists from these sources to verify the users are who they say they are.

Sharing Directories

If you work with others in your office or your home, or if you work on more than one computer yourself, you are already familiar with the reasons to share files. You may be working on a proposal or a presentation and would like the input from someone else in your group. Or you may share parts of the project—you write the script, and someone else compiles the art. Or you may have client data files that everyone in your group needs access to. Whatever reason you have for setting up a network, the first thing you probably want to do is make your files available to others on your LAN.

With the built-in networking features of Windows 95, sharing your data on the network is a very simple process. The first thing you should do is open the My Computer folder. Select an icon that represents a physical drive or a folder and click your right mouse button. At the bottom of the menu is the item labeled Properties. Click this item and you will see some information about your hard drive or folder. The first screen is some general information about the device, including the label, the used and unused space, and the total capacity of the drive. But if you look at the tabs across the top of the window, you will see another choice called Sharing (see Figure 6-6).

Click this tab with your left mouse button. By default, none of the drives or directories are shared when you install Windows 95, so Not Shared is probably selected on this screen. If you select the radio button next to Shared As:, the rest of the options will become available to you. Since you probably do not want to share your entire hard drive on the network, create a folder called Public Files and select it before you go through the steps below.

The first field you need to fill in asks for a Share Name. Whatever name you enter here is what will show up when another user on the network attempts to access your computer. If they browse the network using Network Neighborhood, this name will appear as a directory folder under your computer name. If they use command line utilities to access the network, this is the resource name they will need to enter after the server name, for example, **server****resource**.

There are no specific guidelines for the information your would enter here, but the name should give other users some idea of what this resource contains. If it is your entire hard drive, such as our example here, name it **CDRIVE**. If it contains your project documents, name it **Project Documents**.

How the bottom of this dialog box looks is dependent on the type of access control you set up earlier—share-level or user-level. If you selected Share-level access control, then you will have a couple of fields to enter read-only or full control passwords. Once the passwords are defined, other users will need to type them in whenever they want to connect to that resource.

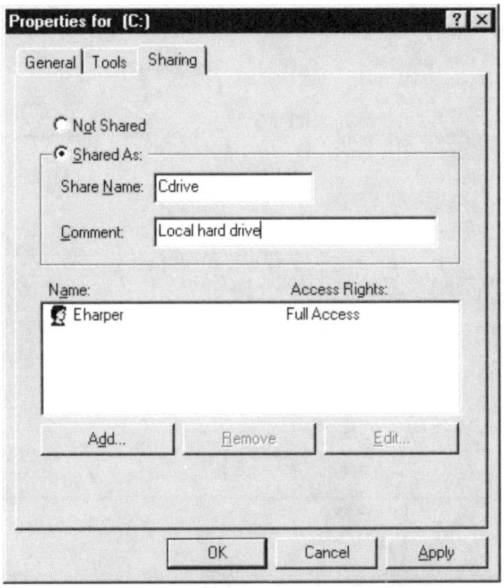

Figure 6-6.   *Sharing properties for local resource*

If you have User-level access control defined, you will see a box that will contain a list of users with associated access rights. Click the Add button to see a list of possible users. Remember, the user list comes from the server or domain you specified in the Access Control portion of the Network setup dialog box. You can be very specific about what users have what access (see Figure 6-7).

You can give some users (or groups) read-only access, others full access. Or you can define custom access rights. If you place a user's name in this box and click OK, you will see another dialog box with a list of possible rights that users may have. As you can see from Figure 6-8, you can get very specific about the kinds of access you want to give users to your files.

Click OK at the bottom of the box in Figure 6-7 and you will see the folder or drive icon change into an icon with a hand holding the resource. This hand means you are presenting this item for others to use on the network. And it is a good way of reminding you which items you have shared.

Sharing Printers

Sharing printers for others to use on the network isn't any more difficult than sharing directories. First, you need to highlight the printer you want to share. Open the My Computer icon, then open the Printers Folder. All of the printers available to your

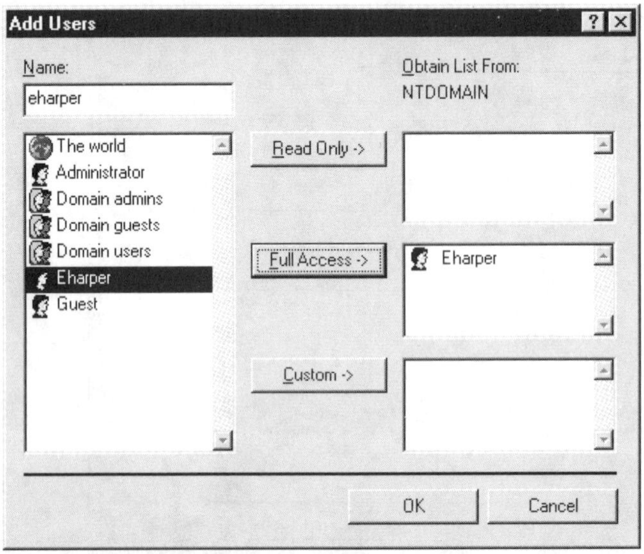

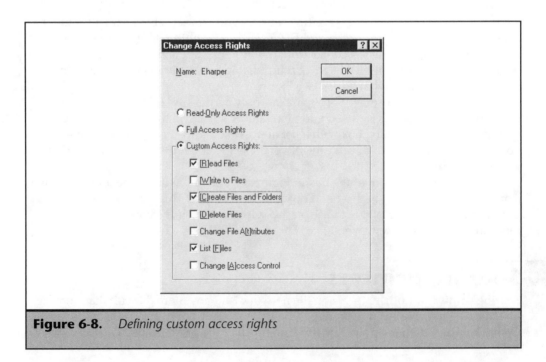

Figure 6-7. *Adding users to share list*

Figure 6-8. *Defining custom access rights*

system should be visible in this window. It doesn't matter if they are local printers or printers you have connected to over the network. The only difference you will see here is the icon. Local printers have a regular printer icon, network printers show a cable connecting to the printer.

Keep in mind that you can only share local printers. If you have access to a NetWare print queue, for example, you cannot share this printer with others, who may not have access to the NetWare printer. There is no gateway for sharing other servers' resources. Windows NT, on the other hand, has such capabilities. If you enable the NetWare gateway on a Windows NT server, Microsoft network clients can access the NetWare print queues through the Windows NT machine. Windows 95 does not have this capability.

To share a local printer, click the appropriate icon with your right mouse button. This will bring up a menu. Now, with the left mouse button, click the menu option titled Properties. Now you will see a dialog box like the one in Figure 6-9.

Notice the two rows of tabs across the top of the window. Click on the Sharing tab to see what sharing options you have available. The window is simple. Either the printer is shared or not shared. Click the Shared As button and enter a descriptive name in the Share Name field. As when you shared local directories, you should assign a name that will mean something to the other users on your network that browse through a list of available printers. "LaserJet" means a lot more to someone

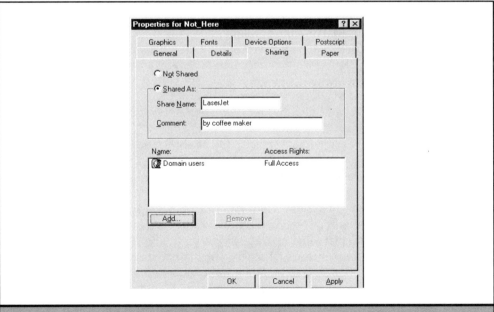

Figure 6-9. *Share properties for local printer*

browsing the network than simply "printer." Put any additional information in the Comment field. Entering **by coffee maker** gives users the information they want as they look for printers to attach to.

The value for the next field is different depending on what kind of security you have enabled for your machine. If you are using share-level security, you will be asked to identify a password for the printer. Then, when users try to attach to your printer, they will need to provide the correct password. If you have enabled user-level security, then you can enter a list of users that are defined in the domain server user list. Unlike when you share local directories, you only have one share option—full access. It doesn't really make sense to give someone read-only access to a printer, does it?

Management Applets

Turning your desktop computer into a server that other users on the network can access carries quite a bit of responsibility. You leave yourself open to all sorts of possible accidents. You run the risk of giving other users access to personal files. The possibility of other users deleting the wrong files or spreading a virus to your system is very real and worth considering before you start sharing your system's resources. The precautionary measures mentioned earlier in the chapter about user and share-level security will avert many problems if executed properly. But there is still a risk of passwords getting into the hands of someone who can do some damage.

Mishaps such as these are not limited to those who carry malicious intent. File use accidents are just as real and probably more common than problems from your enemies. Just keep in mind that no system is 100 percent secure, and Windows 95 was not designed to be a completely secure system.

Besides the security risks associated with setting up your machine as a network server, there is also the risk that when others start accessing your computer's resources, performance of the tasks you are working on will suffer. If other users print to a printer attached to your system regularly, or if they copy files and run applications from your hard drive repeatedly, you will notice a difference in the way your system performs.

Windows 95 was not designed to replace a file or application server on your network. The network server components are to provide a mechanism to occasionally share files with others in a workgroup. If your machine becomes too heavily used, you may want to consider setting up a dedicated machine to handle the more exhausting duties. Deciding what type of system will run on the dedicated machine is beyond the scope of this book. Whether it be NetWare, Windows NT, LANtastic, or something else, you should be aware that other operating systems are better suited to share resources with a large group of users who need constant access.

With that in mind, you should be aware of some tools Windows 95 has that help you manage the way others use your system. One, called Net Watcher, lets you know exactly who is accessing your machine, how long they have been attached, and what resources they are using. System Monitor keeps track of how your system is being used, whether by local application requests or by requests from other systems. Using these tools together may give you the information you need to justify installing another system to handle network server tasks.

Net Watcher

Net Watcher is installed on your system in the System Tools folder. Select Programs from the Start menu, then select Accessories, then System Tools. Inside the System Tools folder is a shortcut to the Net Watcher program. The purpose of this tool is to see exactly who on the network is accessing your system's resources (see Figure 6-10). Net Watcher displays each machine that is connected to your Windows 95 server, the user name of the person logged on to that machine, which shared resources they are attached to, which files they may have open on your machine, how long they have been connected, and how long they have been sitting there idle. That is a lot of valuable information if you are concerned with making sure only those you specify have access to your resources.

Net Watcher lets you view this information three different ways. You can have the utility sort the information by user, as mentioned above. But you can also view the information by shared resources. In other words, you have a list of shared resources on the left side of the screen, then a list of who are using that resource on the right side of the screen.

The third way is by open files. If you want Net Watcher to list only the open files, you can select that option. You should use care with this option, however. Someone can change the attributes of a file without opening it. If you have the View Open Files

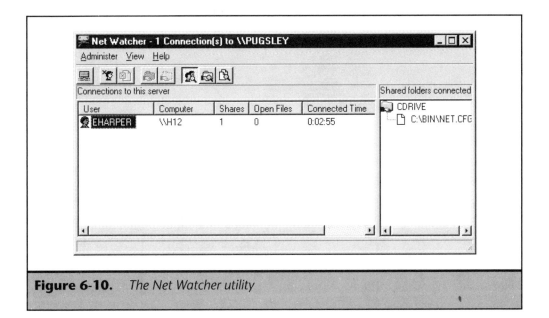

Figure 6-10. *The Net Watcher utility*

option selected, you will never know this has happened. If you are truly concerned about watching who is accessing your system's resources, view the Connections or Shared Folders option instead.

The other thing you can do with Net Watcher is administer other machines on the network. There are a few things you will need to set up on the other machine before this is possible, however. First, you need to open the Passwords program from the Control Panel. One of the tabs across the top of this box is labeled Remote Administration. (See Figure 6-11.) You will need to check the box titled Enable Remote Administration of this server. Then, you may need to edit the list of users who you want to grant this privilege. By default only members of the Domain admins group may administer a machine remotely. If you want to add users to this list, you can click the Add button and enter the additional users' names.

This Remote Administration option only works if you have User-level security enabled. If you are using Share-level security, you will have to change the machine over to User-level so you can read user and group accounts from a domain.

The other catch with monitoring other machines with Net Watcher is that you have to have the same type of sharing services. If one is broadcasting sharing services for NetWare and the other for Microsoft networks, the two systems won't be compatible enough to share the proper data.

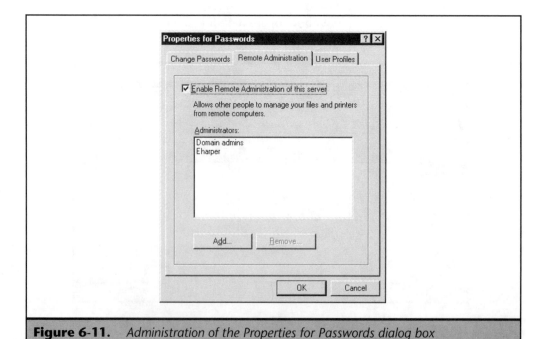

Figure 6-11.   *Administration of the Properties for Passwords dialog box*

Once you have these two things reconciled, you can use Net Watcher to see who is using resources on any other Windows 95 server on the network. To connect to another machine, click the Connect button on the toolbar, or click Administer, Select Server from the menu. This will bring up a dialog box allowing you to choose the other server you want to administer.

System Monitor

The other tool you can use to manage your Windows 95 computer as a server is System Monitor. System Monitor is also found in the System Tools folder. This utility doesn't give you information on who is using the system, but it does tell you how much your system is being taxed by others on the network. That's good information to have so you'll know when to split up resources between other servers on the network or when to dedicate a server to network services.

When you start the System Monitor utility, you will see a graph presenting your system's processor usage (see Figure 6-12).

System Monitor uses an area graph by default, but you can select a bar or line graph if you prefer. You can add many items to monitor, which you will need to do if you want to use System Monitor to look at how others are using your system. To add monitored items, click the Add icon in the toolbar, or select Edit, Add Item from the menu. When you do this, you will see a dialog box that has two windows (see Figure 6-13). On the left is a category list of things you can monitor. On the right is a list of items that pertain to each category. First you highlight a category, then select an item from the list.

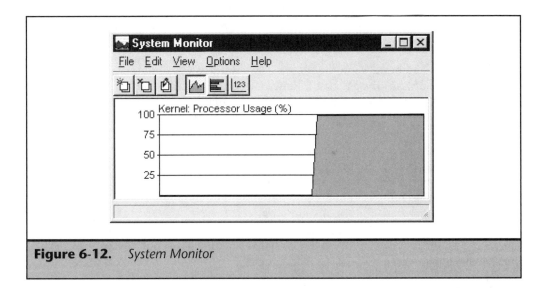

Figure 6-12. *System Monitor*

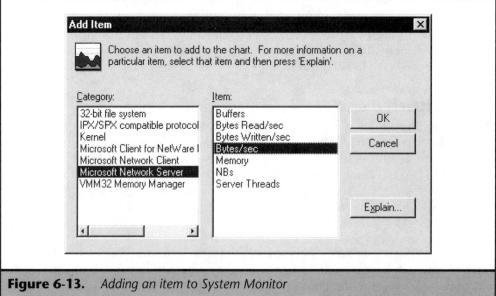

Figure 6-13. *Adding an item to System Monitor*

To see how much file access is taking place on your system, for example, select the Microsoft Network Server category, then select Bytes/sec. This will let you know how many reads and writes other users are generating on your disk. Whenever you select an item in the right window, you can click on the Explain button to find out exactly what it does.

> **TIP:** *You can use System Monitor to measure all sorts of information on your system. In addition to the server example given here, you can also use it to monitor items related to the client, file, protocol, and memory components in your system.*

As with Net Watcher, monitoring other systems is possible, but only if the machine you want to manage has the Microsoft Remote Registry service enabled. This service is not enabled by default, so you will have to do it manually.

To do so, double-click the Network icon in the Control Panel. Click the Add button, then select Service from the Component Type list. In the Select Network Service dialog box, select Microsoft under the list of Manufacturers to bring up a list of Network Services. Select Microsoft Remote Registry from this list, then click the OK button. When you close the Network dialog box, Windows 95 will inform you that you must reboot for the changes to take place. When you do, you will be able to manage this system by other machines on the network.

To begin monitoring another computer on the network, select Connect from the File menu. Enter the machine name in the dialog box that subsequently appears and you will be able to manage items on that computer.

You don't need to have both of these utilities running constantly to effectively manage your system. Sure, if you are very concerned about security and who is accessing your files, you will probably want to leave Net Watcher open all the time. But an occasional look may be all that is needed. If you ever notice sluggish performance on your Windows 95 computer, then System Monitor will be able to tell you if others are accessing your system heavily.

Summary

Although you may not want to use Windows 95 as the primary file, print, and application server in your organization, you certainly can use the server capabilities to share files and printers within a workgroup quite effectively. You should be aware, however, that Windows 95 is not a secure system. It can be set up so that most accidents can be avoided, but if you are worried about someone breaking into the system, you will want to look at a dedicated system like Windows NT.

Also, use the tools provided with Windows 95 to keep track of the ways others are using your system's resources. Net Watcher will tell you who is using what resource and System Monitor will tell you the effect the other users are having on your system's performance. Most of all, if you have never configured your machine to be a server before, keep in mind the responsibilities. If you rush into it haphazardly, you may find yourself on the bad end of an accident.

Chapter Seven

Customizing Your Network Configuration

*"I am not discouraged,
because every wrong attempt
discarded is another step forward."*
— *Thomas Edison*

By now you have experience with Windows 95 as both a server and a client. Now that you know the basics of networking with this operating system, this chapter will teach you how to customize your operating system. You are going to learn the little tips and tricks that will not only make you more productive, but will make using your Windows 95 computer more pleasurable.

The whole user interface (UI) of Windows 95 is designed to let you do your work more efficiently. Microsoft spent a lot of money conducting usability tests to ensure that the product was easy for anyone to learn. Microsoft can't predict every situation and configuration, and so the default settings that are perfect for someone else, might not work efficiently for you. This chapter will help you change those default settings to match your needs. We'll start at the desktop and work our way down.

The Desktop

The desktop is the home base for all your computing activities (see Figure 7-1). It is the screen you look at from the moment you first boot your Windows 95 computer. It may

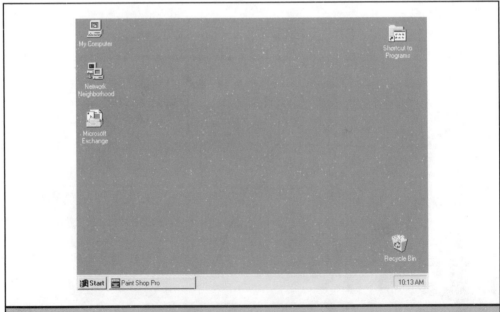

Figure 7-1. *The Windows 95 desktop*

help to think of it very literally as the top of a desk. The Taskbar across the bottom contains the Start menu, which contains program icons. These icons are just drawers out of which you pull information you want to work on. It's essential, therefore, to make sure that you have the proper things in your desk drawers.

The Start Menu

One of the fastest ways to launch a program is to copy that program's icon to the Start menu. You can do this in a few different ways. To enter an icon anywhere in the Start menu structure, do the following steps:

1. Click the Start button.

2. Click the Settings entry.

3. Select Taskbar.

4. Click the Start Menu Programs tab.

5. Click on the Add button.

6. Enter the file name of the program you want added to the Start menu in the field provided, or you can use the Browse feature to search the directory structure to find the file (see Figure 7-2).

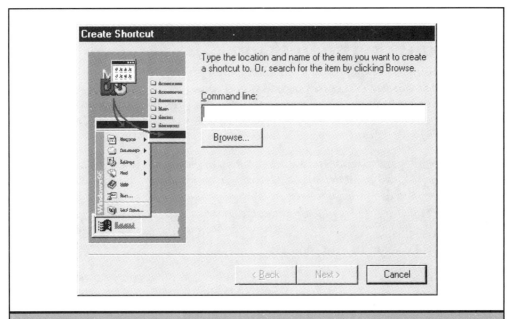

Figure 7-2. *Adding items to Start menu*

7. Click Next.

8. Select the menu on which you want the program to appear.

9. Click Next again.

10. Type the name you want to see on the menu.

11. Click Finish.

Another way to enter an application to the Start menu is to do the following:

1. Right Click the Start button.

2. Click the Open entry.

3. The Start menu folder will open.

4. Drag and drop an icon shortcut to the Start menu folder. The shortcut can be a program file, document file, or folder.

TIP: *Always use the right mouse button when dragging and dropping. That way, you get a menu of choices rather than the default action, which you might not anticipate. Sometimes Windows 95 will move a folder when you meant to copy it.*

However, the easiest way to include a file or folder in the Start menu is to simply drag and drop it to the Start button on the Taskbar. Keep in mind that this procedure adds the item to the first level of the Start menu. Use the above procedures to add an item to a cascading menu.

Placing Icons on the Desktop

Of course adding an item to the Start menu may not provide the best solution to launch the item quickly. After all, it takes a mouse click just to open the Start menu and it is possible to put so many items there that it takes too much time to search for a particular one. Another option is to put icons directly on the desktop. To do this, follow these steps:

1. From an open folder or from the Windows Explorer, use the right mouse button to click the item (file, folder, printer, or computer), hold down the button, and drag the item to the desktop.

2. When you release the button, a menu will pop up asking whether you wanted to move the object, copy it, or create a shortcut to the desktop. Most of the time you will want to create a shortcut.

This can give you quick access to one of the other computers on your network. You can drag a server icon to the desktop then double-click it to quickly open a NetWare volume, a Windows NT folder, or a network CD-ROM.

Taskbar

Don't forget that the Taskbar itself is configurable. By default the installation places it at the bottom of the screen. You may prefer it on the top or one of the sides. To move it to one of these locations, simply click a part of the Taskbar that is not a button and move your mouse to the place on the screen where you want the Taskbar to appear.

You can adjust the size of the Taskbar, too. Move your mouse to the edge of the Taskbar and watch the cursor change to double arrows. Hold down the left button and drag the edge towards the center of the screen to make the Taskbar bigger. Or drag it towards the edge of your screen to hide the Taskbar altogether. If you have several items minimized simultaneously, increasing the size of the Taskbar will make it possible to view more of the icons.

To see other Taskbar attributes, perform the following steps:

1. Click the Start menu.
2. Click the Settings entry.
3. Select Taskbar from the menu. The Taskbar Properties dialog box opens.
4. Click the Taskbar Options tab.
5. Choose the Taskbar properties you like: Always on top, Auto hide, and Show small icons in Start menu. The window will give you a preview of the options you choose (see Figure 7-3).

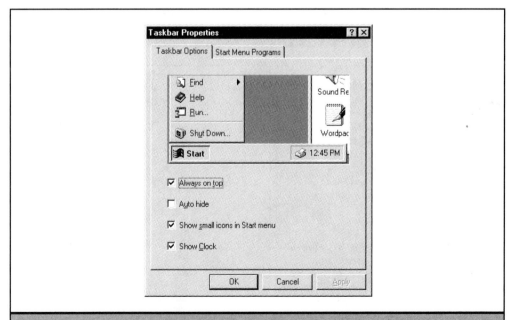

Figure 7-3.   *Setting Taskbar options*

Windows 95 Registry

Any desktop configuration changes you make to your Windows 95 system are ultimately recorded in the Windows 95 Registry. The *Windows 95 Registry* is a database that stores information about hardware and software components. Although it is logically one data store, it actually consists of different files. User-specific information is stored in the hidden USER.DAT file, and system specific information is stored in the hidden SYSTEM.DAT file. When Windows 95 boots, it loads information, based on profiles and policies set up by the system administrator and the local default settings, into the Registry database.

Although it is possible to edit this database directly using the REGEDIT.EXE program (see Figure 7-4), Microsoft discourages this in most cases. To change and configure network settings, use the Network applet from the control panel and the profile and policy tools discussed in this chapter. When you look at the Registry database, it will probably seem a little confusing. Directly editing components could cause your system to function improperly or not at all. Be careful!

User Profiles

Besides the desktop and Start menu, users can configure their machines for a lot of different things. Colors, wallpaper, and network connections are just a few more items

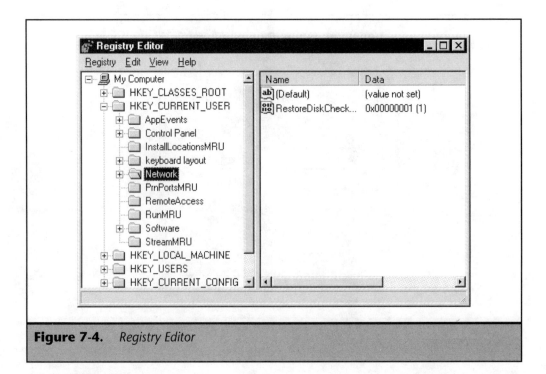

Figure 7-4. *Registry Editor*

that a user can select to make the setup "their own." But what happens if you have different users using the same computer? Or what if the network manager wants to restrict access to certain programs or wants to make sure that everyone is mapped to a network directory using the same drive letter. Windows 95 provides a way for administrators to control these items, often to protect users from themselves. All of a user's configuration preferences and options are stored in a *user profile*. A user profile houses a user's name, password, and Windows 95 preferences.

> **NOTE:** *User profile settings include all the information in the Hkey_Current_User section of the Windows 95 Registry.*

The actual configuration information is stored in a hidden file called USER.DAT. This file is usually stored on your local hard drive, but can be stored on a network server to accommodate the type of user that roams from one machine to another. When a user logs on, Windows 95 checks for that user's profile. If the profile is stored on a network server, Windows 95 searches the home directory on a Windows NT server or a user's mail directory on a Novell NetWare server to retrieve the configuration information.

Normally, Windows 95 will use the same settings no matter who logs on to the computer. If you are going to use user profiles (see Figure 7-5), you have to enable that feature.

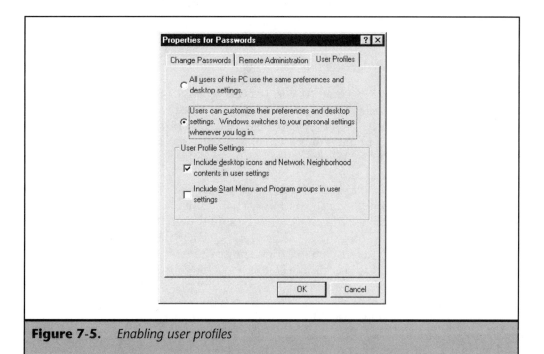

Figure 7-5. *Enabling user profiles*

To do this, you need to

1. Open the Control Panel.

2. Double-click the Passwords icon.

3. Select the User Profiles tab along the top of the window.

4. Select the second option, which states that users can customize their preferences and desktop settings.

5. Select which profile settings to keep customized. Windows 95 gives you the option of A, which includes desktop icons and Network Neighborhood contents in user settings, and/or B, which includes Start menu and program groups in user settings.

Normally this function is turned off so that all users on the PC would keep the same preferences and desktop settings. However, if the network administrator created a system policy that enabled this setting, that would become the default. Once the User Profile option is selected, Windows 95 creates a Profiles directory in the Windows 95 directory. All of the users that log on to this particular machine would have their own directories in the Profiles directory. The USER.DAT file is placed in this directory and three other subdirectories are created—Desktop, Recent, and Start menu.

The settings that can be saved by a user are as follows:

1. Desktop layout, background pattern, font selection, colors, shortcuts on the desktop, and so on.

2. Network settings, including which servers you wanted to be attached to.

3. Application settings, including the menu, toolbar, fonts, windows, and so on.

When the Windows 95 machine boots and a user logs on, the system searches for a profile that matches that user. It first searches for the profile on the local hard drive, then on the network server. If a profile happens to exist in both places, Windows 95 uses the later version and updates the older version. Once the profile is found, the information is loaded into the Windows 95 Registry, and the configuration parameters are set.

If Windows 95 can't find a profile for the user that logged on, it uses the default settings to create a new profile for the user. Any changes made to the desktop are saved in the user profile when the user logs off or shuts down the machine. Changes are saved to the local computer and to the network server, making sure that the latest profile is available if the user logs on to a different machine.

As mentioned above, the user profile is stored in a file called USER.DAT. A network administrator can, however, create a mandatory profile called USER.MAN for all users who log on to a networked system. When Windows 95 checks the network server for a profile and finds the USER.MAN file, it automatically uses that copy of the profile rather than the local copy. If the user makes changes to the desktop or network settings that would affect the profile, those changes are not saved to USER.MAN. Changes *are* saved to the local USER.DAT file on the local machine. Therefore, if the user is not attached to the network the next time he logs on to the computer, Windows 95 will not see the USER.MAN file and will load the changed profile.

If you are a network administrator who would like to create a mandatory profile for your users, do the following:

1. First you must enable user profiles (see the preceding instructions).

2. Customize the desktop of any Windows 95 computer.

3. Copy the USER.DAT file to the user's default home directory if you use Windows NT or to the user's mail directory if you use NetWare, and rename the file USER.MAN.

Once you put the USER.MAN file in the user's directory, you should secure it by hiding it or flagging it read-only so that users can't change or delete the file.

System Policies

As a network administrator, you may want to control the user's environment in ways beyond those defined in the user profile. You may, for example, want to make sure that users don't change the network adapter information in the Control Panel. Or you may want to make sure all of your users use the company logo for their desktop image. All these settings and more can be controlled by the administrator through the Systems Policy Editor. Because the System Policy Editor is the tool you will use to control these settings, you should make sure that users do not have access to it. The best way to do this is to make sure that you don't install it on their computers. The file is called POLEDIT.EXE and can be found in the Windows 95 CD in the Administrator directory. See Figure 7-6.

You can set policies on a user-by-user basis, or on a computer-by-computer basis. The desktop settings you define automatically update the Local_User portion of the Registry, which updates the USER.DAT file. Network and security settings you define automatically update the Local_Machine portion of the Registry, which updates the SYSTEM.DAT file. Although you may have dozens of user and machine settings defined, these are all saved to a single file, usually called POLICY.POL. You can have many policy files and name them whatever you like as long as you use the .POL extension. CONFIG.POL is a reserved file name, however.

Figure 7-7 shows the Policy Editor for a default user.

As you can see, there are five main categories of configuration options that you can set for a user—Control Panel, Desktop, Network, Shell, and System. Each category has one or more subcategories to set specific options. The Network category configures two network controls: file sharing controls and print sharing controls. When set, these options remove the file system sharing and printer sharing options from the computer for the current user profile. Anyone using that user profile will not be able to share these items and the Sharing tab will not appear in the Properties dialog box.

Figure 7-8 shows system policies for a default computer.

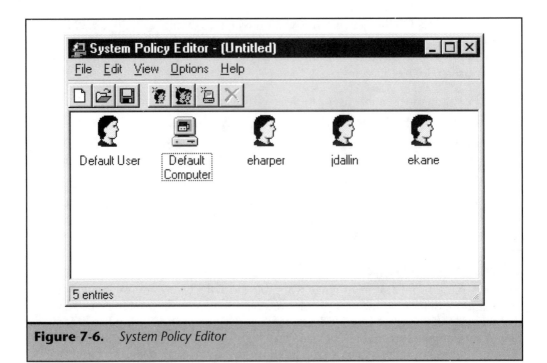

Figure 7-6. *System Policy Editor*

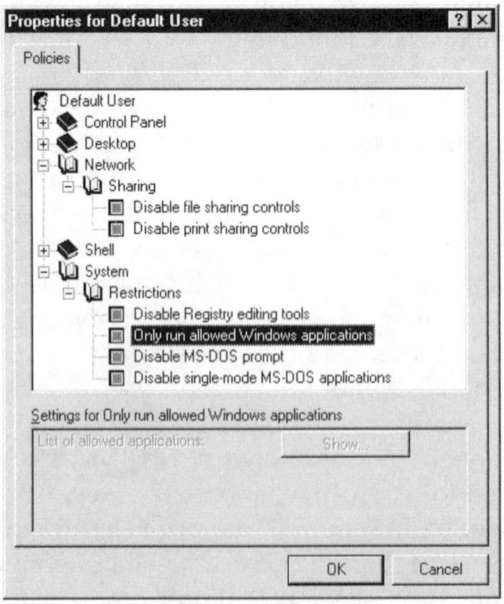

Figure 7-7. *Default User properties*

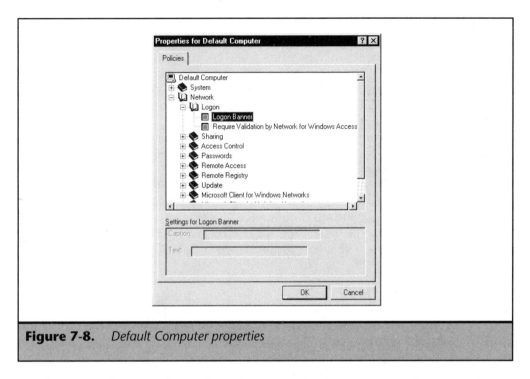

Figure 7-8. *Default Computer properties*

There are only two main configuration categories for a computer: System and Network. The Network category, however, has several subcategories:

- Logon dialog box settings
- Sharing settings
- Access control settings for user-level security
- Password settings
- Remote access settings
- Remote Registry settings
- Update settings
- Microsoft Client for Windows Networks settings
- Microsoft Client for NetWare Networks settings
- Simple Network Management Protocol (SNMP) settings

Once the policies have been created, you should copy the policy file to either the NETLOGON directory of a Windows NT server or the PUBLIC directory of a NetWare server. When the user logs on, Windows 95 checks for a computer policy entry equal to the computer name. If it finds a match, it downloads to the SYSTEM.DAT portion of the Registry the computer-specific policies you defined with the Policy Editor. If it doesn't find a match, it downloads the default workstation policies.

Next, Windows 95 checks for a user policy entry equal to the user name. If it finds a match, it downloads to the USER.DAT portion of the Registry the user-specific policies you defined with the Policy Editor. If it doesn't find a match, it downloads the default user policies. If Windows 95 can't find a server and consequently no policy file, then it uses the default settings for that machine.

Remember, the system information is read first, then the user information. Therefore, if some of the user policies contradict what is defined in the system policies, the user policies will override.

In addition to the .POL files you create with the Policy Editor, Windows 95 lets you create a master system policy file called CONFIG.POL. If Windows 95 finds this file, it will override any settings on the local computer. This way an administrator can make one master system policy file for all users logging on to a server. Remember to secure the policy files you create so that users can't change or delete them.

Policy Editor Modes

When you open the System Policy Editor, you create policy files to be copied to shared server directories. Windows 95 gives you another option. You can open the editor in Registry mode and immediately edit the contents of the Registry database. Changes are realized immediately. If you select Open Registry from the File menu, you will be working with the Policy Editor in Registry mode.

Old Friends: Program Manager and File Manager

So far in this chapter, you have learned a lot about customizing your Windows 95 interface, but maybe you prefer the old interface Microsoft left behind. Many people who use Windows 95 are familiar with other versions of the Windows operating system. Unless you have installed a third-party shell, Windows 3.x users are probably very familiar with the Program Manager. In fact, they may still prefer the Program Manager to the desktop interface presented to them in Windows 95.

Windows 3.x users may not be as familiar with the File Manager. Although a very useful utility, it was confusing to many people, so, according to Microsoft, few people used it. However, many of those who did use it learned how to manipulate the files they were working with very well. They were fast with the File Manager, whether they had to copy a file, move a whole directory, rename a file, or format a disk. The Explorer utility in Windows 95 is supposed to take over many of those tasks.

Explorer has its limitations however. Instead of dragging and dropping a file from one directory to another to copy it, you now have to cut/copy and paste the file. If you want to drag and drop, you still can, but only if you open two incidences of Explorer and put them side by side manually. Both of these options do the same thing, but take more steps to accomplish the task.

However, there is good news for Windows 3.x users who prefer these "old" tools. Microsoft, in their infinite wisdom, didn't just throw the Program Manager and File Manager out the door; they left them in. They may not pop up when you load Windows 95, but they're there if you know where to look.

To launch the Program Manager, simply type

```
START PROGMAN
```

at a command prompt, or select the icon from the Windows 95 folder (see Figure 7-9). It's not exactly like the Program Manager you were used to in Windows 3.x. The groups, when minimized, form more of a bar than an icon. But the concept is the same. If you want to use it because you are familiar with it and are productive with it, then, by all means, do so. You will find the program (PROGMAN.EXE) in the directory where you installed Windows 95. Open up the folder representing that directory, and copy the icon to your Startup folder and the Program Manager will launch for you every time your computer boots.

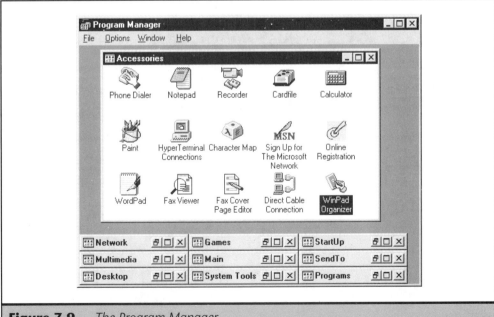

Figure 7-9. *The Program Manager*

The File Manager is there, too. You can start it by clicking the icon in the Windows directory folder or by typing

```
START WINFILE
```

from any command prompt (see Figure 7-10). Except for the title bars, this looks exactly like the File Manager that shipped with Windows for Workgroups. You can still use the toolbar for almost anything you need to do. (Select Customize Toolbar from the Options menu to add the items you like.) It really is a handy tool, but because it's a carry over from Windows 3.x days, it doesn't recognize long file names.

Just because you never used the File Manager (or even Program Manager) in the past, doesn't mean you can't look at them now. You may find them very useful and conducive to the way you like to work.

Hidden Shares

Even though Windows 95 has built-in security checks to limit access to resources you are sharing from your computer, there are a couple problems that still exist. If you are using the share-level security of Windows 95, then you have the problem of assigning a new password for every share. If you want to restrict access to one of the users you

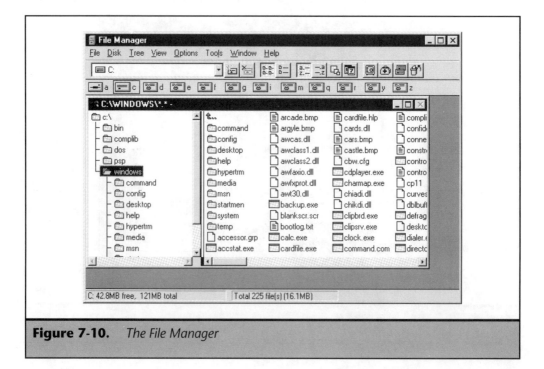

Figure 7-10. *The File Manager*

gave the password to, you have to assign a new password, then inform the other users of the change. User-level security is better, but you may not have a domain controller or NetWare server on your network that you can use to keep track of user accounts.

If other users browse the network and see a shared directory on your machine, they may just get curious enough to break in. Windows 95 is not a completely secure operating system. If people really want to look at that shared directory, and if they are tenacious enough, they will probably succeed. However, if they don't know that the share exists, then their chances of accessing your data over the network severely diminish.

Windows 95 provides a way for you to share local resources, yet those resources won't be displayed as users browse the network. To make a shared resource hidden, simply put a "$" character at the end of the share name.

Login Scripts

If you are attaching to other servers besides Windows 95, then you may have the option of setting up login scripts. These can be very helpful in setting up a consistent configuration. If you are attaching to a NetWare server, you can set up your login script through the SYSCON utility. Although a complete lesson on writing NetWare login scripts is beyond the scope of this book, keep in mind that you can gain a lot of benefits from setting up a script to set environment variables, map drives to network directories, and capture ports to network printers.

If you are connecting to a Windows NT server, you can define any batch file to use for the user login script. You just have to tell Windows NT what the name of the batch file is and where to find it. Do this with the User Manager applet in the Administrative Tools group.

Summary

This chapter has been a hodgepodge of tips to help you configure your Windows 95 system. As a system administrator, you should become very familiar with the System Policy Editor to exercise control over your users' environment. Creating profiles is another way to control environmental settings. Windows 95 gives you much flexibility in configuring your system; you have many options. With these options, your computers should be easy to use and easy to manage.

Chapter Eight

Networking Applets

*"Why is it necessary to drag down from the Olympian fields
of Plato the fundamental ideas of thought in natural science,
and attempt to reveal their earthly lineage?"*

—Albert Einstein, "Relativity, The Special and General Theory"

A s a network operating system, Windows 95 includes a few network *applets*,
which are scaled-down applications, that help you become more productive in
sharing data with your co-workers. In this chapter, you will see a brief
description of the network applets and learn how to use them.

Direct Cable Connections

Even though Windows 95 gives you all the software tools you need to set up a local
area network, you may not always need that much power. Included with Windows 95
is software that lets you network two machines together with a simple serial or
parallel cable. Using software licensed from Parallel Technologies, Inc., Microsoft
provided a tool in Windows 95 that lets you easily share files from one machine to
another. Since it requires no special equipment, it can be quite handy when you are
away from your office, whether you're on an airplane or in a hotel room. Or it can be
an easy way to connect your notebook and desktop PCs.

The Direct Connection network driver uses different types of cables. You can use a
serial cable to connect to the serial ports on your computers, a standard parallel cable,
or a special high-speed parallel cable. To enable this utility, you need to do two things.
First, you need to install it. Second, you need to configure it.

The Direct Cable Connection applet was probably installed for you by Windows 95
when you first set up your machine. However, if you did a custom install and skipped
this utility, you will need to install it now. To install the Direct Cable Connection tool,
follow these steps:

1. Open the Control Panel.

2. Double-click the Add/Remove Programs icon.

3. Select the Windows Setup tab across the top of the window.

4. Double-click Communications.

5. Select the checkbox next to Direct Cable Connection, as shown in Figure 8-1.

This tool doesn't take a lot of disk space, but can be quite handy—especially when you
are away from your network. Incidentally, in order for this tool to be installed, you
will also need to install the Dial-Up Network option. Windows 95 informs you of this
and will select it automatically when you select Direct Cable Connection.

6. Click the OK button.

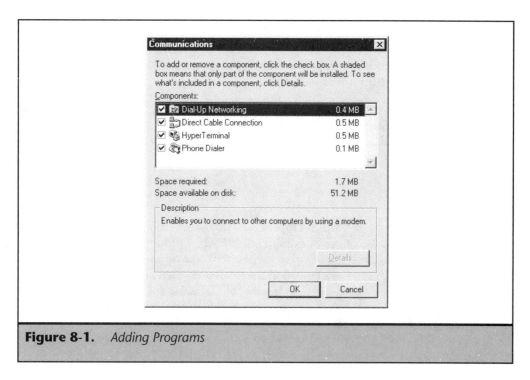

Figure 8-1. *Adding Programs*

Windows 95 will copy the necessary files to your hard disk. Once the software is installed, you will need to enable and configure it. To do so, follow these steps:

1. Open the Accessories folder in the Program group.

2. Select the Direct Cable Connection icon.

3. Follow the Windows wizard in configuring your machine to be a host or a guest.

In order to access the shared directories on someone else's computer, they need to be the host and you the guest. Next you will configure the port.

4. Select whether you want to use a parallel port or a serial port for the connection. Either one will work, but a parallel connection gives you quite a bit better performance.

5. Plug your cable into the other computer.

6. If you have configured your machine to be a host, you will first need to share some folders for the guest to have access. If you have already done so, the folders you already shared will contain the only files to which a guest has access. Also, if you are a host, you have the option of defining a password that a guest would need to enter in order to gain access to your machine. If you wish to do so, select the checkbox next to Use Password Protection, then click

the Set Password button. If you don't enable password protection, the button will be grayed out and unavailable.

7. Click the Finish button and Windows 95 will automatically attempt to make the connection to another machine.

That's all there is to it. Remember, unlike some other serial or parallel file transfer products, this utility works with the network drivers of Windows 95. Only folders you specify to be shared will be available. And the passwords you defined for those shares are still required.

Briefcase

More and more people use multiple computers to do their work. Many people have computers at home that they use to catch up on tasks they didn't get finished at the office. Some users have notebook computers that they take on the road. When they travel, they copy all of the files they need to the notebook, then update the files back on their desk when they return. Keeping track of all the different versions of the different files can be a complicated process. Unfortunately, it's too easy to accidentally replace a file with an older iteration.

To combat this problem, Windows 95 has a utility called the Briefcase. The Briefcase is a folder that is normally installed to the Desktop folder under the Windows 95 directory. It holds files you want to keep synchronized. So if you want to keep a file current on your Windows 95 workstation and another computer, you can simply put it in this folder. There is nothing to enable, but if Windows 95 didn't install it when you first set up your computer, then you should install it now. To install the Briefcase, follow these steps:

1. Open the Control Panel.

2. Double-click the Add/Remove Programs icon.

3. Select the Windows Setup tab across the top of the window.

4. Select the checkbox next to Briefcase File Synchronization.

5. Click the OK button.

Windows 95 will copy the necessary files to your hard disk. Once installed, there's really nothing to configure. To use it, simply drag and drop files from open windows or from the Explorer to the Briefcase icon. If you use a floppy disk to take data home to work on your computer there, drag and drop the Briefcase icon to your floppy drive. When you get home, work on the files—either from the floppy disk, or you can copy the files in the Briefcase to the hard disk.

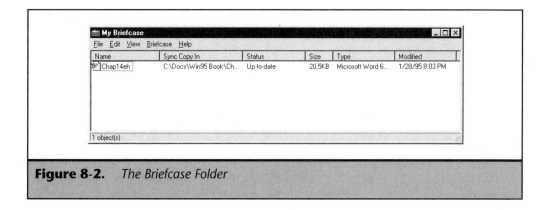

Figure 8-2. *The Briefcase Folder*

If you copied files to the hard disk, before you turn off your computer at home, open the Briefcase window (shown in Figure 8-2), select the files you want to update on your system (in this case, the file in the Briefcase on the floppy drive), then select Update Selection from the Briefcase menu. When you get back to the office, put the floppy disk back in the drive, open the Briefcase folder and select Update Selection from the Briefcase menu.

If you are working on a notebook which is connected to the network, simply drag the files from a Windows 95 server to the Briefcase icon on your notebook. You can work on the files from the Briefcase while you are gone. And when you return, you can update the files.

Even though the Briefcase is a folder like the other folders on Windows 95, it also has the means of tracking where original files are located and updating the oldest files with the most recent copy.

Backup

Whether your are connected to a network or not, backing up your system files is an important administrative task. One of the fastest ways to back up your system is to use a tape drive or another network server. But before you can use the backup utility, you must first install it. Follow these steps:

1. Open the Control Panel.

2. Double-click the Add/Remove Programs icon.

3. Select the Windows Setup tab across the top of the window.

4. Select the checkbox next to Backup.

5. Click the OK button.

Windows 95 will copy the necessary files to your hard disk. To access the Backup application, open the Program folder, the Accessories folder, and the System Tools folder, then select the Backup icon. The screen is split into two sections—directories on the left, subdirectories and files on the right, as shown in Figure 8-3. Select the files or folders you want to back up, then click the Next Step button.

Then you need to specify the destination of your backup files. You may want to back up files to a server. If so, select the server destination and click the Start Backup button. Windows 95 will prompt you with a box where you can enter a backup label. This is a description of the backup so you will know where your files are if you need to do a restore.

If you are worried that others may access your backup data on the server, select the Password Protection button. Windows 95 will prompt you for a password; anyone wanting to restore this data will need to enter this password in order to gain access. When finished, click the OK button and wait for the backup process to complete.

In addition to backing up, you can also compare or restore your files (otherwise what use would the backup be?). To accomplish these tasks, select the backup program and click on the appropriate tab across the top of the screen. As in the backup process, you must select source and destination locations. If you entered a password when you backed up your data, you will need to enter the password when you restore it also.

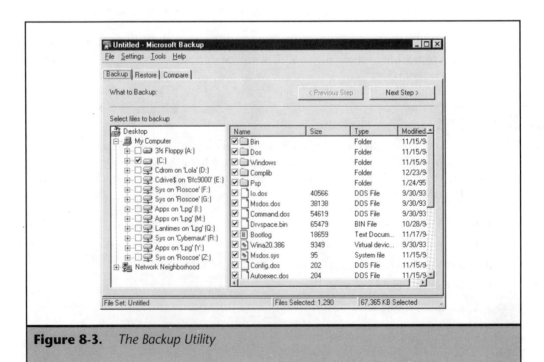

Figure 8-3. *The Backup Utility*

Multi-User Games

Because Windows 95 is so easy to network, many options are open to sharing network applications. Network games are another example of a network application. The Games folder (if it is installed on your computer) is in the Accessories group. If it wasn't installed when you set up Windows 95, please follow these steps:

1. Open the Control Panel.
2. Double-click the Add/Remove Programs icon.
3. Select the Windows Setup tab across the top of the window.
4. Select the checkbox next to Games.
5. Click the OK button.

Windows 95 will copy the necessary files to your hard disk. This book will not list the rules of the games, only how to get them set up. Have fun!

Hearts

When you click on the Hearts game icon, you will see a dialog box asking if you want to be a dealer (start a new game) or join an existing game. You will also want to enter your name. When you click the OK button, you need to wait for others to join your game. They do this by selecting the Join an Existing Game option, then entering the name of the Dealer's computer. When all players (up to four) have joined, the dealer hits F2 and the game begins, as shown in Figure 8-4. If you have less than four players, the computer fills the open slots. If you are a single player, you can start a new game by pressing F2 to play against the computer.

Working with the Briefcase

Because the Briefcase works just like any other folder in Windows 95, you can work on files within it the same way you work on files elsewhere. You can copy, move, edit, and delete files. You can even create files in the Briefcase. To do so, just click the right mouse button over a blank space in the Briefcase window, select New, and click on the desired file type: Text, Image, Sound, etc. You can even create folders, which will let you better organize your briefcase.

However, be careful when creating files within the briefcase. Each file you make within the Briefcase becomes an Orphan, which cannot be synchronized (see Figure 8-5). If you are unsure of the status of a file within the briefcase, just highlight that file, click the right mouse button to open the pop-up menu, click on the Properties button, and select the Update Status tab. If the file is not orphaned, the dialog box will tell you where the original file is and its synchronization status (see Figure 8-6).

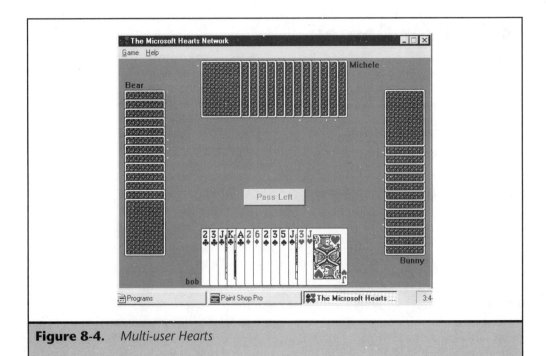

Figure 8-4. *Multi-user Hearts*

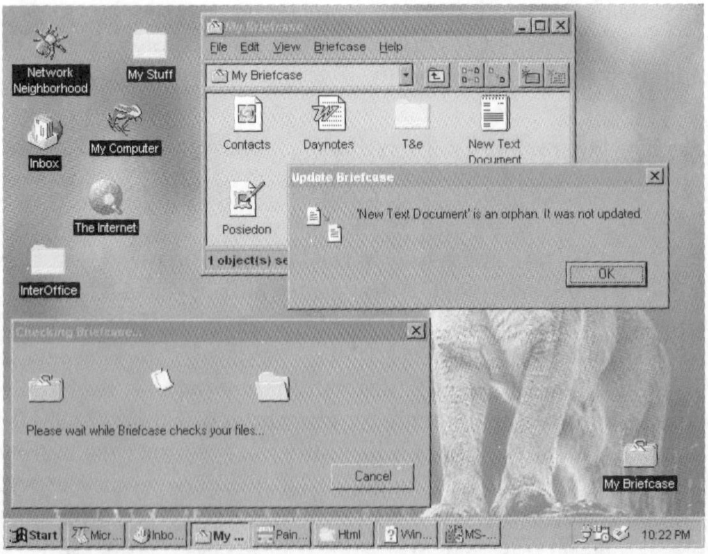

Figure 8-5. *Updating Orphans in your Briefcase*

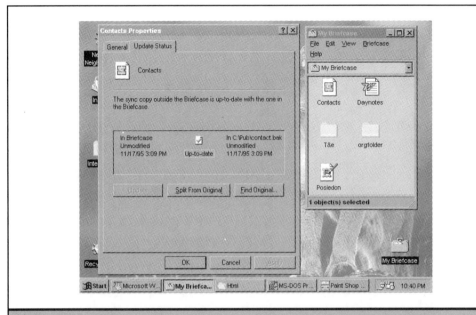

Figure 8-6. *Displaying synchronization information for an object within your Briefcase*

Summary

Windows 95 includes many applets that help you to be more productive or are just plain fun. No doubt, as Windows 95 gains popularity, other products will become available from third-party companies. With the inherent network capabilities of Windows 95, the possibilities are limitless.

Chapter Nine

Networking with Windows NT

"Let us spend one day as deliberately as nature."
—*Henry David Thoreau,* Walden

With the growing popularity of Microsoft's networking products, like Windows NT Server and Windows NT Workstation, you will probably need to at some point connect your Windows 95 computer to these systems. Actually, networking to Windows NT networks isn't much different than networking to Windows 95 networks. You use the same protocols, the same setup techniques, etc. There are just a few other things to take into consideration when connecting to a Windows NT network.

First, you should familiarize yourself with domains. A Windows NT domain is a group of servers that in some ways functions as a single system. They share user accounts with associated rights and privileges and, since the servers function as one unit, you log onto the domain rather than a particular server.

Next, you may want to familiarize yourself with the administration tools provided by Windows NT. Windows NT, like any other network operating system, needs to be regularly administered. Using tools provided by Windows NT, you will be able to manage many of the server's services from your Windows 95 computer.

You should learn about logon scripts so you can customize your setup and remote access service (RAS) connections so you can connect over a modem from just about anywhere you have Windows 95 installed.

Understanding Domains

Most Windows NT networks are organized into domains. With a domain, you can set up some logical user groups for a large number of users. In fact, that is the most common place where you will find domains in use—in large networks. Domains provide, among other things, a common user security model. The user database exists on the primary domain server and can be centrally managed from that site. Therefore, if you want to connect to a Windows NT domain, you need to make sure that you have a user account available.

The good thing about the domain arrangement is that it doesn't matter where on the network you log on. You don't need a special password on each machine that you use. Since the user database is kept at a central location, wherever you log onto the domain, you will have the same rights and configuration. This is especially good for users with portable computers (like notebooks). Since a domain isn't necessarily limited by a geographical location, if you can access your network, you can access your domain.

What Is a Domain?

Since Windows NT uses domains to manage user access to network resources, you should understand thoroughly the domain concept. A domain is a group of servers running Windows NT Server that, in some ways, function as a single system. All of the Windows NT Servers in a domain use the same set of user accounts, so you need to type the information for a user account only once for all the servers in the domain to recognize that account.

In other words, if you set up a domain for your sales department, you might call the domain SALES. The SALES domain would need a primary domain controller that keeps track of the user accounts for the domain. The primary domain controller would be a Windows NT Server machine. Other Windows NT Servers in the domain would probably be backup domain controllers. They would keep a copy of the user account database local, but you wouldn't manage those accounts from these machines. They are there as a backup in case something happens to the primary domain controller. Another benefit is that they help balance the stress of processing logon requests by letting users log onto the nearest domain controller. This can alleviate traffic loads on the primary domain controller, which could become quite heavy—especially first thing in the morning when everyone arrives for work.

 TIP: When users log on, they are logging on not to a machine, but to the domain. It doesn't matter which machine they use to log on. Nor does it matter which of the Windows NT Servers process the logon request. The logon name and password are verified and the appropriate rights and privileges of that account are granted.

But the SALES domain only processes the logon of one department in the company. You probably have other domains, like an ACCT domain for accounting information and a PRODUCT domain for the Production Department. Obviously, some users from each of these domains will need to share information with users outside their own domain. Does this mean you must set up the same user account on each of the domains? No. That would defeat the purpose of dividing your company into domains.

Instead, you can establish trust relationships between domains. What this means is that if the Production domain trusts the Sales domain, users from the Sales domain can be granted permissions and rights in the Production domain—even though they don't have accounts in the Production domain. (See Figure 9-1.) The user account is not duplicated from one domain to another, but the domain controllers communicate to verify account information and grant user access.

Trust relationships can work both ways. In other words, Production can trust Sales at the same time Sales trusts Production. That way, users from either domain share information. This becomes important to you as a Windows 95 user because you can only log onto one domain at a time. And whatever domain you log onto, you need to make sure that a user account with the appropriate access information is set up.

Domains Help Enforce Security

There are really two different ways to secure files on a Windows NT system—share-level security and file-level security. Share-level security only secures the system from users who log onto the system from the network. You set up a directory to share, then grant rights for that share, much like you do in Windows 95. That doesn't protect the system from someone who is sitting at the console, however. It only protects it from people sitting at other machines on the network.

For the full security features of Windows NT, you must format your disk to NTFS. NTFS stands for the NT file system. Windows NT is the only operating system that

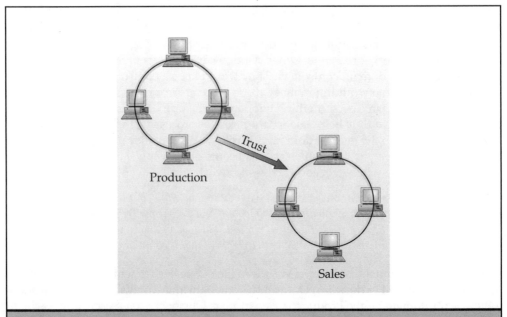

Figure 9-1. *Using trust relationships to link domains*

uses NTFS. DOS and Windows use the FAT (file allocation table) format. Windows 95 uses VFAT, which is a derivation of FAT. The big bonus with the NTFS is that it is capable of setting security options on each individual file. You can actually specify which users have which permissions to each file or directory on the partition.

This applies to users accessing the files from somewhere on the LAN and users sitting at the machine who have logged in with a user account. And you have a few more access options. Instead of controlling read and write access, you can be more specific in your rights. You can, for example, control who can take ownership of a file, who can execute a file (even though they can see it), and who can change the permissions of a file. All of these options are only available if you have installed the NTFS.

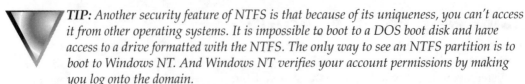

TIP: *Another security feature of NTFS is that because of its uniqueness, you can't access it from other operating systems. It is impossible to boot to a DOS boot disk and have access to a drive formatted with the NTFS. The only way to see an NTFS partition is to boot to Windows NT. And Windows NT verifies your account permissions by making you log onto the domain.*

Domains help security because they provide a central repository for user account information. The network administrator can manage the user accounts by applying associated rights and privileges from the domain controller. Anyone who wishes to have access to any resources within the domain must have a valid account.

Choosing a Protocol

One of the first things you will have to decide as you plan to connect to your Windows NT network is which protocols to use. Here are some general guidelines you can use as you set up your system. Keep in mind that both Windows 95 and Windows NT support multiple protocols on the same network interface card, so you will be able to load just about any protocol you like to connect the two systems.

NetBEUI

If you have a small network of about 20 or so machines, you would be safe using NetBEUI as the transport protocol on your network. The only problem with NetBEUI is that it cannot be routed across networks, so if your LAN ever grows to two or more LANs, you will have to use something besides NetBEUI.

IPX

For small to medium sized networks—say up to 500 workstations, you can use Internet Packet Exchange (IPX). IPX is a fast, routable protocol that is supported by many network peripherals. IPX was, until recently, primarily found on NetWare networks. In fact, if you will be using your Windows 95 as a client in a NetWare environment, you will probably use the IPX protocol. But Novell isn't the only one touting IPX any more. Windows NT workstations and servers now include native support for IPX, as does Windows 95. And since IPX is routable, you can implement it in small systems, yet it is scaleable as your system grows and expands.

TCP/IP

The other protocol you might consider is Transmission Control Protocol/Internet Protocol (TCP/IP). The biggest drawback of this protocol is that with all the addresses to keep track of, it can be very difficult to manage. However, with the advent of Windows NT 3.5, that isn't so much of a problem anymore. Windows NT includes two utilities—DHCP (Dynamic Host Configuration Protocol) and WINS (Windows Internet Naming Service)—that take away many of the problems associated with managing large TCP/IP networks.

Although typically slower than IPX and NetBEUI, TCP/IP is great for large internetworks because of its portability and routability. Almost every operating system now supports TCP/IP and it works so well in large systems that it is the base of the global Internet, the largest internetwork in the world connecting universities, research sites, government offices, and corporations. If it works well on a global scale, it should work in your office. And if you intend on connecting your office to the Internet, you may want to start off with TCP/IP.

TIP: *For more information about selecting protocols along with the pluses and minuses of each, see Appendix A in this book. Here you will get a more detailed description of the protocols available for Windows 95 networking.*

Installing Windows NT Support

Fortunately, setting up your machine for Windows NT support is almost the same process as Windows 95 networking. There are a few differences, which you will see in a minute. First, open the Control Panel, then double-click the Network icon to open the Network dialog box. If you installed support for Windows 95 networking in the past, then the list of network clients should include an entry for Microsoft Network client. If you haven't already done so, add this client support by clicking the Add button, selecting the client component, and clicking the Add button again. Then, when the Select Network client dialog box opens, select Microsoft from the Manufacturers list and Microsoft Network client from the Models list.

If you already have Microsoft Network client support installed, then highlight that entry in the list and click the Properties button in the Network clients dialog box. As the Properties for Microsoft Network dialog box appears, you will notice that it is divided into two sections (see Figure 9-2). The top section, entitled Logon Validation, is where you will enter the name of the Windows NT domain that you want to participate.

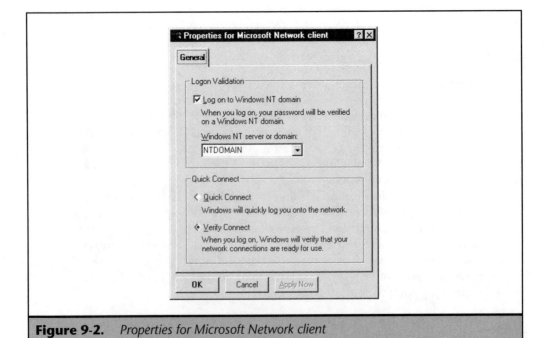

Figure 9-2. *Properties for Microsoft Network client*

You need two things to successfully connect to a domain. First, you need to know the name of the domain. Second, you need a user account in the domain. Your network administrator can take care of both of these for you. If you are the network administrator, then you should know the name of the domain and how to create user accounts with the User Manager tool.

> **TIP:** *It is possible to have Windows NT computers on your network that don't use domains. If that is the case on your system, then you would connect to those machines the same way you would other Windows 95 computers.*

Once you have the name of the domain entered, press the OK button to close the Properties for Microsoft Network client dialog box. The next item you may need to configure is the network protocols you will use to connect to your Windows NT network. Click the Add button, then double-click the Protocols option to open the Network Protocols dialog box.

One of the neat features of Windows 95 is that you can have multiple protocols loaded on the same network adapter at the same time. Since, by default, Microsoft networks use NetBEUI, and you just installed support for Microsoft networking, that item is probably already in the list in the main network dialog box. If you installed client support for NetWare networks, then IPX/SPX-compatible Protocol for Windows may be installed also. If Microsoft NetBEUI doesn't appear in your list, then click the Add button to insert it. When you are finished, highlight that entry and click the Properties button.

When the Properties for Microsoft NetBEUI dialog box appears, you will see a list of network services that Windows 95 assigned to that protocol (see Figure 9-3). You should have two entries—Microsoft Network client and Microsoft Network file and print sharing. If you want to use NetBEUI to access other Windows 95 or Windows NT computers, make sure that the box next to that entry is checked. If other machines will be accessing your computers file and print services over NetBEUI, then check the second box as well. Click the OK button when you're done to close the window.

You may, based on the information presented earlier in the chapter, opt for a protocol other than NetBEUI. If that is so, click the Add button in the Network component type window, select Protocol, and then click the Add button. You will see a dialog box entitled Select Device. Click the Microsoft entry in the Manufacturers list and you will see the protocols you can use to connect to Windows NT machines (see Figure 9-4.).

If you want to configure your system to use IPX/SPX, click that entry and press the OK button. With that entry highlighted in the Network dialog box, click the Properties button to bring up the Properties for IPX/SPX-compatible Protocol for Windows dialog box.

The tab that is active allows you to install NetBIOS support over the IPX protocol. A few applications were written especially for NetBIOS networks, so if you have that need, check the box. Most applications written nowadays are protocol-independent and wouldn't require this support.

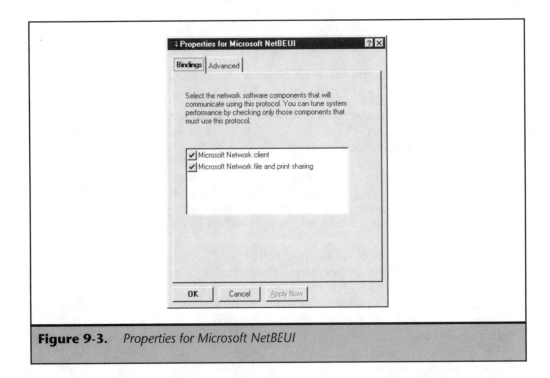

Figure 9-3. *Properties for Microsoft NetBEUI*

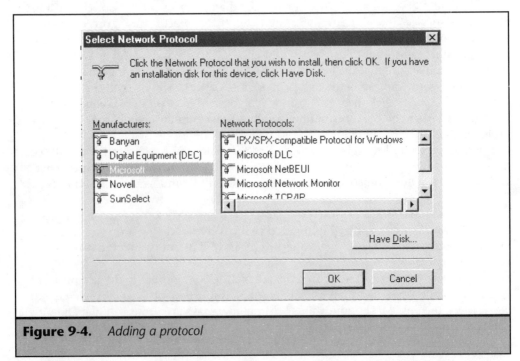

Figure 9-4. *Adding a protocol*

Click the Bindings tab at the top of the window to see what network services are enabled for the IPX/SPX protocol. This list is very similar to the list you looked at for NetBEUI bindings, but may have some additional items (see Figure 9-5). For example, if you installed the Microsoft client for NetWare, then that item will appear in the list. If you want to use IPX/SPX to connect to other Microsoft network devices, make sure the box next to that entry is checked. And, as before, if other machines will be accessing file and print services on your computer through the IPX protocol, make sure the box next to that entry is checked as well.

If you want to disable IPX support for any of these services for some reason, clear the appropriate box. When you have finished configuring these items, click the OK button at the bottom of the window to return to the Network dialog box.

TIP: *It is possible to have the same Windows 95 services bound to multiple protocols simultaneously. This is especially helpful if, for example, you have some Windows NT servers running NetBEUI and others running IPX/SPX. With both protocols enabled on your Windows 95 system, you would be able to attach to both systems simultaneously.*

Now, let's assume that you want to use the TCP/IP protocol to connect to Windows NT systems. Click the Add button, select Protocol, and click the Add button a second time to open the Select Network Protocol dialog box once again. Select Microsoft from the list of Manufacturers and Microsoft TCP/IP from the list of models. Click the OK button at the bottom of the window, then, with that entry highlighted, click the Properties button.

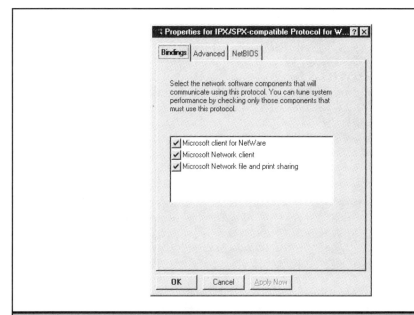

Figure 9-5. *Properties for IPX/SPX*

TCP/IP requires a little more configuration information than either IPX/SPX or NetBEUI, but that shouldn't discourage you from using it if you have the need. Besides, the management problems usually associated with TCP/IP networks have been greatly alleviated by Windows NT. Rather than specifying a static IP address in your configuration, you can use a DHCP (Dynamic Host Configuration Protocol) server to assign the address for you, as shown in Figure 9-6. If you are using TCP/IP on a Windows NT network, it is highly recommended you make use of DHCP. It simplifies the task of assigning addresses considerably.

Working with DHCP is another tool called WINS. This is the tool that associates IP addresses with computer names on a Windows NT network. If your Windows NT system is configured with a DHCP and WINS server, using these services makes TCP/IP networking quite simple. However, Windows 95 is not limited to systems using these tools.

In the Properties for Microsoft TCP/IP dialog box, you can still specify an IP address for your computer. Enter the appropriate IP address and Subnet Mask in the fields provided as directed by the person who administers the TCP/IP network. Be careful to only use the address that is assigned to you. If you accidentally enter an address that another computer is using, all sorts of unpredictable problems can occur.

If your TCP/IP network uses a domain naming system (DNS) server, you can enter the name of that server(s) in this dialog box also. A DNS server is a computer that keeps a list of computer names and associated IP addresses. Rather than keeping this

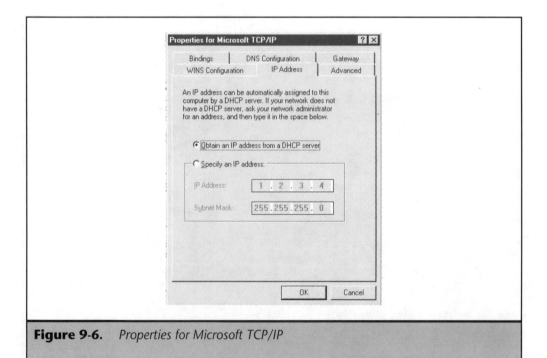

Figure 9-6. *Properties for Microsoft TCP/IP*

information (which can be large and a pain to manage) on your local system, you can simply look at the entries on a DNS server. It's kind of a central repository where this information is kept and administered.

The Bindings section of this dialog box is just like the sections you saw for the NetBEUI and IPX/SPX protocols. Make sure the protocol is bound to the services you need it for and click OK. Choose OK at the Network dialog box.

Now you are ready to connect to the Windows NT computers on your network. You will be able to use the Network Neighborhood to find the files you want. You can map drive letters to Windows NT directories. You can connect to Windows NT printers. You can access files and printers from the command line. There isn't much difference between accessing files on a Windows NT computer and doing the same on a Windows 95 computer.

Enabling User-Level Access Control

Before you close the Network dialog box, there is one more thing you can configure that relates to Windows NT networks. Click the Access Control tab at the top of the window and you will see options for Share-level or User-level access control. Share-level access control is the default option when you first install Windows 95's networking services. If you want to restrict access to a printer attached to your system, you can assign a password to that shared resource. Then, when someone wants to print to your printer, they will have to enter that password or they won't be able to access it. The same holds true for shared directories. If you want to share a directory on your hard drive, you can assign a password. When anyone on the network wants to access the files in that directory, they will need to enter the password to gain access. The problem with this procedure is, if you want to take access away from somebody, you have to change the password, then inform all the other people about the change.

User-level access control is the type of security used in most network operating systems including NetWare and Windows NT. Instead of creating a password for each shared resource, you create a list of users who have access to the resource. The user verification is handled by the network operating system (NOS), not your machine. Windows 95 can use the same user pool that the Windows NT domain uses. It's a lot easier for you, as a Windows 95 user, to administer. If you decide to take access to a resource away, simply remove the user name from the list. You don't have to worry about keeping passwords for every shared resource on your system.

To enable this feature, use your mouse to select User-level access control, then enter the name of the domain whose user accounts you are going to use in the field provided. (See Figure 9-7.) The drawback here is that any user will need an account on the domain controller and will have to authenticate himself or herself to the domain before they connect to your resource.

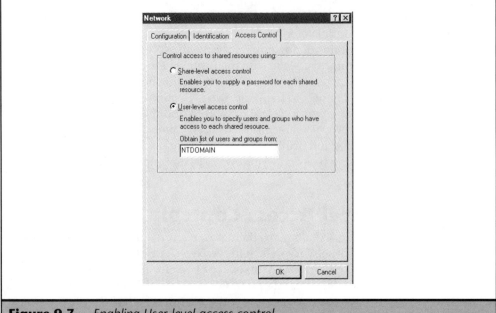

Figure 9-7. *Enabling User-level access control*

NT Management Tools

One of the new features of Windows NT 3.5 is the inclusion of management tools that work on non-Windows NT computers. You can install these utilities to help you manage the server from your Windows 95 computer. The utilities let you do everything from manage user accounts to measuring the performance of your Windows NT Servers. The reason this is so important is because often, for security reasons, network servers are locked in a closet where no one can physically access them. If the server console is the only place you can administer the server, it would be an awfully boring job to sit in a locked closet and watch the server! The obvious problem is that the server isn't monitored at all by the tools it comes with. So Microsoft included some client utilities that you can use on your Windows 95 computer. Of course you must have administrator rights on the domain to be able to use these tools.

> **NOTE:** *The applications shown are for Windows 3.x computers. As of this writing, Microsoft has not finished porting the tools to Windows 95. They will be available in the Resource Kit for Windows NT 3.51.*

User Manager for Domains

User Manager is a tool that you can use on your Windows 95 machine to monitor your domain users. With this utility, you can do everything you would normally do on the server. You can create user accounts, set permissions, logon scripts, and home directories. You can create or delete user groups and add or remove members from those groups. The User Manager for domains on a Windows 95 machine looks and functions just like the User Manager on the Windows NT Server (see Figure 9-8).

Server Manager

Another tool is the Server Manager, as shown in Figure 9-9. It is virtually identical to the Server Manager found in the Administration Tools group on a Windows NT computer. You can see what resources are shared on the servers in a particular domain. You can create new shared resources, delete connections, start and stop services, and send messages to connected users.

Event Viewer

A third very important utility you probably want access to from your Windows 95 workstation is the Event Viewer, shown in Figure 9-10. Microsoft designed Windows NT with this feature so that every important, urgent, or alarming event would be automatically recorded into an event log. If the system encounters problems, you can look into the log to see what service or components failed to execute properly and why. This tool is indispensable when monitoring Windows NT machines, so it's an important one to have for your Windows 95 machine.

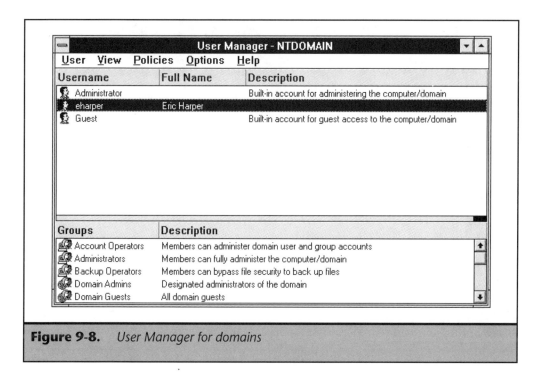

Figure 9-8.   *User Manager for domains*

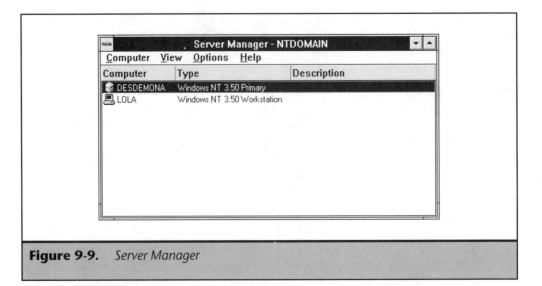

Figure 9-9. *Server Manager*

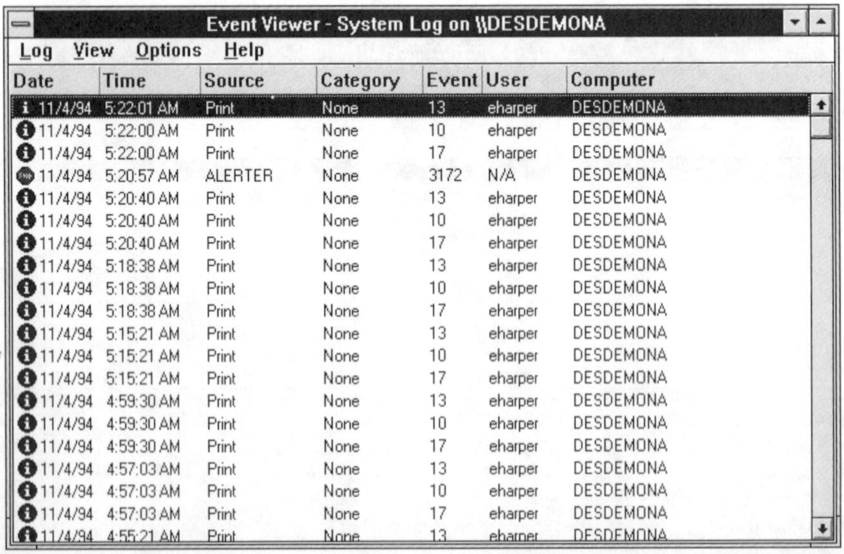

Figure 9-10. *Event Viewer*

Print Manager for Windows NT Server

The Print Manager for Windows NT Server is a little different than the Print Manager you would find on the server (see Figure 9-11). It doesn't have a toolbar, for instance, and you have to specify which printers on which servers you are trying to get information about. But you can get information on print jobs that are being serviced by the Windows NT Server. You can view, delete, or hold the jobs. You can also see who has permissions to the printer.

Logon Scripts

There are many kinds of logon (or login) scripts available in networking. Like NetWare and other network operating systems, Windows NT includes a logon script mechanism that performs certain functions for clients every time they log onto a server. The script can be a batch file with a list of commands and programs that will execute on your Windows 95 computer, or it can be a single executable file—it all depends on what you specify.

The place to define what exactly happens when a user logs in is in the user's profile section found in the Windows NT User Manager utility. Open the User Manager utility, double click a user account to bring up the User Properties dialog box,

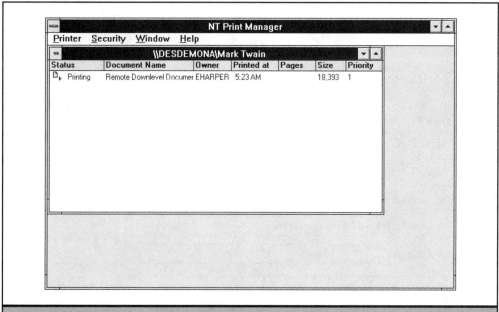

Figure 9-11. *Print Manager for Windows NT Server*

and you will see a Profile icon button at the bottom of the window. Click this button and you will see in the User Environment Profile dialog box a field where you can specify the Logon Script Name (see Figure 9-12). Enter the batch file or executable file (including path) in that field. Then, whenever that user logs on, the logon script is downloaded to their local machine and executed. You can assign a different logon script to each user or create logon scripts for use by multiple users.

The only problem with this setup is that the script is dependent on which machine the user logs onto. If a domain has a primary controller with backup controllers, the user might log onto a backup controller that doesn't have the script. The only way around this problem is to ensure that every controller in the domain has the same set of scripts. Yes, it can be a pain to keep the files current in every controller in the domain, but Windows NT includes a tool that makes it a little less painful.

Called the replicator service, you can actually set up a Windows NT server to keep current copies of a directory on another machine. As the directory's files change, so does the copy on the other machine. The machine where all the scripts are located should be set up as an export server. All of the other controllers should be set up as import computers for this directory. For instructions on setting up and using the replicator service, see the *Windows NT Server System Guide*.

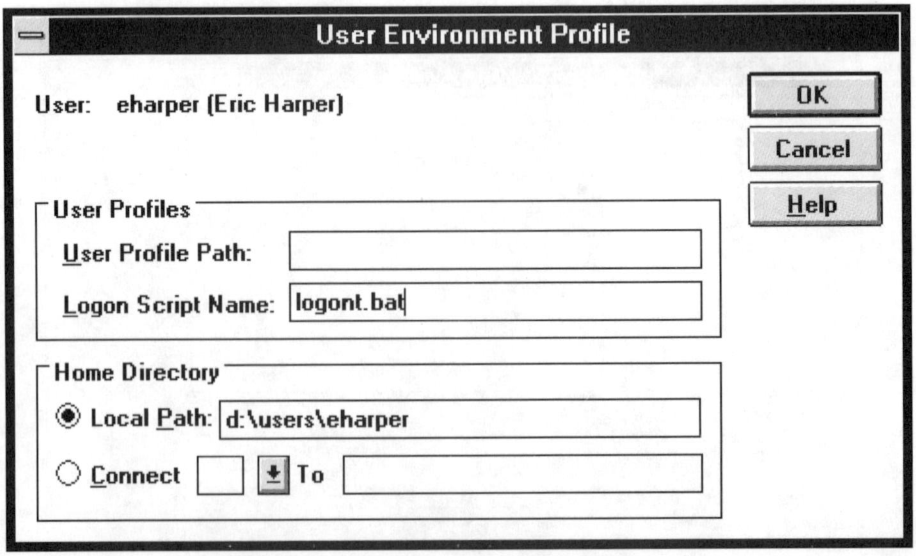

Figure 9-12.   *User Environment Profile*

Using Remote Access Services

You may want to access your Windows NT system, not from the network directly but from a remote location over ISDN or telephone lines. Remote access services (RAS) actually started in Windows NT before it was in Windows 95. You can set up a Windows NT machine as a RAS server and use it to dial into your network from a remote site like your home or a motel room. To set up a Windows NT server for RAS, you simply add the service from the Network icon in the Control Panel. You should consult the RAS guide in your Windows NT documentation for full instructions. It's not a difficult process.

Summary

In this chapter we discussed the know-how you need to have to integrate your Windows 95 system into a Windows NT network, highlighting the protocols, and the client and management tools that are all available to you.

Chapter Ten

Networking with NetWare

Windows 95 and Novell NetWare

You will find that working with Windows 95 in a Novell NetWare environment is quite similar to working in a Microsoft environment. You can log into a NetWare server much like you log into a Windows NT server. You can access file and print services on a Novell server in much the same way as you can on a Windows NT server. And you can share the files and printer on your workstation with others, just as you can on a Windows NT machine. Before Windows 95, however, this last statement would not be possible without the addition of a NETBEUI-based Microsoft network, like a Windows for Workgroups 3.11 network. Novell NetWare has traditionally been a client/server network in which isolated workstations access one or more file and print servers. Workstations could see the NetWare server, but they could not see each other. If these clients wanted to communicate in a NetWare-centric network, they had to adopt a peer-to-peer service such as DR DOS 7, which was formally known as NetWare Lite. With Microsoft Windows 95, NetWare-centric networks contain not just client/server networks, but a combination of client/server and peer-to-peer networks.

This primary benefit of being able to share data across servers and workstations is an integral element in the Windows 95 networking arsenal. However, there are many other benefits built into Windows 95 in a NetWare environment that outweigh traditional MS-DOS and older Windows client capabilities. With Windows 95 on a Novell NetWare network, you can use a single login for all network services; you can share your printer with anyone on the network, or use other's printers in the same manner; you can even gain substantial performance advantages over older network clients.

This chapter will outline these advantages, but more importantly, it will discuss the best methods to access a Novell network and how to best utilize its services from a Windows 95 workstation. We will begin by diving into the complicated matter of configuring the Windows 95 workstation so that it can connect to a Novell network. Here, we will talk about installing different protocols and network clients with the ultimate goal of demonstrating the many options available for communicating over a Novell network. If your workstation is already correctly connected to a Novell network, you should feel free to skip this section and begin reading the section entitled "Getting Started With NetWare." We will continue by discussing the basic methods available for using a Novell network. This section will show you how to view your Novell network, execute programs, and print files through Windows 95's user-friendly Graphical User Interface (GUI). Once you feel comfortable in navigating the network you can move on to the next section, in which we will discuss the more advanced features of the Windows 95 and Novell network. This section will include information about the command line interface: mapping drives, logging in and logging out, etc. Finally, we will conclude the chapter with a discussion of the security and manageability of your Windows 95 workstation on a Novell network.

Features

Windows 95 supports many different third-party networks, such as Banyan VINES, SunSoft, etc., in addition to Novell NetWare. All of these networks can potentially share the benefits of Microsoft's 32-bit Virtual Device Drivers (VxDs) depending upon the level of support provided by each third-party vendor; all networks share the benefits of multiple protocol stack support. But Novell NetWare integration has many capabilities that go beyond these other networks. The main reason for this is the inclusion of a Microsoft client for NetWare with Windows 95. Although you can use your standard Novell network client drivers—NETX.EXE for 3.x or 4.x networks (with bindery emulation) and VLM.EXE for 4.x networks (with NDS support)—and obtain the same level of performance and capability as you would on a Windows 3.1 or MS-DOS workstation, by utilizing the Microsoft client, you can gain access to a superset of capabilities. As mentioned in Chapter 3, "Preparing to Install," these benefits include higher performance, zero conventional memory usage, packet burst protocol support, auto-reconnect capabilities, etc. Beyond those are more general features within the Windows client for NetWare that will not only enhance your ability to work faster and more efficiently, but also to work more effectively with others.

Peer-to-Peer

To take advantage of the ability to share your computer's data with others, you will need to utilize both the Windows 95 client for NetWare and a Novell file server, either 3.x or 4.x. With two or more Windows 95 workstations and a NetWare server, you can immediately and easily share your system's files and printer through an interesting concept called "pass through security." If you institute user-level security within the security section of the Network configuration screen (see Figure 10-1), and you enter the name of a NetWare file server, you can allow users to access your computer based on their security rights as instituted on the NetWare server. Once you obtain a list of users from the server, you can allow each individual differing levels of security on your workstation.

For example, once you have created a user profile based on the user information obtained from the NetWare server, when that user attempts to access your workstation, his/her user name is first validated against NetWare security information. If his/her user name exists upon that server, the Microsoft peer-to-peer client software on your workstation then checks the corresponding security file for any access rights you have given him/her regarding your hard drive and peripherals. If there are any rights, he/she is granted access to your system. This peer-to-peer security scheme works for individual users and for groups as well. For example, if you have a group of NetWare users called "accounting," you could give any user belonging to that group access to your directory entitled "acct_info." Using groups more frequently than individual users will save you a lot of extra time and work in setting up user accounts on your Windows 95 workstation.

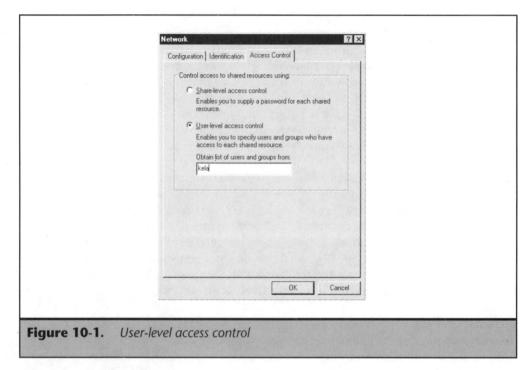

Figure 10-1. *User-level access control*

Access Control

These security features are carried over into the normal client server aspects of NetWare networking under Windows 95. One such feature, which also works with the standard NetWare client, is the ability to log into your Windows 95 workstation and any associated NetWare services with only one password upon booting Windows 95. This is called a Windows Password. From the Password icon within the Control Panel, you can specify the use of a single password. (See Figure 10-2.)

This will allow you to use the initial Windows 95 login screen to access NetWare information on a service by service, or application by application basis. This service provides an excellent solution to the problem of overabundant password requirements. If you are using NetWare 4.x with NDS support, of course, this sort of feature will already be familiar to you, albeit in a different, command line format. However, with NetWare 3.x or 4.x (with bindery emulation), this feature can save a great deal of time and effort by logging you into all of your servers at once, with one password.

Graphical Interface

Through the Windows 95 user interface you can easily access and use your NetWare file and print servers. You can browse the files contained on your file server as if they were local files on your hard disk; you can find out who you are logged in as; you can logout from or login to any server you wish; you can map drives to particular servers, volumes, or even directories; and you can use the Windows Explorer to view and

Figure 10-2. *Change Windows Password*

manipulate services on your NetWare server. All of these tasks can be performed from within Windows 95. This is a great improvement over earlier Microsoft Windows versions, which required you to exit from the Windows program before you executed any NetWare commands like LOGIN.EXE, MAP.EXE, etc. If you entered one of these commands accidentally from an MS-DOS box within Windows, there was a very great chance that your workstation would lock up shortly after you closed the MS-DOS box.

Also, from the Windows 95 interface, you can directly manipulate your NetWare files and directories. For example, by highlighting a NetWare directory and activating a pop-up activity menu (shown below) with the right mouse button, you can open, explore, search, attach a network drive mapping, cut, copy, delete, etc., the contents of the directory.

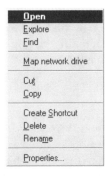

While you access the pop-up menu in the same way for most objects, its contents will differ. Initiating a menu for a text file lets you print that file, change its attributes, and quickly view its contents. You can also execute any programs (files that end in EXE, COM, or BAT).

This object-oriented approach to file management will make your interaction with NetWare very productive because you will not have to learn any new commands or command syntax in order to deal with different files directories, drives, volumes, or even file servers.

Command Line Interface

If you prefer to utilize a command line interface when connecting to your NetWare network, Windows 95 can oblige with a full range of Microsoft networking tools as well as a complete access to NetWare's utilities. The nice thing about the Windows 95 network utilities is that they will work for both Microsoft and NetWare networks. You can access a NetWare server as easily as a Windows NT server. For example, to view your currently attached Network services, you need only type **net view**. This will give you a listing of the network resources available to your Windows 95 workstation.

The command line does not, however, allow you to use the NET START command from an MS-DOS window as you could in previous versions of MS Windows. Windows 95 workstation starts this command with all of your configured parameters before loading the main Windows desktop. If you have installed the Microsoft client for NetWare, for example, Windows 95 will execute a command similar to **net start nwredir** (*nwredir* stands for NetWare redirector).

Thus you will be somewhat shielded from the lower-level functionality of your NetWare network on the Windows 95 side of the command line interface. On the NetWare side, however, you can have full reign. If you want to log out from within an MS-DOS box, you can—although it would not be advisable since all other applications depending upon your NetWare connection would find themselves without network support.

NDS Support

Windows 95, because it directly utilizes NetWare 4.x NetWare directory services (NDS) through VLMs provided separately by both Novell and Microsoft, can give you some additional options when working with NetWare. For example, you can actually log in to the NDS tree (the repository for all network items) and browse the various container and leaf objects. If you want to use one of the objects in the tree, you can simply highlight it and activate the pop-up menu. To utilize one of these items, for example, you must have the proper object rights to access, like a printer or server object.

Enhanced Printing

An excellent part of integrating your Windows 95 workstation with a Novell network comes through the extended printing features available to the Microsoft client for NetWare. You can install a protected-mode 32-bit print server application on your workstation that will allow other, peer workstations to access your printer as if it were a part of a NetWare print server configuration. Since this program reads information directly from NetWare print queues, multiple Windows 95 workstations can dispatch print jobs from a central print queue. For network administrators, this will come as a boon because it means that the overall printing capacity of the Novell network can be increased.

NetWare Installation

Although connecting your Windows 95 workstation to a NetWare network can give you some immediate benefits, there are many steps and decisions for you to make along the way. Again, if you already have your Windows 95 client satisfactorily attached to a NetWare network, you can skip this section and move on to the section entitled "Getting Started With NetWare." The first decision that will need to be made before you connect to a NetWare network has already been made by an administrator. When they created the network, they standardized upon three items: packet drivers, protocols, and network clients. They did this for reasons of manageability and interoperability. If each workstation used a different network client, network administrators could not easily maintain all of the workstations. Similarly, if each network client were to use a different protocol to connect to a file server, most likely only a few would be able to do so.

Therefore, if you are connecting to an existing network, you should check with the administrator concerning the appropriate protocols, network client, and packet drivers you should use on your Windows 95 workstation. Once you have obtained this list, you should (if you have not done so already) install the network interface card you will be using to communicate with the NetWare network.

Installing Hardware

To install a network interface card, you must turn off your computer, remove the outside cover and insert the card into an available expansion slot. You should, at this point, take note of the hardware configuration of your card: its Input/Output (I/O) address, Direct Memory Access (DMA) channel, slot number (if applicable), and interrupt number. If you're not comfortable with this or any other part of the installation, check with the system administrator to avoid any problems. After you have installed your card, boot the Windows 95 workstation. After you enter the desktop environment, you will be presented with a New Device installation picture. This appears automatically whenever Windows 95 detects a change in your system's hardware configuration. If you do not see such a screen, go to your Control Panel and select the icon named Add New Hardware. Follow the Hardware Installation Wizard. (See Figure 10-3.)

If you choose to have Windows automatically scan your system, it will detect your hardware (and hopefully your new card) and present you with its findings. Select the appropriate manufacturer and model of your network adapter card. You will then

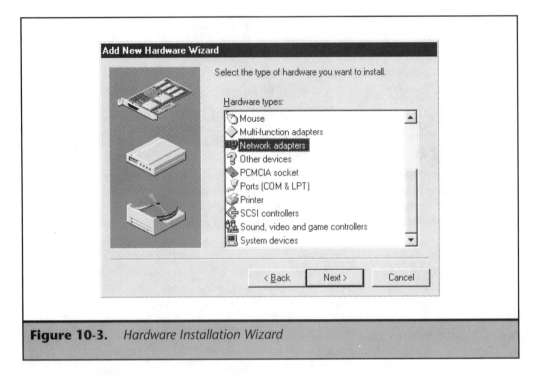

Figure 10-3.   *Hardware Installation Wizard*

need to reboot Windows 95. The next step will be complicated in that you will have to configure the Windows 95's client software so that it can communicate with your network correctly.

Installing Software

After you reboot your workstation, go immediately to the Control Panel and double-click the Network icon. This will bring you to the main network configuration screen, which contains the following elements: Configuration, Identification, and Access Control. First, select your new adapter and click on Properties. Before continuing, you should verify all of the adapter settings, ensuring that you do not have any hardware interrupt or memory address conflicts. If you do, there will be an asterisk (*) before the current settings. (See Figure 10-4.)

Packet Driver Types

To connect with your NetWare network, the first software setting you must consider is the driver type settings, which can be found by double-clicking the Network icon from the Control Panel, highlighting an available adapter, and clicking on the Properties button. Drivers tell Windows 95 how to communicate with your network adapter. And there are three different types of network drivers available within Windows 95: enhanced-mode 32-bit and 16-bit Network Driver Interface Specification

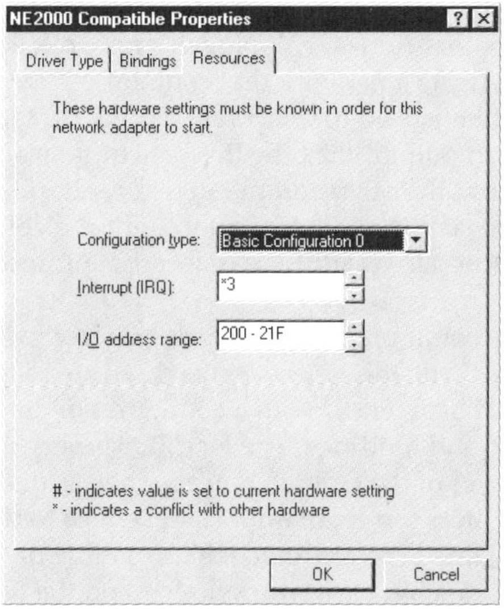

Figure 10-4.   *Network adapter conflict reporting*

(NDIS) drivers, real-mode 16-bit NDIS drivers, and real-mode 16-bit Open Data-link Interface (ODI) drivers. You are free to choose any of these selections, but be aware that unless you possess a 32-bit network adapter card, you will not be able to take full advantage of the 32-bit enhanced-mode client. If you have an Industry Standard Architecture (ISA) computer, do not worry though, since you can simply select a corresponding, 16-bit enhanced-mode driver.

Select the desired driver for your Windows 95 network. Generally, you should initially choose the enhanced-mode driver as it will give you better overall performance. For this example, the enhanced driver will be used. If you experience trouble after installation, you can just choose another, more familiar driver such as the real-mode NDIS or the ODI driver. After you have made your selection, click the button labeled OK to finalize your adapter configuration.

Protocol

You will not have as many possibilities in choosing your protocol as you did in choosing your driver type. This is because the type of protocol you choose is dictated by the type of NetWare network you use. For each type of network, there is a distinct protocol. Banyan VINES networks use a proprietary protocol, Digital Equipment Corp. networks use DECnet protocols, and SunSoft networks use the Transmission Control Protocol/Internet Protocol (TCP/IP). Although these systems usually make use of one protocol, a NetWare network can basically utilize two different protocols,

TCP/IP and Internet Packet Exchange/Sequenced Packet Exchange (IPX/SPX), interchangeably. The majority of NetWare networks will use the IPX/SPX protocols, as it is the default protocol that comes with Novell's network operating system. On the other hand, if you are using a network that contains a large number of UNIX machines, you will most likely need to select the TCP/IP protocol.

To begin, select the Add button, click the Protocol button, and click Add from the Network window. Highlight the Microsoft manufacturer button and then select the IPX/SPX model. Of course, if you wish to use another protocol, either TCP/IP or even NetBIOS Extended User Interface (NetBEUI), select that protocol and click the OK button.

Now you may have to configure your network protocol to better communicate with the NetWare network. To do this, select the newly created protocol and click the Properties button. You will be presented with a configuration page containing three tabs: NetBIOS, Advanced, and Bindings. The NetBIOS is very important to a NetWare network. In the session layer of the OSI reference model, as discussed in Chapter 2, "Networking Basics," NetBIOS serves an important service for NetWare in that it functions alongside the Named Pipes protocol in providing data transport requests, login and logout services, naming of network nodes, and the broadcasting of server names and locations. In light of these services, you should ensure that the "I want to enable NetBIOS over IPX/SPX" button is checked.

The next step is to select the Bindings tab. This is where you set the network services your packet driver will bind to the selected protocol. You should see three entries:

■ Microsoft client for NetWare

■ Microsoft network client

■ File and printer sharing Microsoft networks

You must have a checkmark next to the Microsoft client for NetWare selection. Without this service, you will not be able to connect to any NetWare networks. Only select the Microsoft network client if you are going to be communicating with other Windows 95, Windows for Workgroups, or Windows NT machines. Likewise, the file and print sharing selection should be checked if *and only if* you want other network users to access your files and any attached printer that you may have. The reason why you should only check the services you want is that the more services riding on top of one protocol, the slower your machine will operate as it interacts with other network devices.

Only modify the Advanced Settings tab if you experience problems communicating over the network. Of course, as mentioned in Chapter 4, "Installation Overview," you should verify your network's frame type. For example, if your network administrator has selected the Ethernet 802.2 frame type, you must also select the Ethernet 802.2 frame type. Selecting a frame type different than that used by your NetWare server will prevent you from connecting to the network. This, however, only applies to IPX/SPX protocols. If you chose the TCP/IP protocol, you need not worry about this since TCP/IP relies solely upon the Ethernet II frame type. (See Figure 10-5.)

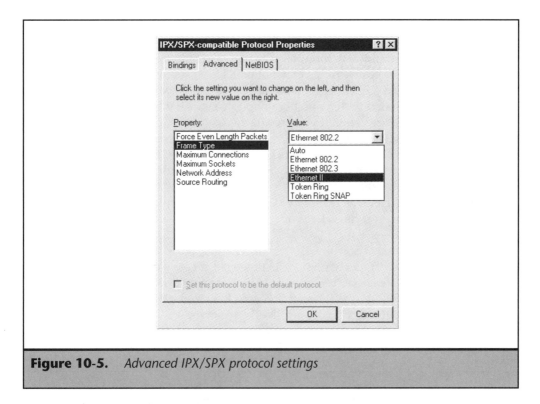

Figure 10-5. *Advanced IPX/SPX protocol settings*

As a general rule of thumb, NetWare 3.x networks will utilize the Ethernet 802.3 frame type, while NetWare 4.x networks will use the Ethernet 802.2 frame type. Novell is migrating to the 802.2 frame type, which is why it appears primarily within NetWare 4.x networks. For more information on these protocols, please refer to Appendix A, "Networking Protocols."

If you have selected more than one protocol, such as both TCP/IP and IPX/SPX, you should ensure that the correct protocol has been selected as the default protocol. For example, if you connect to a NetWare network as your primary service, select IPX/SPX as your default protocol. When you have finished configuring your protocol settings, click the button labeled OK.

The rest of these selections should be left alone unless, after you have connected to the network, you are unable to either log on to a NetWare server or execute a network program. For more information about any problems you may encounter, please refer to Appendix B, "Troubleshooting Windows 95."

Clients and Services

After configuring your network protocols, the Network Dialog window should appear to be filled out with information corresponding to the selections you made within the Protocol configuration. If not, you will need to click the Add button then double-click the client selections, highlight the Microsoft manufacturer and Microsoft client for NetWare headings, and then press the OK button. (See Figure 10-6.)

Do not, however, continue without scrutinizing the contents of these dialog windows because the default settings may not match your network configuration.

First, select the Microsoft client for NetWare entry and click the Properties button. Here you will be presented with a number of options, which depend upon the type of Novell network you are using. If you are attached to a NetWare 4.x network, you should enter the default context in which your workstation resides, the default neighborhood context of your local network, and the preferred tree to which you wish to attach. If you are unsure about any of these entries, you should consult your network administrator. Otherwise, simply enter the two context entries as simple names. For example, a context such as **O=Acme_Sales. OU=Accounting** would be entered as **Accounting**. You can select your preferred NDS tree from a pull-down list of available NetWare trees.

For NetWare 3.x networks, you will only be able to modify the Preferred server and First network drive in this window. The Preferred server simply tells Windows 95 the name of the NetWare server you want it to look for first during its boot processes. During this process, if Windows 95 cannot find your Preferred server, it will simply return an error code and attach to the next NetWare server it is able to locate.

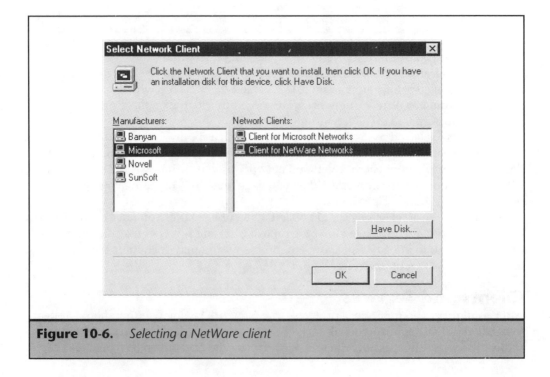

Figure 10-6. *Selecting a NetWare client*

You will probably not need to modify the remaining two selections unless you need to use driver letters for local devices such as CD-ROMs, additional drives, etc. If so, simply set the first network drive to the drive letter immediately following your last local drive.

A second client heading should be the Windows client. Highlight it on the Network window and press the Properties button. If you are using a Windows NT network and you want to use it as a means of user validation on your Windows 95 workstation, place a checkmark next to the Log on to Windows NT domain box and enter the Windows NT server or domain that you want to verify your password and user name. The Quick Connect portion of the screen simply lets you choose whether or not you want to be notified of a network error during the Windows 95 boot process. It also lets you connect to Microsoft without connecting specific drives and devices.

Access Control When you are finished, click OK and then click the Access Control tab from the Network window. The Access Control menu allows you to set your local hard disk security system as either a file by file, directory by directory, share-level access control, or as a user-level access control based system. If you select user-level access control, don't forget to enter a server from which your machine can gather user security information.

Next, click on the Identification tab. The last pieces of information you will need to provide include a name for your computer, the name of the workgroup to which your computer belongs, and a brief description of your computer. The computer name can be anything you want unless your network administrator has chosen a naming standard. The workgroup name must correspond to an existing workgroup, or your computer will belong to a peer-to-peer network comprised of one computer.

After clicking OK to install your newly created Network service, you will be asked to either insert a number of installation disks, as shown below, or provide a location from which Windows 95 can obtain the required network client programs. After installing the required files, you can begin utilizing your NetWare network by simply rebooting your machine.

Getting Started with NetWare

Installing and configuring your network client is the most difficult aspect of connecting your Windows 95 workstation to a NetWare network. After you have completed this phase, utilizing the NetWare network is quite easy. After you reboot your machine for the first time after installing NetWare support, you will notice that instead of seeing a login prompt for a Microsoft network, you will see a screen like the one shown here asking you for a password allowing access to the first NetWare server found by the Windows 95 NetWare client software. You can change the Login Server name to any valid NetWare server name. Likewise, you can change the User Name to any valid NetWare user name.

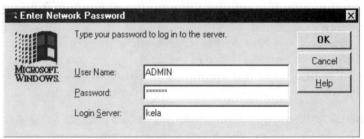

If you used the same login name for your NetWare server as you use for your Windows 95 workstation, you will not be prompted for any more information. But, if you have used a different name, you will initially have to enter an additional name and password for your Windows 95 workstation. Then, the next time you start Windows 95, you will only need to enter one password. Your name and password will be added to the central information repository. Once you have logged onto the Windows 95 workstation and a NetWare network, you are ready to access your network's services.

Basic Techniques

The best place to start networking with NetWare is to access a NetWare server. Since you already logged onto a NetWare server when you started Windows 95, you will be able to see that server by double-clicking the Network Neighborhood icon from the Windows 95 desktop. This window is your main access point for all NetWare services. Here you should see two computers, one having the name of the NetWare server you logged onto after you rebooted your workstation and the other having the name of your workstation. Although these icons look identical, they will allow you to perform very different activities. For example, if you first highlight the NetWare server icon and then click it with the right mouse button, you will notice a small pop-up screen containing a number of options: Open, Explore, Who Am I, Logout, Login As, Map Network Drive, Create Shortcut, and Properties. To learn about this server, click the Properties selection. A window should appear, indicating the name of the server, its make (in this case Novell), its version, revision dates, and copyright information. This window only contains information, however; you cannot change any of the information.

Exploring a NetWare Server

To discover more about your NetWare server, open the pop-up menu again and click the Explore selection. This will launch the Windows 95 Explorer program, which is the same program you use to explore the file system of your local machine. Here, it will simply be directed to begin at the selected file server instead of at your workstation. (See Figure 10-7.)

The Explorer provides you with a wealth of information about your file server. For example, if you highlight your NetWare System Volume and select File and then Properties, you will see a window describing real-time information about this volume, such as its size, number of files, number of folders (directories), and the attributes (Hidden, Read Only, System, etc.). If you would like to explore this volume further, you can activate the pop-up activity menu by placing the mouse pointer on the volume and clicking the right button. This menu will let you further explore the volume, open the volume as a window, map a network drive to the volume, create a shortcut to the volume, or view its properties in the same manner as with the pull-down menu.

Executing Network Programs

The Explorer is an excellent way to view your NetWare server and its installed volumes, but it is also an excellent way to perform network tasks. For example, you can execute programs and batch files from the Explorer. To do this, activate the pop-up menu for the System volume by clicking the right mouse button and then clicking the Open selection—you can also double-click the volume folder icon. Both methods will bring up a folder containing the contents of the System volume. Since Windows 95 is able to directly access NetWare file system information, folders will appear as folders, and files will appear as files. To go a little bit deeper, open the pop-up menu for the a folder containing a program such as Microsoft Word for Windows 6.0 and click the Open selection.

Of course, the Open command can be quickly circumvented by double-clicking the desired object (document, folder, program, etc.). If the object is an executable program,

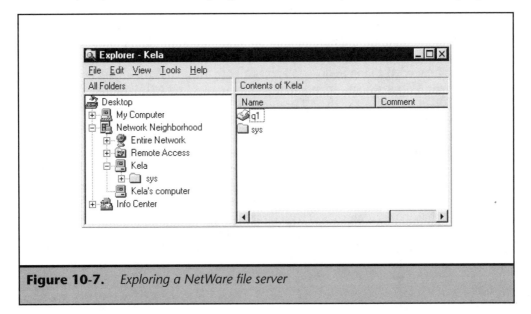

Figure 10-7. *Exploring a NetWare file server*

this will start the program. If the object is a document, double-clicking it will open it in its associated word processing program. Documents that do not have any detectable associations will appear as white sheets of paper like the one shown here. If you double-click one of these, you will be given a dialog box asking you which program you would like to associate with the document. To execute a program, such as the Microsoft Word for Windows installation utility, just double-click the Setup icon and the program will start directly from the NetWare drive.

Accessing Additional Servers

These principles can be applied to any file, directory, volume, or server in the NetWare environment. One object is the same as another to Windows 95. However, the server and its attached printers alone must be dealt with a bit differently than the other NetWare objects. This is because Windows 95 considers NetWare servers and NetWare print queues as separate network devices. Under the Universal Naming Convention (UNC) standard, when you view a NetWare server or print to a NetWare print queue, you are accessing completely separate entities. Before you installed Windows 95, you may have only needed to log in once to access all of your NetWare file servers. You can do this with Windows 95, too, but to do so you must first tell Windows 95 which servers you want to connect with and under which names you want to be registered with those servers.

Before you can connect to your other NetWare servers, you must find those servers, and although you can utilize a command line utility to do this, Windows 95 can tell you which servers are attached to your network. To do this, simply double-click the Entire Network icon within the Network Neighborhood window. This will open another window containing icons that correspond to the available network servers, regardless of their type (Windows NT, NetWare, VINES, etc.). If you see a server icon to which you want to log in, simply open the pop-up menu with the right mouse button and click the Login As selection. This will open a standard network login screen like the one shown next, which will ask you for a user name and password.

Notice the name of the server has two backslashes before its name. Those are the base operators for the UNC standard. You will see these again. As with your initial login screen, you can use any valid NetWare user name or password. You can even ask Windows 95 to save your password for the next time you log into this server. If you are not sure about a user name, just click the Connect as Guest checkbox and then click the OK button. If your network administrator has not deleted the Guest user account, or if he or she has not placed a password on the guest user account, you will be logged into the NetWare server. You will not be able to perform the same functions on it as you would on your initial server, however, as a guest account is generally given fewer access privileges.

Selecting a NetWare Printer

Now that you are able to access NetWare servers and execute network applications, you will most likely want to print from one of these applications. If the printer is attached to your Windows 95 workstation, you can simply select the print option within an application, assuming you installed a printer either during installation or thereafter. To utilize a printer attached to another workstation or a NetWare file server, you must follow a number of steps. First, from the Start button, select the Settings option, click the Printers item and then double-click the Add Printer icon. This will open a printer creation Wizard. This will be no different than installing a regular printer, except for two things. When you are asked which type of printer to install, select Network printer, and on the following screen, when you are asked to enter the network path to the printer, you must use UNC notation to tell Windows 95 the name of the desired NetWare print queue. If, for example, your print queue is named "Marketing," and the server upon which it is installed is named "Marketing_One," you would enter the following:

```
\\Marketing_One\Marketing
```

If you are unsure about either the server or the print queue's name, you can use the browsing facility to look for the appropriate services as you would use the Explorer to search for an appropriate drive and file.

Once you have finished the creation of your NetWare printer object, your next step will depend on whether or not the physical printer you wish to utilize is attached to your workstation. If the printer is attached to another workstation or directly to the network, you can immediately use your new printer. On the other hand, a network printer attached to your workstation must be able to communicate with a NetWare print server. This print server, which runs as a NetWare Loadable Module (NLM), resides upon a Novell NetWare server and communicates with the printers attached to its subnetwork. To enable the printer attached to your workstation to communicate with a NetWare print server, select the Properties item from the pop-up menu associated with the new network printer. In case you have created more than one printer (a local printer and a network printer), you can tell the difference between them by the connecting pipe attached to the network printer. Select the Print Server tab and enable the Microsoft Print Server for NetWare radio button. (See Figure 10-8.) All that remains to create a printer is for you to select the appropriate NetWare Server and attached Print Server.

To use your network printer within an application such as Microsoft Word for Windows 6.0, you can simply click on the print button if you have selected the network printer as your default printer. If not, you should select the Print option from the File pull-down menu and then click the Printer button. This will give you a Print Setup window (like the one shown in Figure 10-9) listing installed printers, which should

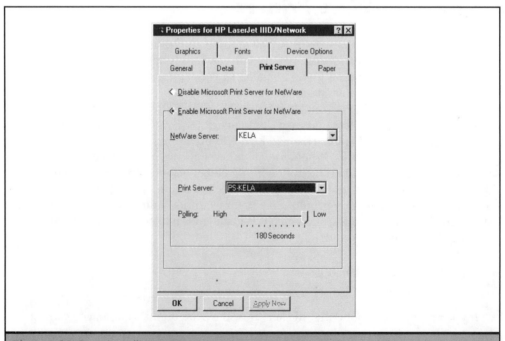

Figure 10-8. *Installing a NetWare print server*

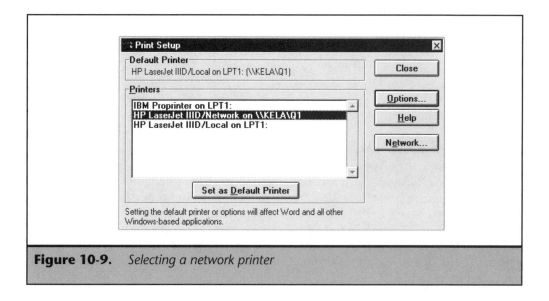

Figure 10-9. *Selecting a network printer*

include your newly created network printer. You can now select the needed printer, and even set it as the default printer.

If you need to temporarily connect to another NetWare print queue, you can click the Network button and search for the NetWare server and attached NetWare print queue, and then add it to one of your printer ports (COM1, LPT2, etc.).

Advanced NetWare Services

Although the graphical user interface of Windows 95 provides thorough network services for Novell NetWare, you may feel more comfortable working from a command line prompt, such as an MS-DOS user interface. You can do this within Windows 95 to perform, for example, a vast number of day to day routines such as mapping network drives, changing contexts (with NetWare 4.x), printing files, viewing directory rights, etc. You can also perform many administrational tasks such as changing user information, managing files and directories, and even remotely managing NetWare servers.

This is possible through Windows 95's Virtual DOS Machines (VDMs). These sessions emulate MS-DOS 8086 machines, are capable of supplying over 600K of memory, and have the ability to run both DOS and Windows programs. Once you have established a Novell network connection, you can execute programs from the command line within Windows 95 just as you did with MS-DOS or Microsoft Windows.

There are, however, many other advanced features available within Windows 95. For example, you can map network drives to a NetWare volume or directory from a graphical user interface. You can also ensure that any created drives are recreated the next time you boot Windows 95.

Mapping Drives

The first task you must accomplish in order to run programs from a NetWare file server involves the creation of a network drive mapping. Drive mappings allow applications to associated drive letters with NetWare resources such as a volume or directory. There are two ways for you to initially do this: either through a command line or through the Windows 95 GUI.

Command Line Drive Mappings

When you log into a NetWare server under Windows 95, three things happen regarding network drives: any network drive mappings specified within your NetWare login script are established, any path statements within your AUTOEXEC.BAT file are instituted as search drive mappings, and any drives previously identified as re-establishable within the Windows 95 GUI are created. Therefore, it is unlikely that you will need to create any drive mappings once you have installed the Windows 95 network client. If need be, however, you can perform any NetWare drive mapping command from an MS-DOS session with the MAP.EXE program. For example, if you want to create a drive mapping for your system volume on a NetWare server, you can enter the following command:

```
MAP G:=KELA/SYS:
```

This will create a relationship between the letter G, the file server named Kela, and its system volume. One nice feature about creating drive mappings in this fashion is that any mapping automatically becomes a part of all other processes within Windows 95. In other words, a drive mapping, once established, will work within each MS-DOS session or executed application automatically. (See Figure 10-10.) However, when you reboot your machine, these command-line-created drive mappings will not be reinstated automatically. You will have to recreate them, as recently discussed.

If you make a mistake in mapping a drive letter, you can remove the drive mapping by executing a command similar to this:

```
MAP DEL G:
```

This will remove the drive labeled G:. However, if any applications are currently using the drive labeled G:, you will receive an error message indicating an error deleting the specified drive.

Microsoft Command Line Utilities

Microsoft Windows 95 clients come with their own set of network utilities that apply to all supported networks such as Banyan VINES, SunSoft, etc. However, with Novell NetWare, these utilities are really only available at the time you boot your

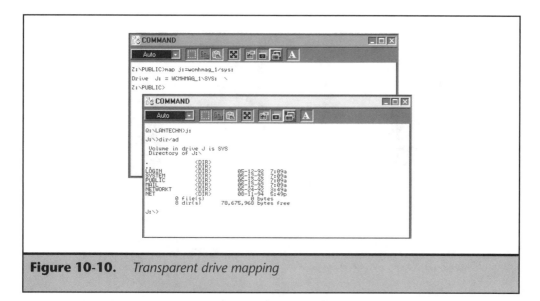

Figure 10-10.   *Transparent drive mapping*

Windows 95 workstation. For example, the NET.EXE command can give you a great deal of information about your NetWare network, such as the number of attached servers and the current mapped drive configurations, but you cannot use it to log on or log off of NetWare servers. That only happens through the initial call to NET.EXE during the boot process. Do not worry, however, because all of the NET.EXE commands are supported through Windows 95's graphical user interface GUI. As a note, you can use Novell's LOGOUT.EXE to log out from a NetWare server, but be careful because if you log out from the server supporting your last mapped drive, your MS-DOS session will have to be terminated.

Mapping Drives with the GUI

If you want to create drive mappings that will be reinstated the next time you boot Windows 95, you must either place those drive mappings in your NetWare login script or execute them from the Network Neighborhood window. To create a NetWare drive mapping, simply open the Network Neighborhood. Open a NetWare server icon from the pop-up menu, highlight a NetWare volume, and again open the pop-up menu. This will display a selection entitled Map Network Drive. Click this selection and you will be given a screen from which you can map a drive. Select the Drive pull-down menu and choose the drive letter you want to associate with the system volume network. (See Figure 10-11.) Once you have done this, you need only to ensure that the Reconnect at Startup checkbox has been checked. That is all there is to it.

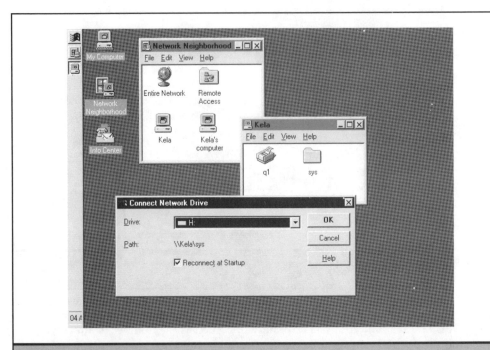

Figure 10-11. *Using the GUI to map the network drive*

Network Management in a NetWare Environment

Once you have created drive mappings for your NetWare network, you can take advantage of the NetWare management utilities that come with Novell NetWare. These utilities will vary from NetWare 3.x to 4.x networks; however, you can manage both versions to the same extent. With NetWare 4.x, for example, you can execute the program called NWADMIN.EXE, a Windows program designed to browse the network objects within NetWare's NetWare Directory Service (NDS). You can use the Explorer to view these objects. Additionally, you can take full advantage of the administrative utilities included with NetWare 3.x. For example, you can use the PCONSOLE.EXE program to manage the NetWare print servers attached to your NetWare network.

You can even remotely monitor your NetWare servers with the RCONSOL.EXE utility. With this, you can view and modify a NetWare server's settings from your Windows 95 workstation. (See Figure 10-12.)

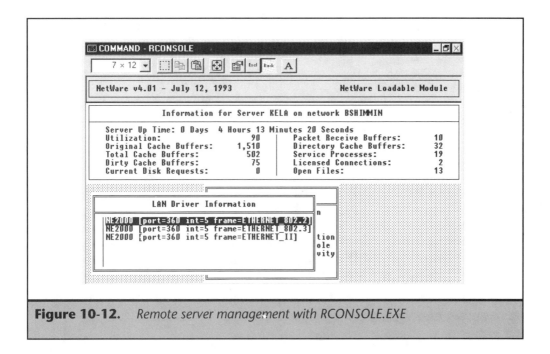

Figure 10-12. *Remote server management with RCONSOLE.EXE*

Security on a Novell Network

Because other Windows 95 workstations have the ability to connect to your
computer over a network, you should institute some security measures. These
procedures parallel those used in a Microsoft network and therefore contain many
Microsoft-specific instructions such as remote access and Microsoft network security
procedures. To create a security system, you should enable sharing on your computer
by selecting your hard drive icon from the Explorer window, activating the pop-up
menu, and clicking on Sharing. Of course, you must have already selected User-Level
Security in your network settings.

To create a security policy, simply select the Add User item and enter a user's
name. (See Figure 10-13.) For each user, you can enable or disable file and print
sharing capabilities. On a computer level, however, you have much more control over
how others use your workstation.

In this way, regardless of who logs into your workstation (either over the network
or locally), you can be assured that your data will be secured and that your system's
setup will remain intact.

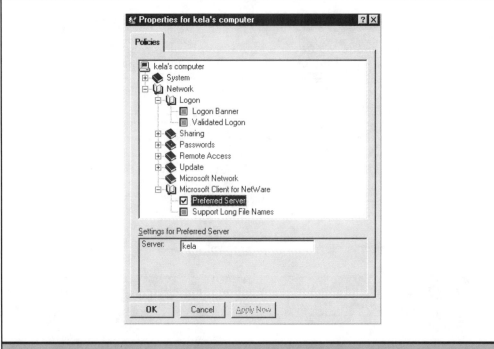

Figure 10-13.   *Preferred Server for NetWare workstation security*

Summary

In this chapter, we addressed the topic of NetWare to Windows 95 connectivity. We
began by describing the most difficult aspect of this integration—the NetWare client
installation. We saw that there are many options available during the Client installation.
Users can choose between NetWare ODI/NDIS drivers for NetWare 3.x and 4.x networks,
or they can choose the Microsoft NetWare client, which offers many benefits. After
installing the NetWare client, we explored the basic tenets of networking with Novell
NetWare by focusing upon Windows 95's graphical user interface tools for accessing,
viewing, and modifying Novell networks. We then approached more advanced topics
such as printer selection and Novell command line utilities, including the MAP
command. And finally, we discussed the best methods for managing the Novell
network from a Windows 95 workstation, as well as the best way to secure that
Windows 95 workstation.

Chapter Eleven

Protocol Configuration

As you may have noticed from the preceding chapters, Windows 95 provides connectivity for a vast number of networking environments, including NetWare, Windows NT, Windows for Workgroups, and UNIX. Windows 95's ability to communicate with so many network operating systems rests in its support for a core set of network protocols (IPX/SPX, TCP/IP, and NetBEUI) and the predominant network transport mediums (token ring and Ethernet). The ability for more than one network operating system to communicate across a common protocol and transport medium is a boon for network administrators wishing to simplify the complexities of network management. For example, a NetWare network, which uses IPX/SPX protocols by default, and a UNIX network, which uses TCP/IP protocols by default, can both function over an Ethernet wiring standard. However, you can use both protocols at the same time if you choose to. In this way, you can simultaneously access an IPX/SPX-based NetWare server and a TCP/IP-based UNIX machine.

Basically, there are two types of networks: multiprotocol networks, which utilize both (or more) protocols; and consolidated networks, which use only one protocol. There are advantages to using one protocol. It makes your workstation operate more quickly because it does not require as much memory overhead as it does to maintain two or more protocols. It also makes your job of installing and maintaining your network connection much easier. However, such a configuration, with one protocol supporting two or more network operating systems, does not occur within heterogeneous networks very often. Such compatibility requires a great deal of forethought and planning, and since most networks evolve over time instead of occurring spontaneously, you will most likely have to manage more than one network protocol.

As a technical precursor to the following chapter entitled "Dial-Up Networking," this chapter will concentrate on what goes into the creation of a multiple vendor network at a generalized protocol level. That is, we will talk about protocols in their basic sense: how you can install and configure them within Windows 95. For a more in-depth discussion, refer to Appendix A, "Networking Protocols."

By learning about protocol configuration and maintenance within a heterogeneous environment, you should be able to connect your Windows 95 workstation to any supported network in any configuration without worry. We will begin by talking about the different protocols supported in Windows 95. They are

- IPX/SPX
- TCP/IP
- NetBEUI

In addition to these three protocols, we will quickly highlight the less pervasive protocols associated with the following network operating systems:

- Banyan VINES

■ SunSoft's PC-NFS

■ Digital Equipment Corp.'s PATHWORKS

For each protocol, we will introduce its history, capabilities, and place within Windows 95. We will then discuss the available configuration options for each protocol, focusing upon compatibility and performance concerns. Where applicable, we will point out any configurations that are inadvisable with other protocols. Also, we will analyze the best configuration for each type of network or combination of networks.

If you are shopping for a new protocol, this chapter will contain information you can use about each protocol's history, performance, characteristics, and intended environment to make an informed decision as to which protocol would be best for your particular environment. For example, if you are using a NetWare network that is connected to the Internet, you may want to change from the IPX/SPX protocol to a more "enterprise-ready" protocol such as TCP/IP. For a thorough and more generalized explanation of these protocols, please refer to Appendix A, "Networking Protocols."

IPX/SPX

IPX/SPX, or internetwork packet exchange/sequenced packet exchange, is really a combination of two protocols, IPX and SPX. Originating from the Xerox Network System (XNS) protocol, IPX evolved in conjunction with SPX around Novell Inc.'s network operating system created in the early 1980s. These two protocols make up the core protocol used by all Novell NetWare network operating systems, including NetWare 2.x, 3.x, and 4.x.

IPX

Because IPX is a connectionless networking protocol, there is no guarantee that each piece of network information (packet) that traverses between a source and destination will complete its journey or that it will arrive in the proper position (sequence). This is not a bad thing, however. To fight off the chaos that would most surely ensue without some sort of send and receive notification from the involved devices, an IPX packet incorporates a Cyclic Redundancy Check (CRC) field that informs a receiving device of each packet's well-being. If a packet is damaged, the receiving device simply ignores that packet and waits for a retransmission, which the sending device automatically does when no receive signal is sent. (See Figure 11-1.)

SPX

The IPX protocol works great for many applications that do not need to ensure that packets arrive in a particular order within a particular amount of time. However, for applications requiring such capabilities, IPX will not provide adequate functionality.

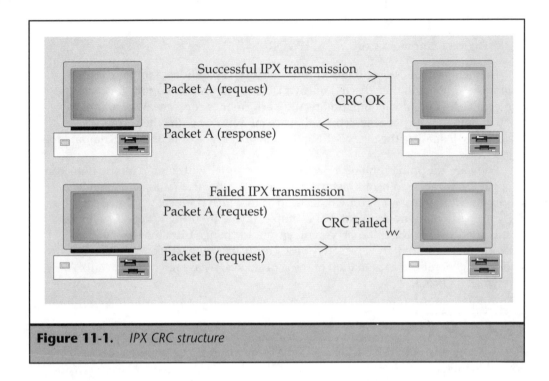

Figure 11-1. *IPX CRC structure*

For example, if a video conferencing system were not able to send and receive packets of information (voice and video) in an appropriate order and in a timely manner, the application itself would become worthless since the video image would appear as jumbled data.

To combat this problem, SPX, which is a higher level protocol that extends the capabilities of IPX, can generate a virtual circuit between network devices. Unlike IPX, when a workstation receives an SPX packet, it is compelled to respond regarding the packet's well-being. If a packet is damaged during transmission, the receiving workstation will wait for it to be resent before accepting subsequent packets from the originating workstation.

IPX/SPX and Frame Types

Because the IPX/SPX protocol is hardware-independent, it can function over many different cable access methods like Ethernet and token ring. It does this through *frame types*, which are merely blueprints for the structure a packet of data will take as it traverses the network. If you double-click your Network icon from the Control Panel window, select the IPX/SPX Protocol item, click the Properties button, and select the Advance tab, you will see a series of arcane-sounding options such as "Maximum Connections, Network Address," etc. Highlight the item entitled "Frame Type." This will display a pull-down list containing a number of options, including the following (see Figure 11-2):

- Ethernet 802.2
- Ethernet 802.3
- Ethernet II
- SNAP

Notice that there is no list for 802.5, which is for token ring networks. Although IPX/SPX will function over token ring, Windows 95 will not support it. This is not due to a flaw within Windows 95, however; it is because Novell networks primarily rely upon Ethernet or even the older ARCNet transport mediums. Token ring networks are usually associated with IBM's LAN Server network, which makes use of the NetBIOS protocol, or with an IBM mini or mainframe computer, which rely upon the SNA (Systems Network Architecture) protocol. Windows 95 does support token ring networks through the DECnet and VINES protocols.

There are many frame types that can work with IPX/SPX. These frame types are standardized by the Institute of Electrical and Electronic Engineers (IEEE). This standards body has defined these frame types according to their purpose and capabilities. And although each possesses individualized characteristics, all will work within a NetWare environment.

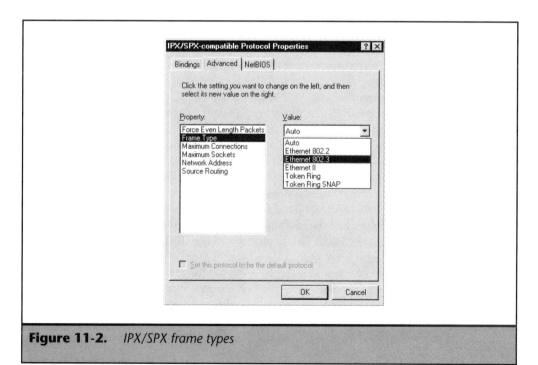

Figure 11-2. *IPX/SPX frame types*

The first frame type for IPX/SPX, called 802.2, was created by the IEEE to provide a means for disparate network operating systems such as those using TCP/IP, XNS, and IPX/SPX to communicate over a common network. Because 802.2 defines the layer of a protocol that is used by Wide Area Network (WAN) hardware devices (routers, for example), it can ensure that all protocols are treated the same as they cross from one LAN to another. For this reason, 802.2 is also the default frame type on Novell NetWare 4.x networks, since the 4.x network operating system targets enterprise-sized networks in which different network operating systems communicate across geographical boundaries. There are other frame types that work well with WANs, however. For example, the X.25 standard allows information to be passed long distances over telephone lines. A very large x.25 network belongs to CompuServe.

IEEE 802.3, which has been called "Raw Ethernet," defines the predominant cable access method used by Ethernet networks. Appearing within Novell networks from the beginning, IEEE 802.3 has found a strong following within the confines of NetWare networks. Chances are, if you have a Novell NetWare 3.x or 2.x network, you will be using the IEEE 802.3 frame type. In addition to Novell networks, another place in which you will find the IEEE 802.3 frame type is within Macintosh networks utilizing a protocol called EtherTalk.

The Ethernet II frame type was the original Ethernet frame type. It can be found within Macintosh networks utilizing the older AppleTalk Phase 1 protocol; however, it is most commonly found in TCP/IP networks running over Ethernet. As such, if your Ethernet network has a large number of UNIX machines, which rely almost exclusively upon TCP/IP, you will most likely need to use the Ethernet II frame type. Also, you will find this frame type on DEC and VINES networks utilizing Ethernet.

The Ethernet SNAP frame type is used predominantly within Macintosh networks. However, you will not likely run into it on your Windows 95-compliant network. This is because most Macintosh networks do not simply coexist with other networks like SUN and LAN Server networks. The Macintosh operating system, over the past few years, has found itself increasingly in the role of a client operating system. Other networks have added support for it, but it, as a network client, has not added support for other networks. If you utilize a Novell network, for example, you can easily connect Macintosh workstations as NetWare clients. However, it is very unlikely that you will attach a NetWare workstation to a Macintosh machine. Therefore, when you choose an Ethernet frame type, even if you share your network with Macintosh workstations, you will not have to choose the Ethernet SNAP protocol. More likely, you will use the IEEE 802.3 frame type because it can support both the Macintosh clients through the EtherTalk protocol and the IBM clients through the IPX/SPX protocol.

In many instances, you will be able to choose from these frame types, since many network operating systems support more than one frame type concurrently. Within a protocol stack, you can run more than one frame type. However, even though you have choices between different frame types on an Ethernet network, the types of network clients and the network operating system will dictate the choice you make. Before you decide upon a frame type, you must consult with your network administrator. He/she will be able to guide you toward the most compatible frame type.

Other IPX/SPX Settings

The most important part of configuring the IPX/SPX protocol is choosing the frame type. If you choose incorrectly, your Windows 95 workstation will not be able to communicate with the network because it will, in a sense, be speaking a different language than the network, as illustrated in Figure 11-3.

The other settings available for IPX/SPX protocols involve adjustments for the manner in which your Windows 95 workstation utilizes its NetWare or other IPX/SPX-compliant network. For example, the Maximum Sockets and the Maximum Connections settings dictate the number of sessions your Windows 95 workstation can maintain while connected to a network. These settings can be found on the same screen as the frame type settings. If you set the Maximum Connections setting to zero, for example, you will be able to create as many sessions as the Windows 95 workstation can support, as dictated by Windows 95 and your workstation's memory/processor capacities. If you choose to limit the number of connections to four

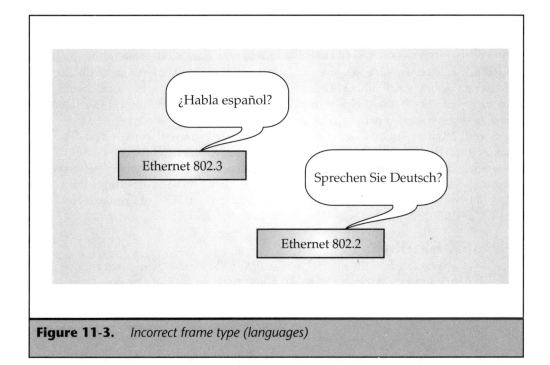

Figure 11-3. *Incorrect frame type (languages)*

or five, you can ensure that you do not risk the loss of your network connection, should you create "one too many" connections.

You can select Force Even Length IPX Packets through the Advanced tab of the Properties for IPX/SPX window (refer to Figure 11-2). This will ensure that all packets leaving your workstation contain the same amount of data. This is a great asset if every workstation relies upon single-length packets, because it will approximate some of the benefits found within cell-switching technologies such as Asynchronous Transfer Mode (ATM) simply by lessening the chances of packet collisions. It does this by filling each packet to a specified limit. If the last packet in a sequence does not contain enough information to fill the predetermined packet size, additional padding is added to the end of the packet. You should leave this setting at No, unless your network administrator tells you otherwise.

The only other setting you should have to deal with is the Network Address field on the same Advanced tab. This will be useful for administration purposes such as the Simple Network Management Protocol (SNMP) offered through Windows 95. If you are on an Ethernet network, this number is "burned" onto your network interface card. The Plug and Play capabilities of Windows 95 should reveal this number; however, if it does not, you can use a configuration tool, which is usually provided with the card. It is a good idea to enter this number, but by no means is it a necessity.

NetBIOS Support

As mentioned in previous chapters, enabling NetBIOS over IPX/SPX is a very good idea if you need to provide compatibility with IBM LAN Server, IBM OS/2, and Microsoft LAN Manager network environments. It cannot be selected as a stand-alone protocol partly because it cannot be routed across WANs. However, it can be encapsulated within other protocols such as IPX/SPX, which is why it is listed as operating "over" IPX/SPX. You should enable this protocol unless you know that none of the applications present on your network utilize NetBIOS. In NetWare environments, NetBIOS has been superseded by Named Pipes support, which, like NetBIOS, establishes a logical connection between two network devices. Named Pipes support can be used for additional activities, such as a means for arbitrating access to network devices like printers through semaphores. However, it is confined to the LAN Server, LAN Manager, and OS/2 environments, while NetBIOS is used on a number of network operating systems. To select the NetBIOS protocol, click on Protocol Settings from the Protocol tab and place a check mark next to the box entitled "I want to enable NetBIOS over IPX/SPX." (See Figure 11-4.)

IPX/SPX Bindings

Once you have established the miscellaneous IPX/SPX settings, you must choose which network services Windows 95 should bind to your IPX/SPX protocol stack. Binding a service to a protocol is a way of adding services to the innate facilities

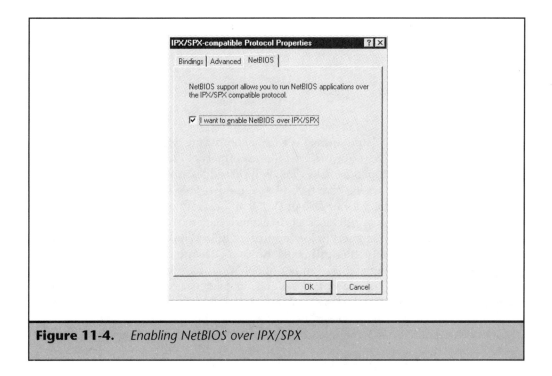

Figure 11-4.   *Enabling NetBIOS over IPX/SPX*

within IPX/SPX. For example, if you choose the Microsoft NetWare client support over IPX/SPX, you will be given the following protocol binding choices:

- Client for NetWare Networks
- Client for Microsoft Networks
- File and Print Sharing Microsoft Networks
- NETBIOS Support for IPX/SPX-Compatible Protocol

If IPX/SPX is going to be your primary protocol, you must bind the Microsoft Client for NetWare to your protocol stack. The Microsoft Network Client adds support for Microsoft networks such as Windows 95, Windows NT, and Windows for Workgroups networks. And the Microsoft Network File and Print Sharing is a special add-on for NetWare networks that enables your Windows 95 workstation to act as a print server for NetWare print queues and a file-sharing machine for other NetWare machines.

Since each service adds overhead to your Windows 95 workstation, you should only enable those services that you will use. For example, if you have the only Windows 95 workstation on a network void of Microsoft products like Windows NT, you will not want to enable the Microsoft Network Client. Likewise, if you are on a Novell network, and you do not want to share your printer or files with other network users, simply deselect the check box next to the Microsoft Network File and Print Sharing box.

TCP/IP

A second network protocol aptly tuned for LAN computing with Windows 95 workstations is the Transport Control Protocol and Internet Protocol (TCP/IP). This protocol, originally developed back in 1969, will provide you with some important capabilities under Windows 95. Like IPX/SPX, Windows 95's TCP/IP Protocol functions as a 32-bit Virtual Device Driver (VxD) and consumes no conventional memory on your machine. A VxD loads into extended memory as a part of extended memory, and it can be loaded and unloaded from within Windows 95. It can therefore be used in conjunction with other protocols through ODI and NDIS drivers. This will give you the option to connect to a number of network operating systems such as NetWare and SCO UNIX for example. However, its biggest asset lies not in its speed or interoperability but in its predominance as the protocol of choice for the Internet.

The Internet, which encompasses the Earth, connecting institutions, companies, and individuals in over 150 countries, has grown from 213 hosts in August, 1981 to over 2,217,000 hosts in 1995—all of which rely upon the TCP/IP protocol. There are many advantages associated with the TCP/IP protocol. It is robust in that it supports many useful protocols such as the File Transfer Protocol (FTP), which enables two TCP/IP-based computers to exchange binary and textual files over a network. It supports the Telnet protocol, which enables one computer to remotely access another computer and execute programs on that computer as though they were local programs. It also supports a sophisticated protocol called Simple Mail Transfer Protocol (SMTP), which will allow you to exchange e-mail containing voice, video, and files with other computers.

If you wish to take advantage of these protocols under TCP/IP, you must either have TCP/IP hosts, which are usually UNIX machines available on your company's network, or you must have access to the Internet. At your office, you will most likely have direct TCP/IP access both to local and remote Internet UNIX machines. However, in some instances, companies either do not have dial-up connections to the Internet or do not have any local UNIX machines. In this case, you will still want to install TCP/IP support, but in communicating with the Internet, your machine will use what is known as Point-to-Point Protocol (PPP).

TCP/IP Installation and Configuration

Despite TCP/IP's powerful protocols and predominant acceptance, installing support for TCP/IP contains some added complexities that make it more difficult to implement than IPX/SPX, but this section will tell you how to install it successfully. In an IPX/SPX network, each server, workstation, and peripheral makes itself known by a signal number that is hard-wired into the network adapter. This "network address" is predetermined at the manufacturing level and requires no additional configuration for a network to take advantage of its addressing capabilities. Since an IPX/SPX network relies solely upon this number for network device communication, you can dynamically add and remove a workstation without having to change any settings on the workstation.

IP Addresses

With a TCP/IP network, on the other hand, the task of adding and removing workstations becomes much more complicated. Under the TCP/IP protocol standard, workstations are known not only by their burned-in network address, but by highly configurable logical addresses known as IP addresses. On a TCP/IP network, an administrator must create and maintain individual IP addresses for each network device (workstation, server, and peripheral) that is associated with the burned-in address. This address contains four sets of numbers, called octets that are offset by periods. An IP address, therefore, looks something like this:

```
124.124.11.1
```

Think of an IP address' hard-wired number as a house number, such as 1243 Del Oro Ave. And think of an IP address' logical component as the name of a house's owner, such as "Mr. Flibble."

There are four types of IP addresses (A, B, C, and D). Each address type identifies a computer contained within one or more networks. Remember, a network is a group of computers, and an internetwork is a group of networks connected through a router or bridge. Each address corresponds to a network of a particular size. For example, the type A address will work in a network consisting of 126 host addresses, while the type C address corresponds to a network containing 2,097,152 host addresses. Although this chapter will not discuss these types in detail, within Appendix A, "Networking Protocols," you will find additional information.

An easy way to understand the notation for these addresses is to view each octet as a refinement of an address. The first octet, for example, can refer to a city; the second octet can refer to a suburb; the third octet can refer to a block, and the fourth octet can refer to a house. As a note, this example works only for a type C address. Before a network can connect to the Internet via TCP/IP, it must apply for a range of IP addresses from the Network Information Center because there are a limited number of addresses available under the current TCP/IP addressing conventions. But even if you do not connect your Windows 95 workstation to the outside world, you should follow either the naming guidelines of your network administrator or create a meaningful standard for future IP addresses.

A second type of address, which really is a part of all types of IP addresses, is the subnet mask address. This address does not point to a machine, however. Instead it points to a group of machines, setting them apart from all other machines. This is necessary, especially within broadcast-based networks like Ethernet, in order to limit the amount of traffic present on the network. For example, a large network can be broken up into two subnetworks through two subnet masks. These masks would prevent packets from leaving one network and propagating to the other unless they were destined specifically for a machine on the other network. For the machines within a subnet to communicate, they must all have the same subnet mask IP address.

Automatic Address Resolution

If you are not sure about the best way to pick a network address, Windows 95 includes a service that will allow your workstation to automatically choose and retain an IP address from a central address server. Called Dynamic Host Configuration Protocol (DHCP), this service resides upon a Windows NT server and transparently allocates an IP address for you when you install the TCP/IP protocol. Think of it as an address broker that assigns and maintains each workstation's address. But the DHCP has the additional benefit of allowing for dynamic allocation. In this way, you can move your workstation from one logical network to another without worrying about obtaining an accurate and valid IP address. Although this sounds difficult to implement, assuming you have created a Windows NT DHCP server, you will only need to specify that you want to obtain your IP address from the DHCP server while installing the TCP/IP protocol. That is it.

Installing TCP/IP Support

With an IP address firmly in mind or a DHCP server successfully installed, you can proceed to install TCP/IP support on your Windows 95 workstation by accessing the Network icon on the Control Panel window. From there, click on the Add button and then double-click on the Protocol selection. Here, you will see a list of network types. Select Microsoft, highlight the TCP/IP selection, and click on the OK button. (See Figure 11-5.)

From this point on, there are many decisions to be made because Microsoft's TCP/IP client comes with additional administrational procedures such as the Microsoft Windows NT Windows Internet Naming Service (WINS) and the Open Software Foundation's (OSF's) Distributed Computing Environment (DCE) Domain Naming Service (DNS).

The first decision to make concerns your IP address. Select the TCP/IP button from the Network window, click on the Properties button, and then click on the IP Address tab. (See Figure 11-6.) This will display two radio buttons: one indicating that you wish to obtain your network address from a DHCP server, and the other indicating that you wish to enter your own IP address. If you are going to enter your own network address, select the Specify an IP address button, and enter the octets one at a time for your IP address and your subnet mask.

Address Resolution   Now select the WINS Configuration tab. This service works like the DHCP service in that it enables your workstation to locate and utilize individual IP addresses. With this service, you do not have to enter the numerical IP

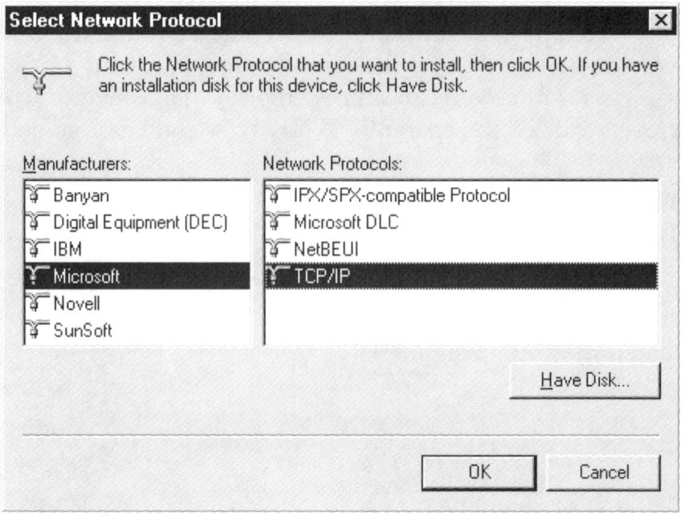

Select Network Protocol

Click the Network Protocol that you want to install, then click OK. If you have an installation disk for this device, click Have Disk.

Manufacturers:
- Banyan
- Digital Equipment (DEC)
- IBM
- Microsoft
- Novell
- SunSoft

Network Protocols:
- IPX/SPX-compatible Protocol
- Microsoft DLC
- NetBEUI
- TCP/IP

Have Disk...

OK   Cancel

Figure 11-5. *Selecting the Microsoft TCP/IP client*

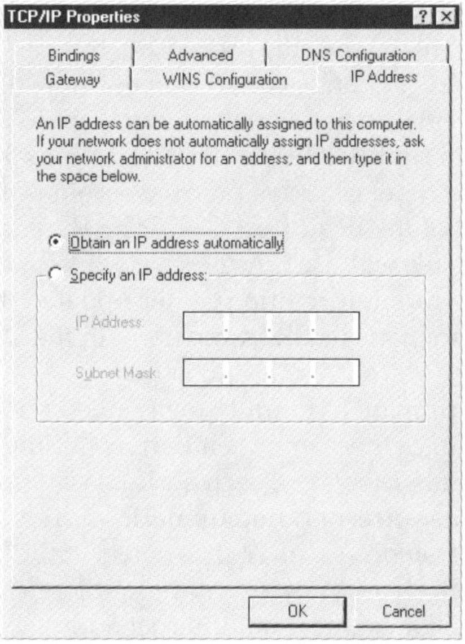

TCP/IP Properties

| Bindings | Advanced | DNS Configuration |
| Gateway | WINS Configuration | IP Address |

An IP address can be automatically assigned to this computer. If your network does not automatically assign IP addresses, ask your network administrator for an address, and then type it in the space below.

- ○ Obtain an IP address automatically
- ○ Specify an IP address:

  IP Address   .   .   .

  Subnet Mask   .   .   .

OK   Cancel

Figure 11-6. *Entering the IP address for your workstation*

address of a network resource. Instead, you can access it through a meaningful name. If you have ever used a UNIX workstation, you will be familiar with the "hosts" file, which contains two columns: the first column contains the numerical IP addresses of the resources you use most often, and the second column contains a linked name. With it, when you access a resource you can simply enter the name, and the corresponding numerical address is utilized transparently. A hosts file could look something like this:

```
132.145.12.1 receiving.acme.com
132.145.10.1 shipping.acme.com
143.122.2.153 bigschool.business.edu
```

Instead of entering a command like

```
telnet 132.145.12.1
```

you could enter a command like

```
telnet acme.receiving.com
```

This method of using friendly names works great for smaller networks. If your Windows 95 workstation is not going to communicate with the Internet or any other IP networks, you will most likely use this procedure. It is easy to set up, and assuming not very many adds, moves, or changes occur on your network, it is easy to maintain. Think of it as a sort of personal address book. If you want to add a new machine to your address book, you can simply edit the hosts text file and add that entry. However, for larger, more changeable networks, this practice becomes unfeasible. There is just no way to keep track of all of the IP addresses. During the early years of the Internet, just such a centralized hosts file was used. As new networks and machines were added to the Internet, the SRI network information center updated the hosts file. When the Internet became too large to manage, SRI came up with the Domain Naming System (DNS) architecture.

What the DNS does is provide a centrally maintained server that reads the mnemonic names and changes them into their corresponding numeric addresses. Through a vast number of name servers, each address sent out over the Internet is automatically resolved to its corresponding numeric address, just as a hosts file. It does this in a hierarchical fashion. Think of it as a tree, at the base of which there is the root. This is the place where all addresses start. From there, the first branching occurs at the organizational level. For example, all Internet addresses contain a final name that indicates the corresponding address' organizational type. Some predominant organizations are listed here:

gov	government
edu	education
com	commercial
mil	military
org	miscellaneous organization
con	country (this changes for each country)

The remaining levels represent the different subcategories found within one of these organizations. The example you saw previously of shipping.acme.com illustrates this in that *shipping* is the specific machine within the company called *acme*, and that the *acme* is the name of a company of the type *com*.

Windows 95 uses a Windows NT WINS server or a DNS server to resolve network addresses. Therefore, it is important that you ascertain an address for one or the other of these two machines. Otherwise, if you enter a command like

```
ftp shipping.acme.com
```

you will receive a message indicating that a host directory lookup failed for the host shipping.acme.com. The WINS support generally applies to a local network. Here, you will have one or more Windows NT machines that resolve network addresses. The DNS server, on the other hand, resides upon the Internet as a UNIX host. To make the WINS service available to your Windows 95 machine, from the WINS tab, select Enable WINS and enter the IP addresses of the desired and secondary WINS machines. If your Windows NT machine that you use to maintain your IP address (the DHCP machine) supports it, you can simply place a check mark in the box indicating that you would like the DHCP server to provide address resolution.

DNS Configuration

To make the DNS service available to your Windows 95 machine, select the DNS Configuration tab and enable DNS support. (See Figure 11-7.) Now, you will need to enter the host and domain name of the desired machine. If you are unsure of these names, contact your network administrator. Now enter the IP addresses of up to three DNS servers you know of. When you make an address resolution request, Windows 95 will search these machines one at a time for your desired address. If, after exhausting its search of these servers it does not find the requested address, it will return an address unresolvable message. Finally, enter the real name and suffix of the DNS server domains to which these machines belong.

The third item required is the TCP/IP gateway option. If your network connects to another network via a gateway, this entry will be necessary for your workstation to communicate across the gateway. You can obtain the IP addresses of the installed gateways from your network administrator. Once you have acquired these addresses,

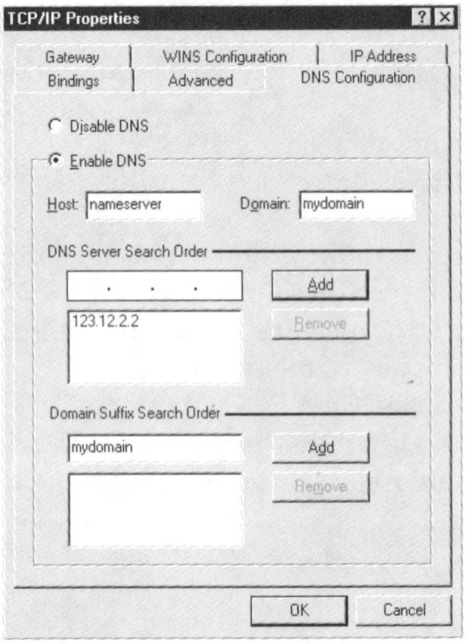

Figure 11-7.   *DNS address screen*

you should determine their distance from your Windows 95 workstation. The reason for this is simple. Each TCP/IP packet only lives for a certain amount of time. Therefore, you should avoid any unnecessary hops, which occur whenever a packet traverses from one logical network to another via a repeater such as an Ethernet hub. Unfortunately, the only way to obtain this information is to either physically trace your cable's path to the gateway (which is usually a router, although it can be a NetWare file server designed to route TCP/IP packets from one network to another) or to capture and view a TCP/IP packet that has traversed from your workstation across the gateway.

Once you have established the proper order, enter those addresses into the space provided in the Gateway tab. (See Figure 11-8.) Place them in order of proximity, the closest gateway residing at the top of the list.

To finish your TCP/IP configuration, select the Bindings tab and place a check mark next to the Windows 95 services you want bound with the TCP/IP protocol. An important consideration to make here is that if you are using more than one protocol stack, such as IPX/SPX and TCP/IP, you should not duplicate efforts over both stacks since each service you bind to a stack takes up valuable workstation resources. Therefore, you should generally check the Bindings tabs on both protocols and ensure that services are not duplicated from one protocol to another. There are instances in which you will want to duplicate services, however. For example, if your network

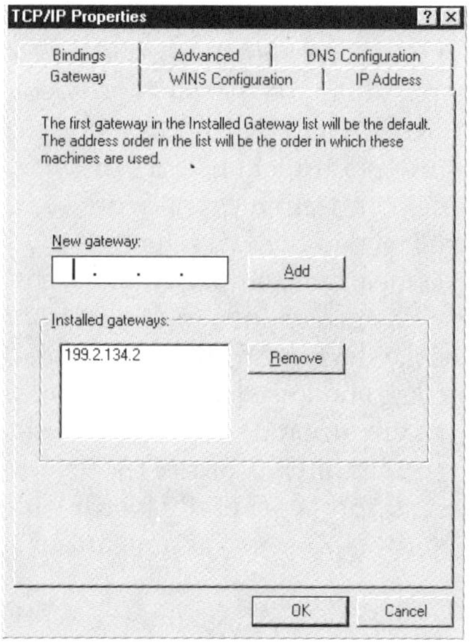

Figure 11-8. *Gateway configuration*

contains two Windows 95 workstations in which one uses TCP/IP and the other uses IPX/SPX, you will have to bind the selection entitled file and print sharing for both protocols. The selections available within a NetWare environment for both IPX/SPX and TCP/IP include

- Microsoft Network file and print sharing
- Microsoft Network client
- Microsoft Network client for NetWare

The Microsoft Network client for NetWare will only appear within the IPX/SPX Bindings tab; however, the other two appear in both. After you have selected which services to bind to the TCP/IP protocol, click the OK button. If you are using more than one protocol, you will now have to decide which protocol will be used by your Windows 95 workstation first. If, for example, you are connecting to a network with a TCP/IP-based UNIX server and an IPX/SPX-based NetWare server, you will most likely want to choose the protocol that corresponds to the server to which you want to initially connect. The secondary server will be available, but when your workstation first searches for network services, the first protocol will be used to establish a network connection.

NetBEUI

Support for NetBEUI within Windows 95 may seem a bit confusing at first because the NetBEUI protocol is closely related to the NetBIOS protocol, which is available in conjunction with both the IPX/SPX and TCP/IP protocols. NetBEUI stands for NetBIOS Extended User Interface. It functions over the network and transport layers of the OSI model and provides connectionless network services. For more information about both the NetBEUI protocol and the OSI reference model, refer to Appendix A, "Networking Protocols." As a means of comparison, IPX corresponds to the network layer of the OSI model, and SPX corresponds to the transport layer.

As a non-routable protocol, which means that it cannot be routed between logical networks, NetBEUI is finding less and less of a market. However, many legacy networks and smaller networks rely heavily upon its services. For example, Microsoft Windows for Workgroups defaults to the NetBEUI protocol for peer-to-peer communication, and Microsoft LAN Manager supports primarily NetBEUI. Both Windows 95 and Windows NT provide NetBEUI support as a means of communication with these systems.

Although NetBEUI is not suitable for large internetworks, you may choose to install it for compatibility. To activate the NetBEUI protocol, select Add and double-click the Protocol button from the Network Configuration window. Highlight the Microsoft selection and click the Microsoft NetBEUI selection. (See Figure 11-9.)

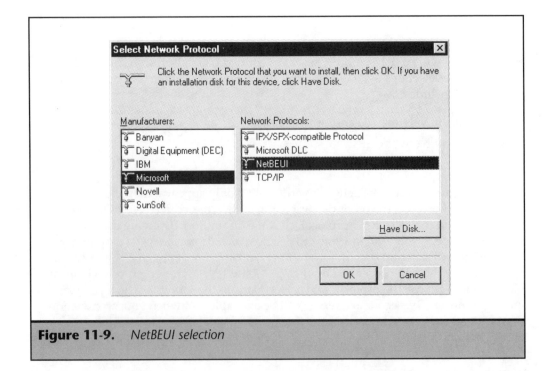

Figure 11-9. *NetBEUI selection*

Configuring NetBEUI

There is not much required to configure NetBEUI. Basically, you can change the number of sessions available on your Windows 95 workstation, the number of network control blocks available to your NetBEUI sessions, and the services to bind to your NetBEUI protocol. After you have selected the protocol, you should select the Properties option. From here, you should select the Advanced tab. Do not change the network control blocks or the session limitations unless you have determined a specific need for such changes. The sessions option defaults to 10 active sessions, and under most circumstances this should be fine. On the Bindings tab, you will find the Microsoft network client and the Microsoft file and print sharing selections. If you are going to use NetBEUI as a primary protocol, for example, to connect to a Windows for Workgroups network, you should enable both items. Otherwise, unmark them. Your applications will still be able to take advantage of them and your machine will not be burdened with the additional duties of supporting the main client software twice.

Other Protocols

Other, less predominant protocols are supported in Windows 95. They include Banyan VINES, SunSoft's PC-NFS protocols, and Digital Equipment Corp.'s PATHWORKS. If you require one of these protocols, Windows 95 will not require any additional software. You can simply install them as you would IPX/SPX or TCP/IP.

Banyan VINES

As a UNIX-based network operating system, Banyan VINES can support a large number of servers over a wide geographic area. Although VINES only occupies a little over seven percent of the total network operating system market (far behind Novell's 70 + percent), it commands over 25 percent of the enterprise-sized network market. This is due, in part, to VINES' global naming service, called StreetTalk. Similar to Novell's NetWare Directory Services, StreetTalk will enable your Windows 95 workstation to access network devices regardless of their location. Once you have installed StreetTalk, for example, you will be able to refer to a device by a common name instead of a network address without having to define its name in a hosts file, as with UNIX.

To install support for Banyan VINES, select the Add button and double-click the Protocol button from the Network window. Highlight the Banyan selection, and then highlight the Banyan VINES protocol. Now, all that remains is to configure the services you want to bind to your Banyan VINES protocol. As with the other protocols, your choice will depend on which services are already riding over other protocols. If VINES is your only protocol, by all means, select both the Microsoft client and Microsoft file and print sharing options. Otherwise, ensure that you do not double your network adapter card's efforts by running these options over two or more protocols.

SunSoft PC-NFS

Developed by Sun Microsystems, the Network File System (NFS) protocol has one purpose, to provide transparent disk access regardless of a disk's physical location. With NFS, a local workstation can access a remote workstation's hard disk as though it were attached to the local hard disk. This protocol arose out of the need to share files between connected UNIX workstations in an engineering environment. NFS is an important protocol because it can provide your Windows 95 workstation with access to the hard disks of many remote machines, assuming of course that those machines utilize NFS as well. NFS is widely distributed upon most brands of UNIX such as SCO, Sun Solaris, BSD, etc. Like the ftp protocol found in TCP/IP, NFS will let you view and retrieve remote files, but it adds some substantial capabilities such as:

- Create, rename, and remove files
- Acquire file attributes
- Create, read, and remove directories
- Read and write files

To install support for NFS, click the Protocol button from the Configuration tab of the Network window. Then select the Add button, highlight the SunSoft item and select the PC-NFS protocol. Just as with the Banyan VINES protocol, your only option once you have installed the NFS protocol is to bind network services to the protocol stack. In order to take advantage of the file systems of other machines, you should check the Microsoft client file and print sharing option.

DEC PATHWORKS

This protocol serves to connect PCs to enterprise networks. You can find PATHWORKS on a wide variety of network operating systems and platforms. The primary goal behind PATHWORKS is to connect heterogeneous clients in a client/server architecture. With PATHWORKS, you can simultaneously access OS/2, Macintosh, DOS, Windows, and UNIX workstations. When it was originally created, PATHWORKS functioned on top of LAN Manager. Now, however, you can access NetWare, LAN Manager, UNIX, and VMS. One nice feature of PATHWORKS is its built-in ability to connect workstations in a peer-to-peer as well as a client/server architecture.

If you choose to install PATHWORKS, click the Add button and double-click the Protocol button in the Network window. Then highlight the Digital Equipment Corp. (DEC) option, and choose the appropriate protocol driver. Windows 95 comes with protocols for both token ring and Ethernet. It also supports PATHWORKS v 4.x and 5.x.

To configure PATHWORKS, there is very little required. As with the three previous protocols, you need only select the desired network services you wish to bind to the PATHWORKS protocol stack. (See Figure 11-10.)

Summary

This chapter addressed the elements necessary to install and configure different protocols such as IPX/SPX, TCP/IP, NetBEUI, Banyan VINES, SunSoft PC-NFS, and DEC PATHWORKS. Each protocol is generally associated with a single network operating system. For example, IPX/SPX is associated with Novell NetWare, while NetBEUI is associated with Microsoft LAN Manager and Windows for Workgroups. IPX/SPX actually evolved around NetWare as the offshoot of Xerox's XNS protocol. The configurations possible within IPX/SPX are many and varied. You can choose the Ethernet frame type, the number of logical connections, and whether or not to enable NetBIOS support.

This chapter then continued to address the many features available from the TCP/IP protocol and its relationship to the worldwide network called the Internet.

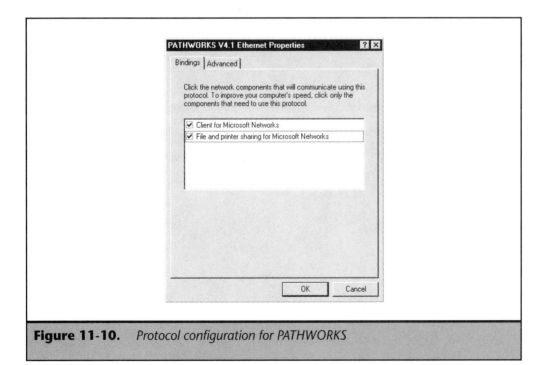

Figure 11-10. *Protocol configuration for PATHWORKS*

Windows 95 contains the ability to solve the problems associated with IP address resolution through either a WINS or a DHCP server residing upon a Windows NT machine. The basic address structure of an IP address was discussed, and the best way to administer an IP address was discussed.

The relevance of NetBEUI was assessed as it related to current and legacy networks. The NetBEUI protocol is generally associated with Windows for WorkGroups networks. The chapter concluded with a discussion of the remaining supported protocols (Banyan VINES, NFS, and PATHWORKS).

Chapter Twelve

Dial-Up Networking

"Where is the wisdom we have lost in knowledge?
Where is the knowledge we have lost in information?"
　　　　—T.S. Eliot, Choruses from 'The Rock'

Windows 95 is perhaps the only operating system outside of Apple Computer Corp.'s Macintosh System 7 to provide a complete and robust networking suite of networking tools. Like System 7, Windows 95 does not require any additional software. To begin networking with Windows 95, you need only configure the operating system. However, to take advantage of these networking options, you need a network interface card and some computers with which you can network. For example, how do you network from your home or from your laptop when you are on the road?

Windows 95 has all the answers. With Windows 95, you can connect your home or laptop machine to a world of network services through a modem. No software is needed. You can log on to your Windows 95 or Windows NT workstation at work and take full advantage of all your office capabilities. You can exchange e-mail over many online services, such as CompuServe. And you can connect your Windows 95 workstation to the world's largest collection of networks, the Internet. Through the Internet, you can take advantage of many informational services, and can even join real-time conversations with other Windows 95 users around the world. (See Figure 12-1.)

In this chapter we will discuss how Windows 95 can help you connect to the world of online services and remote networking. First we will show you how to use Windows 95's built-in remote access server to connect to your company's network from home. We will then show you how to send and receive e-mail from your Windows 95 workstation with its built-in Microsoft Exchange E-mail client. And finally, we will discuss how you can connect to the Internet and Microsoft's worldwide network.

In each section, we will outline the steps necessary to set up a service, including additional requirements you may need to complete in order to use each service. For example, to use Windows 95's CompuServe connectivity capabilities to send and receive e-mail, you must first have a CompuServe account. However, not every service requires you to set up an account in advance. To access company e-mail through the Microsoft Exchange mail client, you will also need to have an account on the services you wish to access. Using the Microsoft network, however, does not require any prearrangements. You can simply let Windows 95 dial the network, configure your account, and download the necessary software in a matter of minutes. In all instances, we will let you know if you need to do any preliminary tasks.

In all sections, we will focus primarily upon the telecommunications aspect of Windows 95's remote access products. This model of networking assumes that you are a user with two Windows 95 workstations, one at work and the other at home. The work machine, of course, will most likely be connected to a network of some kind in addition to a modem. The home computer will be connected to a telephone line via a modem (preferably a fax modem).

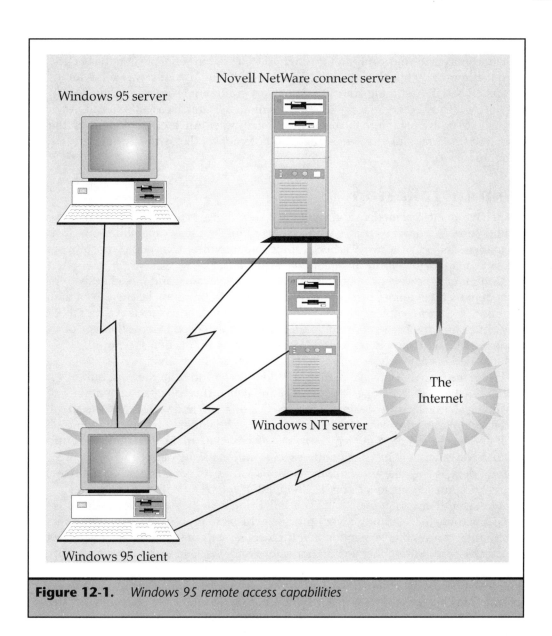

Figure 12-1. *Windows 95 remote access capabilities*

Before You Begin

Before you begin using the Windows 95 remote access products, you must install a modem. If you have already installed a modem, however, you should skip to the next section labeled "Remote Access."

There are two basic types of modems: internal and external. The external modem usually connects to your computer through the 9 or 25 pin serial port on the back of your computer, while the internal modem resides within your computer as an expansion board. Assuming your serial ports are configured correctly—they do not interfere with any other devices—an external modem is much easier to install. All you will need to do is plug it into the back of your computer. An internal modem, on the other hand, will require you to ensure that it does not conflict with any other computer devices.

Modem Installation

If you have an internal modem and you do not know how to check for incompatibilities, do not worry. Windows 95 comes with excellent Plug and Play capabilities. Just install the modem and let Windows 95 check for incompatibilities. You should consult your modem's manual for specific installation instructions.

Don't forget, however, to obtain either the modem's name and model or the type of modem that it emulates before you continue. This is important because even though Windows 95 comes complete with support for over 200 individual modems, your modem may not be one of those supported. In this case, you will need to have the type of modem that it most closely resembles. Most modems can function as a popular and ubiquitous modem type such as a "Hayes compatible" modem.

When the modem is installed, turn on Windows 95 and from the Start button's pull-down menu, click Settings and then Control Panel. This will open a window containing an icon labeled Modems. Double-click this icon and you should see an installation Wizard that can guide you though the remainder of the installation.

If you have a standard modem, such as a Hayes compatible, then press the button marked Next. This will instruct Windows 95 to automatically detect and configure your modem. It will take a few minutes for this process to complete, so do not worry if your computer seems to lock up. If it remains silent for more than two or three minutes, simply press CTRL-ALT-DEL. This will bring up a dialog box from which you can terminate the autodiscovery process, which attempts to obtain configuration information concerning your modem. If this occurs, start the program again and select the check box indicating that you do not want Windows 95 to scan for your modem.

For a nonstandard modem, or a modem that was not detected by the previous autodiscovery routine, place a check mark in the same box to enter your modem information by hand and then click the Next button. From the next screen, you can either select the type of modem that reflects your type of modem or install your own configuration disk by clicking the Have Disk button. (See Figure 12-2.)

Select the correct port to which your modem is attached. This is usually either COM1 or COM2. Click the next button and finish the modem installation. You will now be presented with a screen containing your new modem configuration. At this point, to ensure that your modem does not conflict with any other resources, click the Diagnostics tab. You will see a screen containing your modem and available communication ports. To see additional configuration settings, click the More

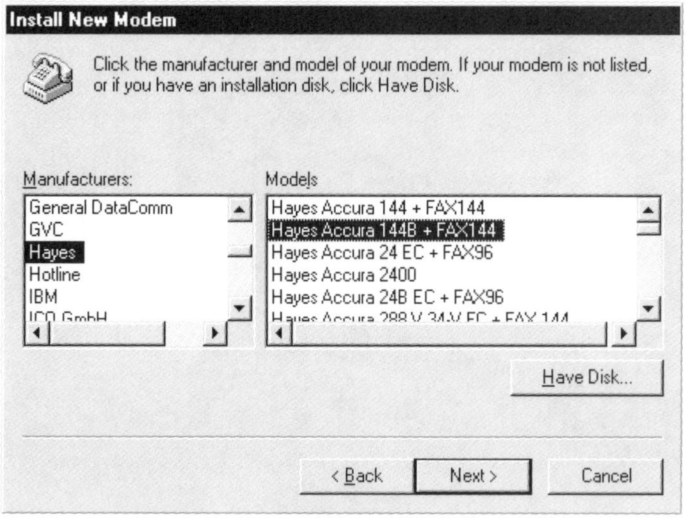

Figure 12-2. *Modem configuration screen*

Information button. (See Figure 12-3.) If there is a connection problem, this screen will tell you what the trouble is.

At this point, if there is a problem, go back to the General Settings tab and click the Properties button. This will open a settings window from which you can change the modem's communication port, modem speed capabilities, speaker volume, etc.

Once you have installed your modem, you will not have to add or reconfigure another modem, regardless of the Windows 95 application you use. Through a feature called Unimodem, a modem becomes available to all certified Windows 95 applications. In this way, if you install a new remote access package, it will simply use the existing Unimodem settings just as a newly installed word processor takes advantage of a previously configured printer under Windows 3.1.

Remote Access

Once you have installed your modem, the first thing you can do is connect your Windows 95 workstation with another Windows 95 workstation. Additionally, you can connect with Windows NT, Windows 3.11, and even third-party remote access products such as Novell's NetWare Connect. By connecting your computer with an office-based Windows 95 workstation, you can accomplish many of the tasks you

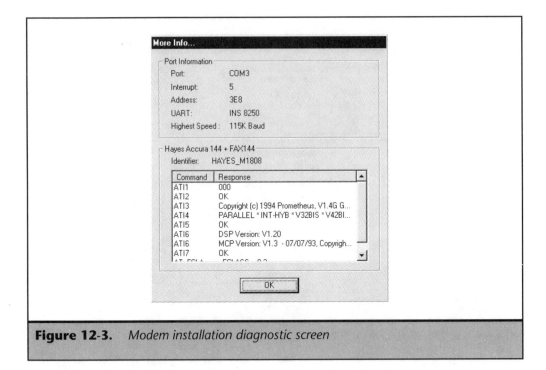

Figure 12-3. *Modem installation diagnostic screen*

normally perform at work while you are at home. For example, you can receive and send mail, access a database, or download a spreadsheet.

Windows 95 accomplishes this feat by providing remote access services. This type of connectivity lets you access all of the items on your desktop and network. If you have a file on your office computer that you need to work on at home, you can simply use the remote access services to retrieve that file. You can even open that file right on the office workstation from your remote computer. For example, you could connect to your office computer and use a copy of Microsoft Excel on your remote workstation to open, edit, save, even print a spreadsheet file on the office computer.

Dial-Up Protocols

Windows 95 can accomplish such feats by tunneling standard network protocols over the phone line. First, Windows 95 uses a protocol common to dial-up networking called Point-to-Point protocol (PPP). Over this protocol, Windows 95 transports your standard application protocols such as Internet Packet Exchange/Sequenced Packet Exchange (IPX/SPX), Transmission Control Protocol/Internet Protocol (TCP/IP), NetBIOS, and NetBIOS Extended User Interface (NetBEUI). (See Figure 12-4.) When you execute an application while connected to a remote machine, information passes through these protocols from the application to the modem. On the other end of the connection, they pass back up this stack of protocols to an application.

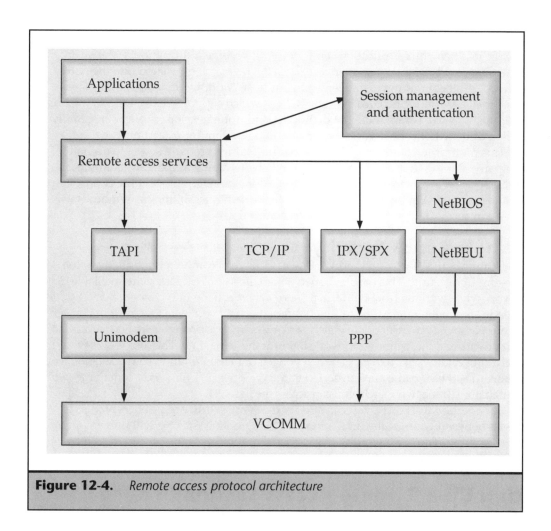

Figure 12-4. *Remote access protocol architecture*

Additionally, Windows 95 comes with telephony support built-in. This will let you connect your Windows 95 workstation to your company's PBX system. Using Microsoft's Telephony Application Programming Interface (TAPI), you can use your modem to handle two-way communication over an ISDN telephone line. This in essence lets your computer dial out while another computer dials into your computer.

Remote Access Concepts

When you installed Windows 95 at your office, if you were connected to a network such as Novell NetWare, you installed one of the above protocols, most likely IPX/SPX. On your home computer, however, because Windows 95 will not have detected any network hardware, you will have no such protocols. This is fine. The way Windows 95's remote access works is it connects your local computer with a remote host computer over PPP. When your application sends network-specific information to the host, it is sent over PPP; however, when it reaches the host, it is translated into the native network protocol through a gateway on your host Windows 95 workstation. This is true for all networking protocols except TCP/IP, which supports native PPP commands and functions. All commands that do not depend upon network services are simply routed directly to the host Windows 95 operating system for execution.

This multiprotocol routing can provide full-featured remote access to a small company wishing to use the host Windows 95 workstation as a dedicated remote access server. However, it only supports one connection. For more connections, you should consider Windows NT. It can provide the same capabilities as Windows 95, but it can support up to 256 simultaneous connections.

Remote Access Security

One feature both Windows 95 and Windows NT have in common is the ability to use pass-through security. This enables you to obtain the same network rights available to you at work while working from home. In essence, when you log into your office workstation, it sends your login information to a NetWare server as if you were logging into that server. If your password and user name match NetWare's information, you are given access to the network and the Windows 95 workstation at the same time. This also works with Microsoft Windows NT networks. When you log in to the Windows 95 workstation, your password and user name are transferred to the Windows NT file server containing your user account. If the two match, you can access the network.

For additional security, you can specify that your password be encrypted as it passes between your local workstation and the remote host. This will prevent anyone from "sniffing" your password with a device that intercepts the password as it travels across the phone lines or a network.

Setting Up a Remote Access Session

The first thing you must accomplish to connect your local workstation with a remote host is specifying which machine is to act as the host and which is to act as the remote client. A nice thing about Windows 95's remote access capabilities is that the same software is required for both the client and the host computers. In this way, you can interchangeably work remotely with your home and work computers. To switch your local client to a remote host, for example, you simply click one button. However, before you can manage your connection this easily, you must install and configure the remote access software. The first step is to install and configure the remote client software. Then you should install and configure the remote host software.

Installing the Local Client Access Software

When you installed Windows 95, if you had a modem installed, the installation program would have automatically copied the remote access files to your hard disk. If not, you will have to install them by hand. Assuming you have installed a modem, go to the Control Panel window and double-click the Add/Remove Programs icon. This will open a settings window containing dialog boxes for the installation and removal of both Microsoft Windows 95 and third-party applications. Select the tab labeled Windows Setup. You will see a scroll box containing a list of software applications available for installation. The boxes containing check marks represent items currently installed on your computer. You can select and deselect any items you want, but to enable remote computing applications, you must double-click on the Communications item and place check marks next to the items labeled Hyper Terminal and Dial-Up Networking. (See Figure 12-5.) You should also select the Microsoft Exchange option.

Once you click the OK button, you will be prompted to insert the disks necessary to install your software. All that remains is to restart the computer.

Configuring the Local Client Access Software

Now that you have installed the appropriate software, click the Start button, the Programs button, and then the Accessories button. From here, click the Dial-Up Networking button. This will open a window similar to the printer window, containing a template icon labeled Create New Connection. When you double-click it, you will open a new connection Wizard. Notice that it defaults to the modem you just installed. If you need to make changes to the modem that will apply only to this connection session, feel free to do so because your changes will not affect any other applications.

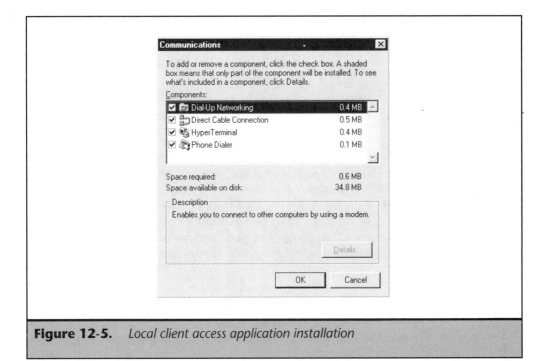

Figure 12-5. *Local client access application installation*

For example, you may want to change the volume of the modem, stop bits, parity, baud rate, or flow control. Keep in mind, however, that in most cases, you will not need to change any of these settings. To do so may interfere with your connection. In many ways it is best to leave these setting alone on both the local client and the remote host. In this way, you ensure that both computers are going to be able to work together seamlessly.

After finishing your changes, click the Next button. This will open a dialog box asking you for an area code, telephone number, and country code. If you need to enter any different numbers to access an outside line or to turn off call waiting, do not enter them here. There is an excellent feature designed just for those contingencies. If you need to dial long distance, for example, Windows 95 will automatically enter the number "1" when it places the call. Select finish. This will create a second icon in the Dial-Up Networking window. That is all there is to it.

Installing and Configuring the Remote Access Software

To install and configure the remote access software, you must perform the same tasks as you did when you installed the local client. One nice aspect of the Windows 95 remote access product is that it can act simultaneously as a host and a remote client. When you install Dial-Up-Networking, your machine automatically becomes available as a dial-up server. This does not mean that it can maintain two connections, however. It means that if you plan to use both computers interchangeably, then you can configure each to be a server once, and thereafter, call from one to the other regardless of which machine acts as the client or host. Moreover, once you have set up each workstation, you never need to reconfigure them unless you turn the service off. This means that you can close the Dial-Up Networking window or reboot the workstation without worrying about terminating your service. It will always be available.

Choosing a Server Type With Windows 95, there are number of server types that can exist on a host server. You can enable it as a PPP server, a NetWare Connect server, a Windows NT server, or even a Windows for Workgroups server. If you are just connecting remote and local Windows 95 machines, you will need to choose the "PPP: Windows 95, Windows NT 3.5, Internet" selection from the pull-down menu under the Server Types button. This is the most flexible type of server, as it provides connectivity for many different types of server configurations. (See Figure 12-6.) If you have a NetWare network, however, you may want to choose the NetWare Connect server type as it will provide you with pass-through security through a NetWare file server.

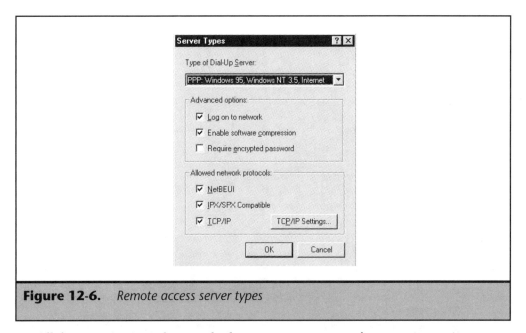

Figure 12-6. *Remote access server types*

All that remains is to choose whether or not you want software compression and an encrypted password to be passed between the host server and the client. The password is a good idea, but unless you are using an older modem that does not contain any software compression algorithms, do not select software compression. You will experience fewer problems.

Enabling Device Sharing   The last thing you will have to configure before you use the remote access software is file sharing. This tells your Windows 95 workstation which files, directories, drives, and even printers are to be made available to remote users. For example, if you intend for others to use your Windows 95 workstation, you can limit them to only a specific drive or directory. To activate sharing, open the desktop icon labeled My Computer, and click once on your hard disk's icon. Then, clicking once with the right mouse button, activate the pop-up menu for the hard drive and click the Properties selection. This will open the settings window containing three tabs labeled General, Tools, and Sharing. Select the Sharing tab, and click the radio button called Sharing. (See Figure 12-7.)

You can share a drive in three ways. You can let people read the effected information; you can let them have full access to the that information; or you can provide full access only through select passwords. Your choice should depend upon how you will share the data on your host computer.

Using Windows 95 Remote Access

Having completed the installation and configuration requirements for Windows 95's remote access product, you will find using the product refreshingly simple. To begin using the remote access software, simply open the Dial-Up Networking window and

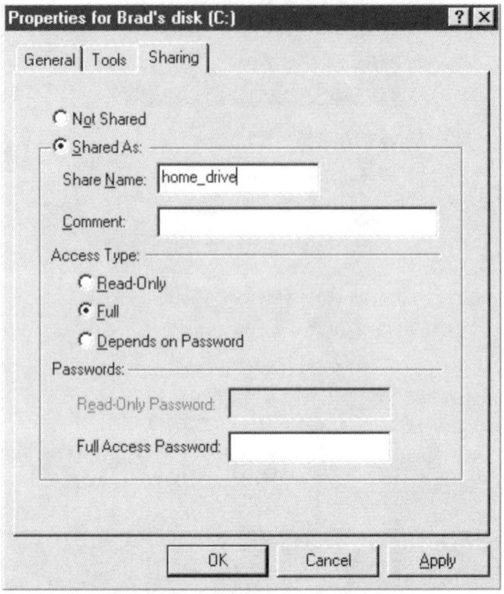

Figure 12-7. *Device sharing window*

double-click the newly created remote session icon. This will open a dialog box in which you will be required to enter a password and name. If there are any last minute changes to be made to either the modem configuration or the remote server, make those changes here. They will be saved for the next time automatically. If you have configured both machines with the same settings (passwords, names, server-types, etc.), you should not have to make any changes.

When you are ready to begin, simply click the Connect button. The workstation will call the remote host and check your name and password against either its own user list or the list of a Windows NT or NetWare file server. The first time you make a connection, it will ask you for the name and password, however, so be prepared to have the password you used in setting up the host computer ready.

If all goes well, you will see a confirmation dialog box, indicating that you have connected with the other machine. Notice that the only thing that looks different is the menu bar, on which there is a representation of a modem next to the clock. This will tell you the status of your connection. (See Figure 12-8.)

Nothing else will appear changed. This is because in a remote access session, you only "access" data and services on the host machine. All of its drives, directories, files,

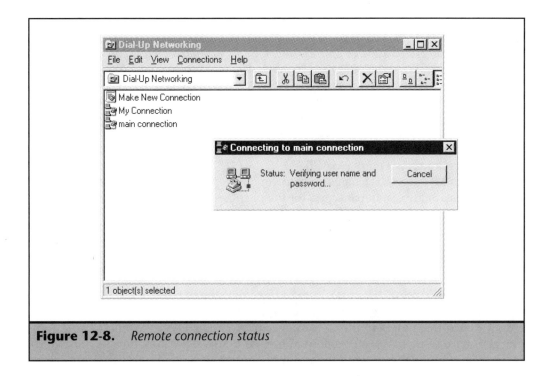

Figure 12-8. *Remote connection status*

and printers (depending upon your security setup) merely become extensions of your own local desktop.

To access those extensions, you can simply open your network neighborhood, in which the host machine will appear as though it were a network file server. Or you can open the My Computer icon on the Windows 95 desktop. The remote system's information will appear in the same way your information will appear.

Remote E-Mail with Windows 95

Your Windows 95 workstation can connect you with any network services available on your remote host computer through the remote access server. But if you do not have a direct telephone connection between your work computer and your home computer, you can still stay connected to important information in the form of built-in electronic mail (e-mail) services.

To this end, Windows 95 comes with a very powerful e-mail application called Microsoft Exchange. This application can give your Windows 95 workstation access to other computers through e-mail.

Microsoft Exchange

Microsoft Exchange is a suite of applications that act primarily as a single interface through which you can send and receive many different types of information. Through what Microsoft calls a *Universal Inbox,* Microsoft Exchange can access common message types from different vendors. For example, with it you can access e-mail from Microsoft Mail, Lotus, cc:Mail, etc. Furthermore, it can exchange e-mail with online services such as CompuServe. Microsoft does this through a standardized information communication interface called simple Messaging Application Programming Interface (simple MAPI).

Although Microsoft Exchange can help you connect your networked Windows 95 workstation to many e-mail packages, for the purpose of this chapter we will discuss only those aspects of Microsoft Exchange that pertain to remote, dial-up networking.

MAPI

The basic building block of dial-up e-mail under Windows 95's Exchange package is MAPI. It is a standard architecture to which e-mail vendors can tailor their applications in order to provide consistency between applications. Currently, this technology is used as compatibility insurance between disparate e-mail platforms. For example, a company may have a Davinci e-mail system in one office while maintaining a Microsoft Mail e-mail system in another office. Normally, because these two messaging platforms were built by different vendors—and use different messaging transports—you would not expect them to communicate. With a gateway providing a bridge between MAPI and non-MAPI applications, such as Davinci, you could send and receive e-mail from one to the other.

This works great for integrating two disparate installations, but it does not allow users a choice of messaging front ends. If your workstation connects to a Davinci messaging system, you must use Davinci's front end application. You cannot choose to use the Microsoft Mail front end to access the Davinci messaging system. With Windows 95's Exchange Universal Inbox, however, you can use a single front end to access either of these two messaging systems.

An excellent example of the capabilities of MAPI is the CompuServe online service MAPI driver that is available for Windows 95. If you have a CompuServe account, you could exchange e-mail with any MAPI-compliant messaging system from the Universal Inbox via the network. And from the same interface, you could exchange e-mail with CompuServe via the phone line. This means that you will no longer have to go to a number of e-mail interfaces in order to send and receive mail. You can do all of it from the Exchange interface.

Installing Support for Microsoft Exchange

When you installed Windows 95, you were prompted to install Microsoft Exchange. If you choose not to install Microsoft Exchange at that time, you must install it by hand.

If you are unsure whether or not you installed Exchange, an easy way to check is to click the Start button and then the Programs button. If you have installed the program, you should see a selection labeled Microsoft Exchange. If you do not see this option, go back to the previous section describing the installation of dial-up networking software before continuing and set up your software.

Once you have installed the Exchange software, you will be ready to access a wealth of capabilities including

- Rich text e-mail including full use of fonts, colors, bullets, etc.

- Full Object Linking and Embedding (OLE) support, including visual editing and cross-application drag and drop capabilities. This lets you create a spreadsheet, for example, and drag it to a word processor, where it can be printed and saved as a part of a document.

- A built-in remote mail feature that uses TAPI to support all major modem types and network protocols. TAPI helps Windows 95 utilize many different types of modems.

- Object-oriented file-system capabilities, which allow you to drag files to and from the Exchange client. This lets you easily mail a file to someone by dragging a file from a file folder to the Exchange e-mail interface.

- A customizable toolbar with integrated shortcut options.

- Blind Carbon Copies (BCC). A BCC message can be sent to an individual without alerting that individual as to the originator's identity.

- Intelligent message responses that automatically indent replies.

- The ability to connect to multiple mailboxes and files simultaneously. With Microsoft Exchange, you can send and receive mail over different mail systems at one time, such as CompuServe, Internet, and Microsoft Mail.

- Integration of the Windows 95 registry to enable a single, master password.

Using Microsoft Exchange

If your host computer that you access is attached to a network containing a Microsoft Mail messaging system, you can dial into your network directly from Microsoft Exchange to send and receive messages. If you have already installed a remote access driver, you will only need to compose and then send an e-mail message to take advantage of this capability. Windows 95 will automatically prompt you one time for the name of your host post office. After that, whenever you select to send all outbound messages, Windows 95 will automatically detect each message's destination and send it to the appropriate post office or online service.

Microsoft Exchange as a CompuServe Client

Even if you do not have a Microsoft Mail application, you can use the Exchange server built into Windows 95 to power a small workgroup of mail users. In either case, one of the greatest benefits of Microsoft Exchange is its ability to exchange information with the worldwide CompuServe online network. This is a very powerful capability because through CompuServe you can send and receive mail over virtually any network service, such as MCI Mail and the Internet.

The way Exchange communicates with CompuServe is quite ingenious because it does not require a separate communications package to create a remote session with the CompuServe network. It works transparently within the Exchange client through a MAPI driver that initiates the dial-up connection in the background.

To install support for CompuServe, open the Mail and Fax icon from the Control Panel and click the button labeled Add. This will show which services you can add to the Exchange client. Select the CompuServe Mail icon and click OK. (See Figure 12-9.) If the CompuServe icon does not appear, click Have Disk. By installing CompuServe suppport, you will not only be able to send and receive CompuServe mail, but you will be able to automatically update the Exchange address directory with the contents from your CompuServe directory. This includes any changes as well. So if you make any changes to the CompuServe directory, the Exchange directory will also be aware of those changes.

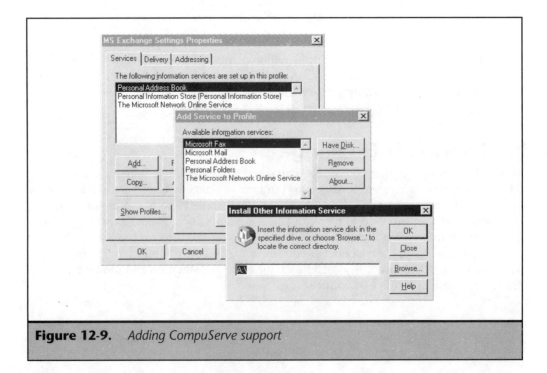

Figure 12-9. *Adding CompuServe support*

The Exchange program will then ask you to enter a description of this service as well as the location of your Exchange post office. If you are installing support for CompuServe on your home computer, you will want to enter the post office location that is in your Windows directory. For example, you would enter **C:\ WINDOWS\ MYMAIL** as the location name. You will then be asked to enter your password. If you have installed the CompuServe information manager (either the DOS or Windows version), Windows 95 will automatically detect its CIM.INI file, which contains login information such as your name, account number, encrypted password, and access numbers. It will automatically update Exchange with this information.

If you do not have the CompuServe Information Manager (CIM) application available, you will be prompted to enter the needed information manually. All that remains is to follow the dialog boxes through the remainder of the installation. You may want to evaluate, however, if you want to delete messages on the CompuServe service once they have been retrieved to your local machine. If you plan to access CompuServe both at work and at home, you should choose not to delete the retrieved messages because you will still have access to those messages at work even if you have retrieved them at home.

Using CompuServe   It is a very simple task to use CompuServe mail from your Windows 95 Exchange e-mail client. Just click the Start button, then Programs, and then Send A New Message. This will bring up an e-mail editor. Here you can use Microsoft's *Rich Text Editor* to create your message. When you enter the addressing information, enter it the same way you would if you were connected to CompuServe. To send an Internet message, for example, you would enter the standard CompuServe notation:

internet: *address*

as shown in Figure 12-10.

The first time you enter this address, you will be asked to select its appropriate type from a list of possible CompuServe message types and give the address a proper name. And that is it. Just select Send Message from the File pull-down menu to send the message and Windows 95 will automatically call CompuServe and mail your message.

Windows 95 Internet Support

One of the strongest features of Windows 95 is its ability to connect you with online information, and in no way does it demonstrate this better than in its Internet connectivity capabilities. Through an Internet MAPI driver and Microsoft Exchange, your workstation can communicate simultaneously with the Internet. Additionally, through its built-in Internet client, you can connect to Microsoft's Internet access service and take full advantage of the Internet, downloading files, participating in newsgroups, chatting in real-time with other Internet users, and even browsing the World Wide Web through Microsoft's downloadable browser (available at http:/www.microsoft.com).

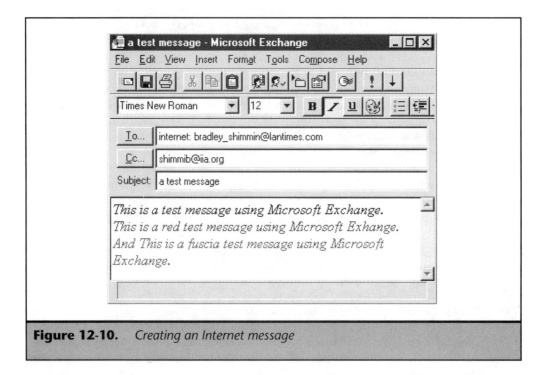

Figure 12-10. *Creating an Internet message*

Internet Mail

Available separately, Microsoft's Internet mail accessory features rely upon Windows 95's built-in Exchange service to provide you with the following capabilities:

- Support for the Internet standard for electronic mail: Simple Mail Transport Protocol (SMTP).

- *Windows Sockets* compatibility to create simultaneous Internet sessions over TCP/IP and PPP.

- Simultaneous use of dial-up PPP and LAN-based protocols such as TCP/IP and IPX/SPX.

- Multipurpose Internet Mail Extensions (MIME) to send and receive video, image, voice, text, and graphics.

- Built-in *uuencode/uudecode* support for translating binary files to and from ASCII.

All of these features will help you navigate the Internet via e-mail more effectively. Through MIME support, for example, you can receive a sound clip from a friend and, by simply clicking on it within your Exchange client Inbox, play back the sound.

The same holds for pictures. Normally, when you send someone a picture over the Internet, you must change the picture from a binary format into an ASCII format so that it can safely navigate any gateways it must cross on its way across the Internet. This method requires you to execute the uuencode command to change it into ASCII when you send the message. It also requires the receiving party to translate it back into a format suitable for viewing through the uudecode command. Similarly, because Windows 95 utilizes the recognized simple Mail Transport Protocol (SMTP) you can be assured that no matter who you send your e-mail to, they will receive it.

Adding Internet Mail Support

To create support for dial-up Internet e-mail support, you must add it to your Exchange client just as you did with support for CompuServe mail. First, open the Control Panel, double-click the icon labeled Mail and Fax, and then click the Add button. This will bring up a screen of possible mail services. Click on Have Disk and insert the appropriate disk. Click OK to bring up a Wizard that will help you through your installation.

This service requires you to already have an Internet connection, but do not let the number of tabs and fields intimidate you in this configuration window. The most difficult piece of information you will need to come up with is your e-mail host server's name and the phone number used to connect with that server. This information should be easily attainable from your Internet access provider. To complete the configuration, enter your e-mail account information, including your mail account name, password, and mail server name. (See Figure 12-11.)

Figure 12-11. *Internet Mail Service configuration screen*

Next, select the Connection tab and specify the type of connection you desire. If you are on a network that has a direct connection to the Internet, you can simply leave the connection information on its default setting marked LAN connection. For a dial-up connection, you must change it appropriately, click the Connect Options button, and enter your logon name and password. When you are done, click the Edit button and enter the phone number of your Internet access service.

All other configuration options should work fine for most Internet mail services and accounts. But feel free to modify any of them as they pertain to the manner in which Microsoft Exchange handles your incoming and outgoing mail. For example, from the General tab, if you click the Advanced Options button, you can instruct Exchange to transport your attachments as either MIME or simple text.

You may also want to modify the default action Microsoft Exchange takes when you open the Inbox. For example, if you instruct Exchange to open the Inbox with your Internet connection as the default task, your machine will automatically dial the Internet if you have any mail to be sent. If you want to select a specific startup configuration for the Inbox, therefore, simply make your choice from the settings window that you activate from the Microsoft Exchange Profiles icon.

Once you have installed the Internet mail client, whenever you address a message, you can specify which service it is to be routed through, such as CompuServe or the Internet. That is all there is to it. You do not have to change the way you address your e-mail; you do not have to change the way you create the text in your message. All services appear as one within your Windows 95 Exchange client.

Dial-Up Microsoft Network Services

Of course, if you connect your Windows 95 workstation to a network that has a direct connection to the network, the built-in TCP/IP protocol will provide you with immediate and complete Internet access. If you have no such connection, however, do not worry. Windows 95 comes with the software needed to connect your workstation with the Internet over a phone line. A service called the Microsoft Network (MSN) can communicate with over 2.5 million other computers spread throughout the globe through e-mail, newsgroups, and the World Wide Web. Additional Microsoft Network-centric services such as bulletin boards, chat rooms, and file libraries are limited to Microsoft's private MSN network.

Connecting to the Microsoft Network

It is quite simple to connect with the Microsoft network. You do not need any special software or hardware beyond a modem. If you installed the Microsoft Network, double-click on the Sign Up for the Microsoft Network icon. This will open a dialog box in which you will have to enter personal information and payment method. To enter a local access number, you need only enter your area code and the first three digits of your local telephone number. The MSN software will then dial the network, verify your account, and transfer the necessary applications back to your workstation.

Figure 12-12. *MSN dial-up procedure*

This will also download the closest access number to help you avoid long-distance charges. All that remains to use the Microsoft Network is to reboot your Windows 95 workstation and double-click the new desktop icon labeled Microsoft Network. This will dial the network, log you in, and present you with an initial login screen. (See Figure 12-12.)

Designed around the Windows 95 object oriented user interface, the Microsoft Network functions as a series of folders, files, and windows. By double-clicking the Categories picture from the initial login screen, for example, you will be presented with a standard window containing many bulletin boards, documents, and services. (See Figure 12-13.)

When you double-click one of these items, you will either start a program or open another window. In either way, if you click on the original Categories window, you can access another program or window, just as you would with a local application on your Windows 95 desktop.

Summary

In this chapter, we have discussed the many dial-up networking features available in Windows 95. Without having to purchase or add any additional software, you can take

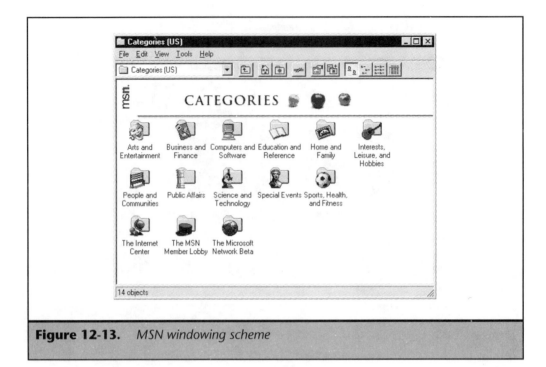

Figure 12-13. *MSN windowing scheme*

control of the computer at your office, send and receive mail with on-line services, and even take a tour of Microsoft's idea of the Information SuperHighway.

For example, you can access files, printers, and application services on a remote network via Windows 95's dial-up PPP. You can send mail to online services such as the Internet or CompuServe directly from your Microsoft Exchange e-mail client, which is also included with Windows 95. And finally, you can connect with Microsoft's online services and exchange files, programs, and ideas with other Windows 95 users around the world. The only thing you need to access these services is a modem.

Chapter Thirteen

Plug and Play

"Work consists of whatever a body is obliged to do.
Play consists of whatever a body is not obliged to do."
—Mark Twain

Even though it's roughly the same size and weight, your computer bears little resemblance to your household appliances. Your microwave cooks, your toaster toasts, your television entertains and educates. But what does a computer do? Well, it's a little more complicated. It educates and entertains, just like your TV, but most people have a hard time using it. Why is that?

The PC Problem

When you turn on your television set, do you see a message on your screen telling you the tube is warming up? Does it tell you who the manufacturer of the circuit board was? Does it tell you what kind of VCR you have hooked up and whether or not it's responding? If you plug a new cable box in, do you have to load a new driver on your TV? No. Your television set just works.

When Microsoft set out to revamp the Windows operating system, it made ease of use a priority. It spent a lot of time and money redesigning the user interface to make it simpler for people who are new to computers. But even with the new interface, inserting a new scanner or fax card takes more knowledge and skill than most users possess. You have things to worry about like interrupt conflicts, port addresses, SCSI termination, and DMA channels. The computer is very particular about how it communicates with all the peripherals, and you have to get it just right or it won't work.

But beyond the occasional reconfiguring of computer hardware, more and more people are buying notebook computers. Many of these portable systems have docking stations that stay at home or the office with an external monitor, keyboard, mouse, network card, etc. Depending on whether the notebook is plugged into the docking station or not, things like video resolution and network options may change. The software on the notebook needs an effective and seamless way to handle the possibility that a system may change configurations several times a day.

Suppose you have a meeting in the morning and you want to take your notebook with you. Without turning it off, you pull it out of the docking station, losing your network and modem connections. While at your meeting, you take notes which you would like printed when you return to your office. When you get back to your desk and plug your notebook back into its docking station, it senses the resources that are available again. The documents you sent to the printer at your meeting start printing. Now that your modem is available again, your computer automatically calls a service and gets your e-mail. Not once all day did you have to worry about loading the right drivers or compensating for connections that weren't really there.

What Is Plug and Play?

To make this scenario a reality, Microsoft, Compaq Computer Corporation, and Intel Corporation launched an effort to create an architecture that would make reconfiguring computer hardware as easy as switching channels on your TV. This effort is known as Plug and Play.

Ideally, this is how a Plug and Play system is supposed to work. You buy a new Plug and Play SCSI adapter to install in your system. You pop the top off the computer, slide the card in, and plug in the cables. When you put the top back on and turn the machine on, the system recognizes the new card. It assigns interrupts and DMA settings automatically. When the operating system boots, it also recognizes the new card and automatically loads the appropriate drivers. No jumpers or switches to mess with.

But, in order for a computer to fully implement this Plug and Play strategy, it needs a combination of the right hardware and software. Initially, the motherboards need to be aware of the cards that are inserted into the bus expansion slots. Then, the cards you insert need to communicate with the other cards in the system to find out what configuration options are available to them. Also, the software needs to be aware of the hardware configuration so it can effectively communicate with all the system components.

Plug and Play promises to deliver the benefits in those examples. And Plug and Play is designed to be backwards-compatible with the systems already in existence. If you buy a new SCSI adapter, for example, you want it to work in your system, even if your motherboard isn't Plug and Play ready.

Windows 95's Role

Plug and Play is an open standard and support is not limited to Windows 95. However, this is the first operating system to take advantage of this new technology. In order to fulfill the Plug and Play promises, a computer must be able to perform dynamic configurations. Windows 95 supports all of the configuration management, resource arbitration, and device enumeration functions defined by Plug and Play. *Resource arbitration* is the process of allocating interrupt request (IRQ) signals, direct memory access (DMA) channels, I/O port addresses, and memory addresses to system components that require these resources. *Device enumeration* is the process by which the system components and their available resources are identified. The information is placed in the Registry.

In fact, with Windows 95, hardware and software configurations of both Plug and Play and legacy systems are stored in the Registry. This availability of configuration information helps to make a Windows 95 PC much easier to manage. Especially since access to the information is made available both locally and remotely.

PC 95

Plug and Play-ready hardware solutions are already appearing on store shelves, but Windows 95 is the first computer operating system to implement the Plug and Play standard. To ensure a computer has all the Plug and Play components necessary, Microsoft defined the PC 95 specification. *PC 95* refers to a computer consisting of three key elements—a minimum set of hardware components, Plug and Play components, and Windows 95. All three of these elements are necessary if a manufacturer wants to use the Microsoft Windows 95 Logo on its machines. If the logo is present, Windows 95 is preinstalled and the system has passed the Windows 95 Hardware Compatibility Tests (HCT). This lets users know the computer will be easy to use and configure.

Benefits

It's hard to quantify the benefits of Plug and Play. If computers are easier to use, then maybe more people will not be afraid to use them. This could create more demand which would drive the whole computer industry. Right now, many users are intimidated by the complexities of their PC. In fact, if many users did not have to learn to use a computer on the job, they probably would not dare buy one for home use. And the idea of upgrading your PC components? Forget it—too frustrating.

The biggest benefit is for the people who have to install new hardware components. Plug and Play removes most of those problems. Adding new devices to your PC will no longer be a painful process. A user can easily install or connect Plug and Play devices to the system, and the system will worry about allocating the hardware resources. Users will not be required to set jumpers or switches to set IRQs, DMA channels, or I/O port addresses.

Besides ease of use for the average computer user, Plug and Play has another benefit. Product managers and network administrators save on support costs when Plug and Play machines are implemented. A network administrator can install a new network or video card easily—perhaps even letting the users do it themselves. The administrator won't have to worry about what other components are already in the system and what resources they have. Just throw the card in and turn the machine on. On a Plug and Play system, Windows 95 will do the rest.

Device Manager

As mentioned above, Windows 95 keeps hardware and software configuration information in the centralized database known as the Registry. However, viewing and editing the Registry by ordinary means (i.e., REGEDIT) can be confusing and intimidating. Since viewing device information is beneficial to persons managing a computer system, Microsoft has provided an easier tool—the Device Manager.

To access this utility, double-click on the system icon and then select the tab labeled Device Manager (see Figure 13-1). This utility lets you see all the devices configured in your Windows 95 system. Additionally, it lets you view the properties of each device, and shows you which resources each device is using. If applicable, you can even change the resource settings. For a legacy system, this only changes the software information. You must still configure the card, setting the appropriate jumpers. For Plug and Play devices, changing the information here dynamically changes the settings of the card.

Notice the "View devices by..." along the top of the screen. By default, Windows 95 displays the devices by type. SCSI controllers are grouped in one area, drives in another. If you wish, you can "View devices by connection." This lists the devices with their associated adapter or controller cards. For example, if you had a SCSI tape drive and CD-ROM, these devices would be listed under the SCSI controller card to which they were connected.

To view the properties for any device listed, simply highlight the item, then click the Properties button. Figure 13-2 lists the hardware resource properties of a network adapter. As you can see, Windows 95 shows the I/O port address, interrupt, and DMA channel for which this card was configured. If you wanted to change any of these settings, you would highlight the resource, then click on the Change Setting button.

Notice the Conflicting Device List towards the bottom of the window. If any of the resource settings listed above this window conflicted with any other device in the

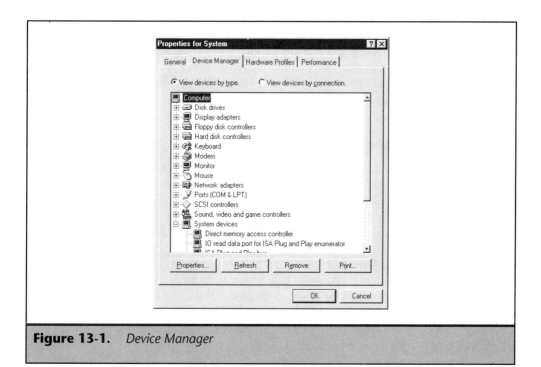

Figure 13-1. *Device Manager*

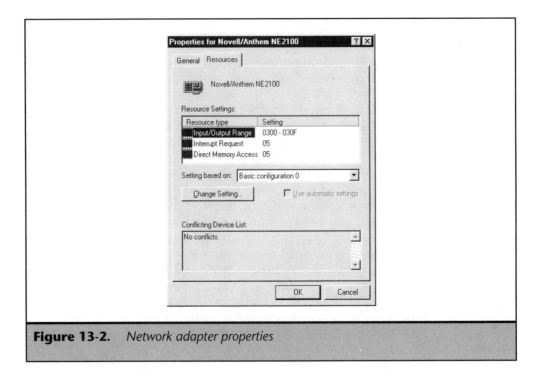

Figure 13-2. *Network adapter properties*

system, Plug and Play or not, that conflict would show up here. In this box, you see the advantage of Windows 95 and the Registry. Because the device information is stored in the Registry database, Windows 95 can automatically identify and resolve device resource conflicts. Identifying conflicts will help users and network managers overcome many of the problems associated with installing new devices.

Support for Legacy Systems

Plug and Play works on a variety of PC architectures—ISA, EISA, PCMCIA, VESA local bus, and PCI. But does implementing a Plug and Play strategy mean you have to buy all new hardware components for Windows 95 to take advantage of Plug and Play? No. Windows 95 is compatible with existing systems.

If a user wants to install a new device on a legacy PC that already has existing components, Windows 95 is often aware of those components (even if not Plug and Play) and will alert you to possible problems. For example, if the system has a sound card using IRQ 5 and you go to install a new network adapter, Windows 95 will tell you that IRQ 5 is already being used and you must select another option.

Remember, Windows 95 keeps track of hardware device information in the Registry. It knows which devices can and cannot be reconfigured and gives resource preference to the legacy devices which cannot.

Summary

The complexities of computers on the market today make it difficult to reconfigure and manage a system. A user wanting to install new system components or upgrade the ones in place is often faced with the challenge of interrupt conflicts, DMA channels, port addresses, and so on. And mobile users whose PC configurations often change many times a day are faced with the challenge of constantly keeping the software abreast of any changes. The Plug and Play specification was designed to overcome these problems.

By dynamically configuring and allocating system resources, a Plug and Play Windows 95 computer gets rid of the frustrations and apprehensions often associated with upgrading or changing a system's structure. Windows 95 tracks the resources in use by system components and keeps the information stored in the Registry. This helps make Windows 95 a very easy system to manage.

Appendix A

Networking Protocols

King—"What mean you by this?"
Hamlet—"Nothing but to show you how a king may go a progress through the guts
of a beggar."

—Shakespeare, Hamlet, *act IV, scene III.*

U nderstanding how your Windows 95 workstation communicates with and takes advantage of network services such as file, print, and application services relies upon the concept of network protocols. Without protocols, you cannot print a file on a network printer or open a file on a file server.

This appendix will discuss protocols from the ground up to show you the benefits of each type of protocol. We will begin by addressing a core concept that will make a protocol's purpose much more clear. It is a model, called the Open Systems Interconnection (OSI) model, from which each protocol can be broken down into understandable parts. We will then apply this model to the TCP/IP protocol in order to illustrate how a protocol works in reference to the OSI model.

What Protocols Are

Protocols allow you to perform many tasks because they, in their most basic sense, are rules. They dictate the manner in which two machines communicate over a network. When a computer requests a file from a file server, for example, both computers must agree upon a great number of rules such as the amount of data to be passed between the workstation and the file server, the addressing information for the packet carrying the information, the error-checking routine used to ensure the information arrived successfully, and the timing procedures sent to ensure that the packets carrying the information arrive in the right order.

In a manner of speaking, a protocol helps applications communicate with Network Interface Cards (NICs) as well. This forms a two-tier connectivity model: one level defines the connection between NICs; the second level defines the connection between applications.

Since many network operating systems utilize different protocols, you may find yourself in a position to decide which protocol to use on your Windows 95 workstation. Each protocol grew out of a different need; therefore each is designed to function within different networking environments. For example, there are some protocols that work better in a WAN environment, and there are those that function better in a LAN environment. Network Basic Input Output System (NetBIOS), as an example of a LAN protocol, originally provided connectivity for IBM and Microsoft networks as a stand-alone protocol. Currently, however, it is commonly used within other protocols such as IPX/SPX to provide compatibility and additional features to its host protocol. TCP/IP, which performs equally well in both WAN and LAN environments, evolved in the opposite direction, beginning life as a foundation technology behind what is today's world-wide collection of connected networks, the Internet.

What Protocols Do

As mentioned previously, protocols help network hardware (NICs) and software (applications) work together in harmony. To do this, a protocol must provide three services:

- Timing
- Semantics
- Syntax

These items may sound at first like grammatical terms for a language. In a way they are grammatical terms, but instead of describing the manner in which words are combined within a sentence, they describe the way informational elements are combined within a network connection. The basic building block for this communication is a *packet*, which is basically a single chunk of information that is transferred between two connected computers. When a computer asks for a file, it receives the file not as one chunk of data, but as a vast number of small packets of information. (See Figure A-1.)

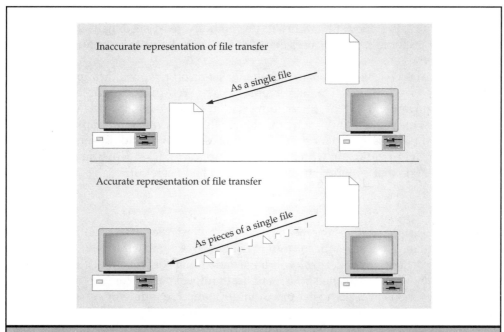

Figure A-1. *File transfer with packets versus file transfer as an entire file*

Packet-based communication accomplishes two things. First, it ensures that in cases where a large file's information is corrupted as it crosses the wire, only a very small portion of the file is corrupted. This means that instead of resending the entire file, a computer need only send the corrupted packet(s). Second, it allows greater amounts of network traffic from greater numbers of workstations to traverse the same section of cable. In its most basic sense, this really keeps a workstation from having to wait for a large packet to pass across its cable before sending or receiving its own information.

A consequence of sending a file over the network as a large number of packets, however, is that it becomes very confusing for a receiving NIC to reconstruct a file from the myriad of packets that pass across its section of cable. For example, what happens when a packet is lost? What happens if a packet arrives out of sequence? And what happens if a packet arrives in an unreadable format?

Timing

A protocol answers these questions through timing. Although timing can have many meanings within a protocol, its basic function is to ensure that NICs agree to a time factor in sending and receiving packets. For example, when a TCP/IP packet leaves a machine, it is given a certain amount of time (called *time to live*) in which it must reach its destination. Once a packet leaves a machine, it is marked with a time stamp that indicates its life expectancy. If it reaches its destination after exceeding its life expectancy, it is ignored. This ensures that a workstation does not listen for a missing packet forever.

When a station receives a packet, it generally sends off a reply indicating that the packet was received all right. If a packet reply does not return to the sending station within a certain amount of time, the sending station assumes that the packet was lost. It then resends the packet. This is why the time to live ratio is so important. For if a packet arrived late at a workstation, and it were accepted as a valid packet, what would the receiving station do with the second, duplicate packet sent from the originating station that assumed the original packet had been lost?

Semantics

In grammar, *semantics* defines the meanings behind words. For example, the word "romantic" can have the semantic meaning of one who is demonstrative in his/her feelings of love. Like language, protocols have words that contain a specific meaning. These words, however, are called *fields*. A typical protocol packet contains a number of fields, each one housing a particular piece of information required for successful communication. For example, each packet contains source address and destination address fields. These fields tell the receiving station, for example, where to send a successfully received packet reply. (See Figure A-2.)

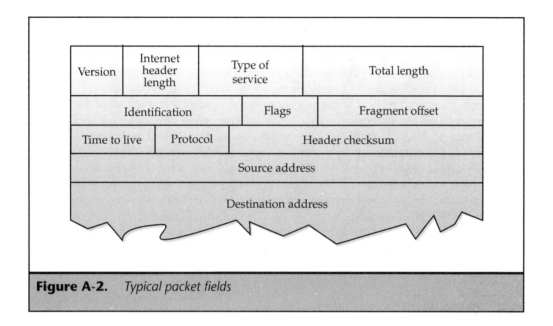

Version	Internet header length	Type of service	Total length		
Identification		Flags	Fragment offset		
Time to live	Protocol	Header checksum			
Source address					
Destination address					

Figure A-2.   *Typical packet fields*

There are many fields in addition to these, including total packet length, checksum number, type of service of the packet, version of the protocol, and packet identification. Therefore, as you might imagine, it is vitally important for both machines to agree upon which fields contain what information, or which words contain which meanings. Since packets arrive as binary 1s and 0s, this agreement on field semantics is crucial; without the agreement, one machine might mistake a destination address for a source address and thereby render further communication impossible.

Syntax

Syntax, another grammatical term, defines the order and length of the fields within each protocol packet. This works in conjunction with semantics to provide a meaningful packet structure by ensuring that each field starts at a certain position within a packet, and that each field means the same thing over time. For example, within an IP packet's header information, the source and destination addresses must appear at the same location within the packet, and they must mean the same thing from one packet to the next. This feature closely corresponds to semantics in that each relies upon the other. Without proper syntax, the meanings of the individual fields within a packet would be worthless. Without proper semantics, the order in which the fields appeared within a packet would also be worthless.

The OSI Model

To better understand how semantics, syntax, and timing enable your Windows 95 workstation to communicate over a network, you should consider the International Standards Organization (ISO) Open Systems Interconnection (OSI) model. This model, which was introduced in 1983, defines a generalized model describing all of the functions required for network communications. It describes how NICs interact, how applications and NICs interact, and how applications interact with each other. Beyond this, the OSI model is meant to help software manufactures create network software that is *open*—in other words, software that can operate across heterogeneous network adapters and across heterogeneous operating systems regardless of the network hardware/software manufacturer. For example, through current network protocol drivers, you can simultaneously load two or more protocols on any network interface card, regardless of vendor. The TCP/IP protocol could be made by the Santa Cruz Operation Inc.; the network adapter could be made by Intel Corp.; and the IPX/SPX protocol could be made by Novell Inc. All can coexist without modification.

OSI Layers

The model is comprised of seven layers. All of the layers together form an entire packet. Each layer represents a different point of interaction between two network devices such as computers, printers, file servers, etc. The seventh layer, the application layer, defines the manner in which two network applications interact. When two e-mail applications (such as X.400-compliant applications) communicate over the network, they exchange program specific information over the seventh layer. Similarly, the first layer defines the manner in which two network adapters interact. It handles the electrical specifications of the wall sockets, wiring, and other hardware required for networking. The seven layers of the OSI model are

- Application
- Presentation
- Session
- Transport
- Network
- Data Link
- Physical

Each layer provides services to the layer directly above it. And all layers provide support for one another. Although each defines a separate function, layers four through seven are primarily responsible for the interoperability mentioned previously, while layers one through three create the physical connection between two network devices. Since all OSI model layers work with one another and with corresponding layers on other machines, they are called *protocol layers* and make up what is called a *protocol stack*.

This naming convention causes some confusion because a protocol layer and a protocol, such as TCP/IP, do not completely make up the communication between network machines. Novell NetWare's primary protocol, IPX/SPX, for example, is actually a combination of many protocols. SPX resides within the transport layer, while IPX resides within the network layer. This takes up only two of the seven layers. The remaining layers are made up of different NetWare-specific protocols such as the NetWare Core Protocol (NCP), which actually resides within the transport, session, presentation, and application layers simultaneously. Other layers contain protocols like the Logical Link Control (LLC) protocol (data link layer) and the NetBIOS protocol (session and transport layers). Therefore, to say that a network's protocol is IPX/SPX is accurate yet incomplete, as there are many other protocols contained within these protocol suites.

Even more confusing, not all network protocols adhere to the OSI model standard. In a perfect OSI-world, each layer exists in isolation. That is, each layer functions without affecting the surrounding layers. Although each communicates with its neighbor, no layer is dependent upon another. If a specific protocol manufacturer changes a layer—such as the internet protocol within the TCP/IP stack—no other layers would require any changes in order to continue functioning with the new protocol. If Novell decides to change IPX/SPX, network adapter card manufacturers should not have to change any of their software in turn.

This modularization works in most situations. However, some protocols, such as NCP, NetBIOS, and the UNIX-based File Transfer Protocol (FTP), refuse to reside within one layer. Protocols like NCP, which expand over more than one layer, break the OSI model's idyllic structure by not providing modularity at the layer level. This does not imply that NCP is flawed, or that the OSI model is flawed. It simply means that Novell, in orchestrating their network communication protocols, chose to give one protocol multiple responsibilities as they are defined within the OSI model.

In many cases, these renegade protocols act as single modules because they do not affect any of the other protocols. For example, the UNIX-based protocol, Telnet, which provides remote control of one machine by another, spans the application, presentation, and session layers. But neither it nor the lower layers are dependent upon each other. You could replace the standard Telnet application and protocol at any time with a different version without repercussions.

Application Layer

The application layer, as mentioned previously, is responsible for allowing network applications to work together. This is where the most meaningful information is passed. Applications such as e-mail, databases, schedulers, etc., all use the application layer to transfer information.

An example of a network protocol that defies the OSI model standard by handling the duties of more than one layer is Novell's NCP. It is responsible for a vast number of network services ranging from simple file transfer to user authentication and network security. When you copy a file from a NetWare file server to your Windows 95 workstation, the XCOPY.EXE program that you use to copy the files carries on a complicated discussion with the file server over NCP. First it asks if the requested file exists. Packets containing NCP information are then bandied back and forth as yes or no questions concerning the whereabouts of the file, your rights to access the file, and availability of the file (whether or not it is in use by someone else). When your Windows 95 workstation receives the "all clear" for the file transfer, the file is sent one piece at a time over NCP packets.

NetWare-specific management applications such as NWADMIN.EXE and FILER.EXE also take full advantage of the NCP protocol in obtaining network data and providing a means for network administrators to manage all aspects of a NetWare network. Using NWADMIN.EXE you can, for example, add and delete users from any workstation.

Another illustration of an application layer protocol is the X.400 standard. Used as an application interface for e-mail compatibility, X.400 defines the way in which an e-mail message passes from one computer to another. Regardless of whether or not you are using TCP/IP, IPX/SPX, or NetBEUI, X.400 applications pass through the application layer. (See Figure A-3.)

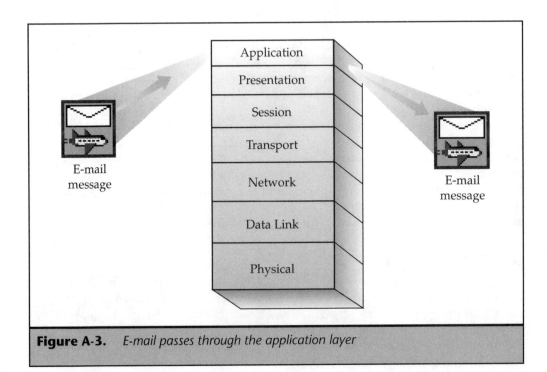

Figure A-3.   *E-mail passes through the application layer*

X.500

An application layer protocol vitally important to X.400 connectivity is the directory services protocol known as X.500. Also created by the ITU, X.500 allows workstations to access and share network resource information such as user names, file server addresses, e-mail addresses, and printer locations. Like the White Pages, X.500 is really just a list of useful information. However, instead of being organized linearly, it is organized in a tree with each branch, or level, corresponding to a domain. (See Figure A-4.) The common X.500 domains are

- Organization
- Division
- Department
- Workgroup
- Object

The levels are nested: each level contains the following level, starting with Organization. Therefore, an organization can house divisions, a division can house departments, etc. This hierarchy makes it easy for your Windows 95 workstation to find network resources because it provides a unique location name for every resource

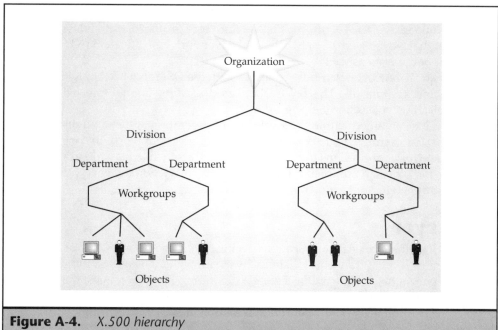

Figure A-4.   *X.500 hierarchy*

on the network. If your Windows 95 workstation is attached to a Novell Inc. NetWare 4.1 network, for example, you can use its NetWare Directory Services (NDS) to find any other user's e-mail address on the NetWare network, regardless of that user's geographical location.

Although not truly X.500 compliant, Internet applications provide other application layer services that can help you find information. If you connect your Windows 95 workstation to an Internet UNIX host via a TCP/IP, PPP, or SLIP connection, for example, you can enter the command **whois** at the UNIX command prompt, followed by the name of a user you wish to locate; you'll receive a list of names and e-mail addresses of all users matching your search. This information is housed on a number of X.500-like directory name servers belonging to the Defense Data Network (DDN) Network Information Center. The **whois** command establishes a session between your workstation and a DDN NIC server.

Presentation Layer

The presentation layer houses protocols that handle the format of the network application data. Residing beneath the application layer and above the session layer, the presentation layer takes data from the application layer and formats it for network communication. This layer provides the protocol syntax previously mentioned. The presentation layer orders the application data into a meaningful format for the session layer, which sends it across the network.

Many popular LAN protocols incorporate this layer into the application layer. For example, NetWare's IPX/SPX utilizes the NetWare core protocol for both layers. The predominantly UNIX-based TCP/IP utilizes the Network Filing System (NFS) protocol for both layers as well.

One protocol, however, that fully complies with the OSI model is Apple Computers Inc.'s AppleTalk. This protocol utilizes the Apple Filing Protocol (AFP) to format application layer data. (See Figure A-5.)

This layer is contained within the workstation's operating system and resident applications. For example, your Windows 95 operating system works in conjunction with your network applications to format special characters like tabs and graphic images, among others. Additionally, this layer is responsible for any encryption techniques applied to application data.

Session Layer

The first OSI element beneath application specific layers, the session layer provides the upper-most level of transport reliability by creating and closing communication sessions between the sending and receiving machines. When you request that a file be sent from a NetWare file server to your Windows 95 workstation, for example, the session layer initiates a communication session that lasts for the duration of the request.

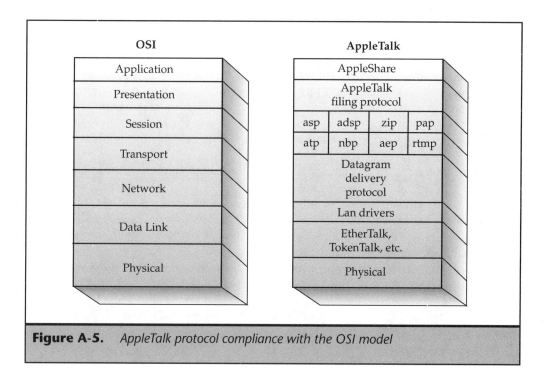

Figure A-5. *AppleTalk protocol compliance with the OSI model*

In creating a communication session, the session layer lays out the terms and agreements to be withheld during the session such as the size of the packets to be exchanged and whether or not to transport data at full or half duplex speeds (for Ethernet networks). If something goes wrong with the transmission, this layer passes information along to the remaining layers, indicating the action required to remedy the problem.

Transport Layer

The transport layer ensures that communications established in the session layer take place correctly. In this way, it ensures point-to-point communication between two machines. If a packet arrives at its destination in an incorrect order, for example, the transport layer is responsible for notifying the station that the packet was received incorrectly. This layer also manages network traffic rates. If the network is too congested, the transport layer throttles back the rate of packet transmittal to reduce the number of lost—and subsequently re-sent—packets.

The most common network protocols found at this level in the OSI reference model are TCP/IP's Transmission Control Protocol (TCP), Novell's Sequenced Packet Exchange (SPX), and NetBIOS/NetBEUI.

Network Layer

The network layer is a very important layer for larger networks because it manages connectionless communication between machines. In other words, it contains information about the sending and receiving machine's home network. When machines on separate networks—different physical segments of a network, called *subnets*—wish to communicate, the information housed in the network layer allows packets from one network to travel to another network through a mechanism known as *routing*.

Routers, which connect subnets together, rely upon the network layer to route traffic between subnets. When a packet leaves your Windows 95 workstation on its way toward a distant subnet across the Internet, for example, it is handed off from router to router on the way to its destination. These routers do not know much about the actual destination of your packet, however. They simply know about the subnets to which they are connected. (See Figure A-6.)

This capability to forward only outbound traffic from one subnet to another is very important for larger networks such as the Internet because it eliminates unnecessary traffic passing from subnet to subnet. The protocols that reside at this level in the OSI reference model are TCP/IP's Internet Protocol (IP) and Novell's Internetwork Packet Exchange (IPX).

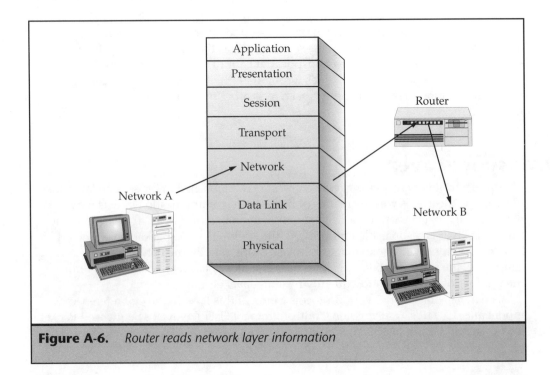

Figure A-6. *Router reads network layer information*

Data Link Layer

This is a very important layer in the OSI reference model because it actually forms the data sent down through the protocol stack into packets to be sent out over the network through the next, and final layer, the physical layer. The data link layer is responsible for forming packets that conform to a specific network access method. If you have attached your Windows 95 workstation to a token ring network, for example, the data link layer forms the data into a format recognizable to a token ring network. Other access methods include Ethernet, Fiber Distributed Data Interface (FDDI), Asynchronous Transfer Mode (ATM), and ARCNET.

It is at this layer that your Windows 95 operating system talks to the hardware in your computer. Assuming you are connected to a network via the Ethernet access method, when you installed Windows 95, you chose to install either a Network Driver Interface Specification (NDIS) or an Open Data-link Interface (ODI) to communicate with your network interface card.

These driver specifications, developed around 1989, allow you to load more than one protocol on your Windows 95 workstation. For example, if you wanted to simultaneously communicate with the TCP/IP-based Internet and an IPX/SPX-based NetWare local area network, you could choose to install both protocols either during installation or afterward through the protocol configuration menu.

You are able to choose both protocols because each protocol layer is very well defined. Therefore, if you installed Windows 95 with NetWare ODI drivers, each time you boot up, you will automatically load a number of drivers:

```
LSL.COM
NE2000.EXE
IPXODI.COM
TCPIP.EXE
NETX.EXE
```

This sequence of commands loads the network software necessary for your Windows 95 workstation to communicate using both TCP/IP and IPX/SPX. Interestingly, these commands span the second through the fourth layers of the OSI reference model. The LSL.COM command loads the Link Support Layer (LSL) software that manages the ODI connection at the data link layer. The NE2000.EXE command loads the driver that enables your software to talk to the network interface card. It also resides in the data link layer. The IPXODI.EXE command loads the ODI software responsible for accommodating more than one protocol as well as the IPX portion of the NetWare protocol stack. Therefore, this command represents both the data link layer and the network layer. The TCPIP.EXE and NETX.EXE commands load the remaining software for the TCP/IP and SPX protocol stacks. They represent the transport layer (SPX and TCP) as well as the network layer (IP).

Physical Layer

This layer, as previously mentioned, represents the actual connection between your software and your hardware. It really does not have anything to do with protocols, except that it defines the access method used by the data link layer. It is handled differently for each type of access method, FDDI, ATM, token ring, and Ethernet. In defining this connection, it is the initial reporter of network errors to the higher levels; it is the first layer to monitor network performance; and it is the first layer to synchronize network packets.

OSI Benefits

As mentioned previously, the benefits of the OSI layered model are twofold: first, they help users and vendors visualize and compartmentalize network communication procedures; second, the OSI model gives vendors a hierarchical method to produce hardware and software that is interpretable with other vendors' hardware and software. This gives vendors the opportunity to concentrate on one or more layers of the OSI model without having to worry about the other layers.

For example, an e-mail vendor can write an e-mail package that can send and receive messages across the network without having to write the communication software responsible for such connectivity. Likewise, a hardware vendor can create a network interface card without worrying about the manner in which an e-mail application must communicate with their hardware.

IPX/SPX, an Example of Protocol Layers in Action

The best way to understand how these OSI reference layers operate in connecting your Windows 95 workstation to the network is to chart the course of a network command as it is sent from your workstation to a network service provider such as a NetWare file server.

This will demonstrate the manner in which data passes down the protocol stack (from layer seven to layer one) on the sending workstation and up the protocol stack (from layer one to layer seven) on the receiving workstation. For this demonstration, imagine using the IPX/SPX protocol to open a file from the Explorer program in Windows 95.

Network Communication

Open your Explorer program in Windows 95, double-click the Network Neighborhood icon, double-click on a NetWare volume folder, and then double-click on a text file such as a Microsoft Word document. This action will invoke a number of communication sessions between your Windows 95 workstation and the NetWare file server. The Windows 95 operating system sends the command to a NetWare file server.

NetWare Is a Redirecting Network Operating System

In most cases, you will not have to enter a command like **open** or **print** at a command prompt with Windows 95's Graphical User Interface (GUI) Explorer application. Without the GUI of Windows 95, you would have to enter a command at the MS-DOS command prompt such as **WP myfile.doc** to open the MS-DOS version of WordPerfect with the *myfile.doc* file as the initial document. (See Figure A-7.) However, the point is that in both cases, the same commands are sent across the network; all network commands on a NetWare network, for example, rely upon the resident protocol such as IPX/SPX.

The way Windows 95's GUI and the DOS command line work is simple. When you enter a command, the command processor on your workstation searches the local hard disk for the command. If it cannot find the command, it transfers control to the network software, which then searches the NetWare file server's hard disk for the desired program. At the point where the command ceases to search the workstation's hard disk and begins to search the file server, the IPX/SPX protocol stack goes into action, wrapping the command into a package that is able to traverse the network to the NetWare file server.

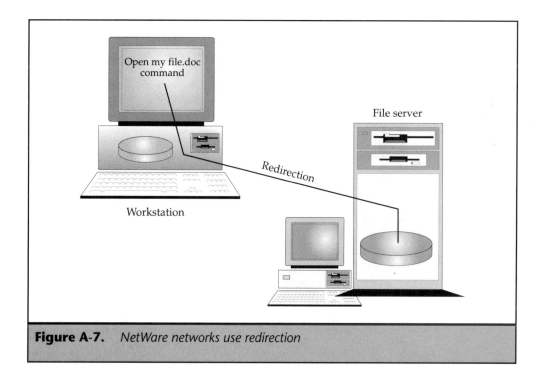

Figure A-7. *NetWare networks use redirection*

Not All Layers Are Created Equal

Once the data is placed into the hands of the IPX/SPX protocol stack, it is passed
down through the OSI reference model stack on its way from the Explorer program to
the network cable. As the data passes from one layer to the next, each layer adds its
own information to the data. Each layer also formats the data to accommodate the
next layer.

Although each bit of information destined for a networked computer passes
through each protocol level as defined in the OSI reference model, each protocol suite
contains a family of protocols that correspond to different layers. Some protocols
overlap layers, while others occupy only a portion of a layer.

In the IPX/SPX protocol suite, all network packets are encapsulated in the
connectionless IPX protocol, but within that packet, other protocols can reside in order
to carry out specific functions. This means that when you issue the network command
Open file, your data will travel across the network always as an IPX packet, but
that packet can contain NetWare Core Protocol (NCP) information, Sequenced Packet
Exchange (SPX) information, NetBIOS information, or named pipes information.
(See Figure A-8.)

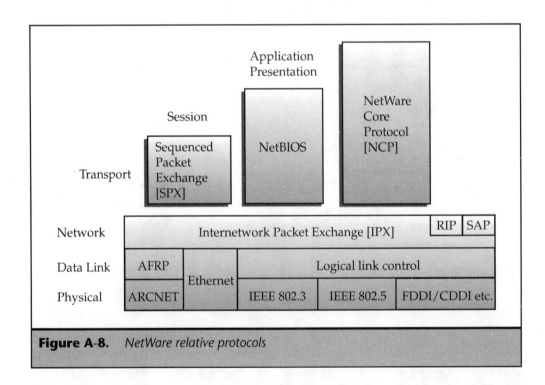

Figure A-8.   *NetWare relative protocols*

Application Layer

The command **Open file** is first redirected to the application layer of the
protocol stack. There it is translated into a language that NetWare can understand,
namely NCPs.

NCPs   Novell's NetWare core protocol represents a proprietary set of commands
used to access and manipulate a NetWare file server. These commands let you make
and break connection between your Windows 95 workstation and the file server. They
let you find and open files residing on a NetWare file server. They also let you print to
a network printer. Virtually all communication between a client and server on a
NetWare network occurs over NCP packets.

   Although the NCP protocol technically spans both the application and
presentation layers of the ODI reference model, its practical abilities reach beyond
these two layers and into the transport and session layers. This is possible because the
NCP protocol, as a member of the IPX/SPX protocol suite, contains some of the
session-control and sequencing mechanisms normally found in the SPX protocol.
Therefore, by tightly integrating the NCP and the IPX protocols, NetWare can forego the
overhead associated with a "thicker" protocol stack fully utilizing NCP, SPX, and IPX.

   Normally, however, only the first two layers of the ODI reference model are
collapsed into the NCP protocol. Once your data passes into the NCP layer, it is
translated into a command the NetWare file server can understand and then passed
directly to the session layer.

Session Layer

Having skipped the presentation layer, the NCP information is passed to the session
layer, which is controlled by two special protocols, NetBIOS and Named Pipes.
NetBIOS, for the most part, is a compatibility protocol originally designed to provide
peer-to-peer communication between applications written specifically for IBM's
NetBIOS protocol. It is not a fully functioning NetBIOS protocol stack, however. It is
simply a translation routine that provides interoperability between NetBIOS-specific
applications and a NetWare network.

   Named Pipes support provides a similar level of compatibility as NetBIOS. It can,
however, be used to create a full range of network services such as logging in and out
from a network machine. For example, some application server software packages
reside on a NetWare network but do not contain any built-in NetWare networking
capabilities. These applications must allow users to log in and authenticate with the
application server. They therefore use Named Pipes support to let users attach to their
services. (See Figure A-9.)

   If the data requires support for these two protocols, the appropriate information is
added to the network packet and then passed down from the application and
presentation layers.

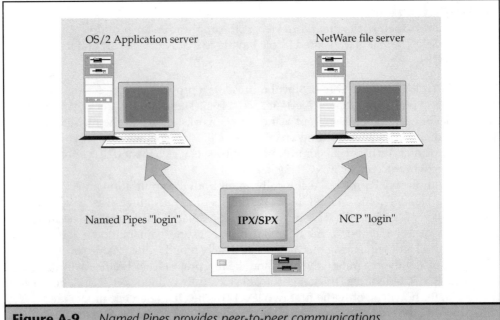

Figure A-9.   *Named Pipes provides peer-to-peer communications*

Transport Layer

When the command information passes through the transport layer of the OSI reference model, it is given the information required to ensure that once it arrives at its destination, it will be recompiled into its greater whole in the right order. It is here that the information can be given this sort of help from the SPX protocol. SPX is a connection-oriented protocol. It does not assume that the receiving station actually received any packets. Like NCPs, NetBIOS, and Named Pipes, SPX packets utilize the services of the IPX protocol to obtain the initial connectivity between your Windows 95 workstation and the NetWare file server. However, the SPX protocol adds a service capable of maintaining a virtual connection between the two machines. It does this by listening for a response from each packet, indicating whether or not the transmission went all right.

Network Layer

Once the **Open file** data that has passed through the application, presentation, session, and transport layers has been correctly formatted and given the information needed to reach its destination, it passes into the network layer. It is subsequently encapsulated into a packet capable of actually traveling over a network cable. For the IPX/SPX network, the information is encapsulated into an IPX packet. IPX packets, unlike connection-oriented SPX-enhanced packets, do not guarantee that your command will reach its destination. It simply sends out information and assumes that it will arrive at its destination. In working this way, IPX can deliver at rapid transport speeds because it only uses approximately half as much bandwidth as connection-oriented protocols.

To ward off the chaos that can ensue without proper assurances of packet delivery, the IPX protocol builds into each packet a Cyclic Redundancy Check (CRC). If the receiving machine looks at the CRC and discovers that there has been a problem, it notifies the sending station of the error, which then resends the packet. Conversely, if the sending workstation does not receive an acknowledgment that the destination workstation received the packet, it re-sends the packet.

Data Link Layer

Now in the shape of an actual packet of data, your command enters the data link layer of the OSI reference model. At this point, it is formatted into a frame type that can accommodate your network cable type, such as Ethernet, ARCNET, FDDI, and Token Ring. It is also here that your data is formatted to accommodate the ODI or NDIS specifications.

Physical Layer

Once past the data link layer, your newly formed packet enters the physical layer, its last stop on its way to the network cable. At this point, the IPX/SPX protocol no longer controls the way your packet traverses the network. It is up to the physical layer to ensure that your packet reaches the network interface card to subsequently travel across the network cable. It is this same process that lets you utilize a modem through the RS232 port on your Windows 95 workstation.

Reversing the Communication Process

Once your newly formed NCP packet containing the **Open file** command passes through the network interface card, it finds its way to its destination. Actually, in most network environments such as Ethernet, your packets are simply sent to all machines attached to your subnet. Only the workstations with a network interface card number that matches the destination address within your packet actually act upon the command. All other workstations simply ignore the packet.

As the packet passes into the network interface card, the information added to your command data is stripped away in the opposite order in which it was applied. That is, what was added at the network layer is analyzed before data added at the application layer. This gives the receiving workstation a chance to resolve lower-level problems such as a faulty network connection before spending a great deal of time processing the higher levels of the protocol stack. In this way, if it spots a problem (such as a bad CRC), it can simply not respond if the packet does not use the SPX protocol, or respond that a problem occurred if the packet contains the SPX protocol. (See Figure A-10.)

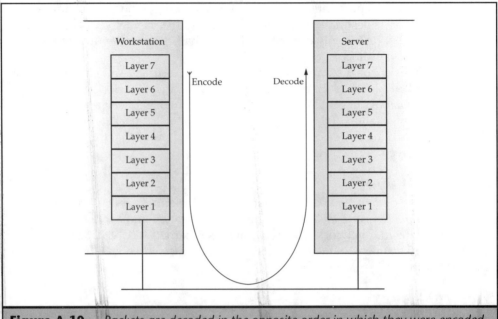

Figure A-10. *Packets are decoded in the opposite order in which they were encoded*

After moving up through the protocol stack, your **Open file** command is passed along to the NetWare file system as an NCP request to open the desired file. If your user name has been granted the rights to access that file, the file server then sends an NCP response indicating that it is all right to open that file. The response then goes through the same formatting stages as your request to open the file.

Summary

The act of sending and receiving a sequence of two packets to determine whether or not you have access rights to a desired file is just a small part of the entire process involved in locating, verifying, authenticating, opening, sending, acknowledging, closing, and terminating the communication session. Each of these events requires at least one series of two packets. In general, requesting that a file be opened and its contents retrieved from a file server can require virtually thousands of packets.

In this appendix, we discussed the nature of networking protocols from two standpoints: the OSI reference model, which defines a series of seven layers required for two networked machines to communicate effectively; and an example of the OSI reference model at work in the NetWare-centric IPX/SPX protocol.

Appendix B

Troubleshooting Windows 95

"A child said, what is the grass? fetching it to me with full hands:
how could I answer the child?...I do not know what it is any more than he."
—*Walt Whitman, Leaves of Grass*

Windows 95, as an advanced, 32-bit operating system, is replete with powerful features such as built-in networking software, Plug and Play capabilities, and an integrated e-mail client. Consequently, it, as any complex system, is subject to failure.

What to Do When Things Go Wrong

This appendix will take you through some of the potential failures (or problems) you may encounter and provide you with some practical solutions to those problems. Since many of the problems listed in this appendix refer to specific hardware and software configurations, you should first check your system for any similarities between your problem and the problem listed before making any changes. If your configuration does not match that of an example problem, please seek technical support directly from Microsoft.

Most problems listed in this appendix, however, are not prescriptive in nature and therefore can be used as templates from which you can solve many different problems. For example, instead of describing the steps required to fix a conflict between an NE2000 and a 3C509 network adapter, most examples in this appendix will illustrate the basic steps required to determine similar problems between any set of adapter cards.

A Quick Table of Contents

Because this section contains a large number of loosely related problems and solutions, a table of contents follows.

Windows 95 Installation has failed and you want to return to MS-DOS
Path statement not recognized
Windows does not load
Boot failure
Applications do not function over more than one network segment
Remote Access Server (RAS) does not work
Internet service connection does not work properly
Network interface card driver does not load
Windows 95 slows during disk operations
Unwanted banner and blank form printing under NetWare
Windows 95 will not work with Windows NT

Booting Problems

Since your first introduction to Windows 95 occurs during installation, it is at that time you will first encounter problems. As with any new product, a failure is most likely to occur during the first days of use. For example, when you reboot Windows 95 for the first time after installation, it may not start properly because you selected an incorrect video adapter driver. The solutions listed below should help you solve these and other types of problems.

Problem: Windows 95 Installation Has Failed and You Want to Return to MS-DOS

In most cases, Windows 95 should install on your workstation without a hitch. However, in some circumstances you may not be able to complete the installation, or when you reboot your machine after installation, it fails to boot. If you have unsuccessfully attempted to fix the problem, you may want to uninstall the Windows 95 operating system and return to the MS-DOS operating system. To uninstall Windows 95, you can insert your start-up disk, reboot your machine, and run uninstal.exe. But, since Windows 95 replaces MS-DOS, even if you delete the Windows 95 program files, your computer will not boot to MS-DOS. You can find yourself in this situation even though you have chosen to save your original system configuration during installation, if you have changed or deleted these configuration files.

Solution: Reinstall the MS-DOS System Files

In most cases, these steps can get you back to MS-DOS; however, if you are using Windows 95's built-in disk compression to make your hard disk hold more data, you should not try any of these as they will render all of your data useless. To return to MS-DOS after compressing your hard drive, you should try to boot to Windows 95's version of MS-DOS using the F4 key while booting. It will load the drivers needed to make your compressed hard disk accessible.

To return to MS-DOS, you will need a bootable floppy disk containing the following files:

SYS.COM
COMMAND.COM
FORMAT.COM
EDIT.COM
ATTRIB.EXE

These files will help you remove the Windows 95 system files and return your computer to normal. The file SYS.COM transfers the files required to boot MS-DOS to your hard disk. The COMMAND.COM file is the main boot file required by MS-DOS.

It contains all of the internal commands you need to perform basic file and directory operations such as viewing directory contents and copying files. The FORMAT.COM file removes all files on your hard disk and makes it ready for the MS-DOS operating system. In most cases, you will not need this utility. However, it is good to have it handy in case you are unable to restore the MS-DOS operating system. The EDIT.COM file is an editor you can use to edit the AUTOEXEC.BAT and CONFIG.SYS files located on your hard disk. Finally, the ATTRIB.EXE file will enable you to make the hidden Windows 95 system files visible so you can delete them.

Try SYS.COM to Install the MS-DOS System Files

The first thing you should try in restoring the MS-DOS operating system is to install the MS-DOS system files with the SYS.COM file. To do this, boot to DOS with your boot disk, and from the command line type the following:

```
SYS C:
```

Press the return key. If you see a message indicating that the system has been successfully transferred, you should remove the boot diskette and reboot your workstation. If all goes well, your workstation should boot to MS-DOS.

Use ATTRIB.EXE to Remove the Windows 95 System Files

If that does not work, you may need to remove the hidden Windows 95 system files from your hard disk. To do this, again boot to the floppy diskette and go to the root of your hard disk. There, type the following:

```
ATTRIB *.*
```

This command will list all of the hidden or system files used by Windows 95. (See Figure B-1.)

You do not need to get rid of all the hidden and system files (denoted with the S and/or H flags). The files you should remove are the SYSCMDR.SYS, SCDOS.SYS, and WINBOOT.SYS (if present). To remove these files, use the ATTRIB.EXE file to remove their hidden and system status. For example, to remove the WINBOOT.SYS file, enter the following:

```
ATTRIB -S -H WINBOOT.SYS
```

You should then delete this and other system files with the DEL command. Now you should be able to transfer the MS-DOS files to the hard disk with the SYS.COM file.

```
C:\>attrib *.*
   A   SHR      IO.DOS         C:\IO.DOS
   A   SHR      MSDOS.DOS      C:\MSDOS.DOS
   A            COMMAND.DOS    C:\COMMAND.DOS
       SHR      DRVSPACE.BIN   C:\DRVSPACE.BIN
   A   SHR      SYSCMNDR.SYS   C:\SYSCMNDR.SYS
   A   SHR      SCDOS.SYS      C:\SCDOS.SYS
   A    H       BOOTLOG.PRV    C:\BOOTLOG.PRV
       SHR      DBLSPACE.BIN   C:\DBLSPACE.BIN
   A    H       BOOTLOG.TXT    C:\BOOTLOG.TXT
       SHR      MSDOS.SYS      C:\MSDOS.SYS
   A            CONFIG.SYS     C:\CONFIG.SYS
   A   SH       DETLOG.TXT     C:\DETLOG.TXT
       SH       DETLOG.OLD     C:\DETLOG.OLD
        H       SETUPLOG.TXT   C:\setuplog.txt
   A            COMMAND.COM    C:\COMMAND.COM
       SHR      IO.SYS         C:\IO.SYS
   A            AUTOEXEC.BAT   C:\AUTOEXEC.BAT

C:\>_
```

Figure B-1.   *ATTRIB.EXE results*

Use FORMAT.COM to Reformat the Hard Drive

If these techniques do not restore your MS-DOS operating system, you may need to reformat your hard disk. However, this will destroy all of the hard disk's information, programs, text files, directories, everything. Therefore, only use this alternative if nothing else works. To format your hard disk, boot to MS-DOS from your floppy diskette and from the command line type

```
FORMAT C: /S
```

The /S option tells FORMAT.COM to transfer the files required to boot MS-DOS to your hard drive after it has finished formatting.

After typing the command, press RETURN. You will then be asked if you are sure you want to perform the requested operation. Press the Y key to continue. Once the operation has completed, you will be asked to enter a volume label. Your machine should now boot to MS-DOS.

You can then use the EDIT.COM file to either create or edit your AUTOEXEC.BAT and CONFIG.SYS files to ensure that your MS-DOS environment is set up correctly.

For more information on how to do this, consult your MS-DOS documentation (you can also restore your files from backup).

Problem: Path Statement Not Recognized

If you maintain more than one operating system on your workstation prior to installing Windows 95, you may find that upon rebooting your machine to run Windows 95 for the first time, it does not load at all. This can be caused by a number of things, such as corrupted files, but most often in a multi-operating system environment it is caused by a path statement problem in the AUTOEXEC.BAT file.

Solution: Check AUTOEXEC.BAT for Improper Path Statement

In most cases, when you install Windows 95 it correctly assesses your AUTOEXEC.BAT's path statement, which contains the locations that the operating system is supposed to look for programs not found in the directory in which a command is executed. For example, if you execute the command FORMAT A: from the root of C:\ with no path statement in your AUTOEXEC.BAT file, you will receive a *bad command or file name* message. With a path statement that tells the operating system to look for a program, you can execute the command FORMAT A: from any location.

When Windows 95 analyzes your AUTOEXEC.BAT file's path statement, it replaces the current location for current system files, such as FORMAT, with the location of its own system files. However, if you use a secondary batch file, such as WINPATH.BAT to initialize path settings for Windows 3.1 for example, Windows 95 will not be able to see this file and will simply place its path statement in the AUTOEXEC.BAT file. Now, if the WINPATH.BAT statement runs after the actual Windows 95 path statement, you will not be able to run Windows 95 properly because it will look in the wrong places for system files.

To check for this problem, you can simply edit your AUTOEXEC.BAT file and ensure that the Windows 95 path statements are correct. A proper statement, for example, would look like this:

```
PATH=C:\WINDOWS;C:\WINDOWS\COMMAND;C:\WINWORD;C:\EXCEL;C:\PKWARE
```

The first two items are required for Windows 95 to operate properly, while the remaining items can refer to any location. It is important that this order be preserved since directories are searched from left to right within the path statement. For example, if you execute FORMAT A: from the root of C:\, Windows 95 will first search your current location for the program. If it cannot find the program, it will first search the C:\WINDOWS directory and then the C:\WINDOWS\COMMAND directory, which is where the file FORMAT.COM actually resides.

Problem: Windows Does Not Load

When you boot Windows 95 for the first time, you should be presented with a login screen. However, if something has gone wrong with your configuration you may be stuck with a blank screen. The most common reason for such a problem concerns network drivers. For example, if you specify a network interface card that conflicts with another device, such as a modem, you may not be able to boot into Windows properly.

Solution: Boot Windows in Fail-Safe Mode

The quickest way to remedy this problem is to boot Windows 95 in fail-safe mode. This will load the Windows 95 environment without loading any device drivers that may be creating conflicts. To boot Windows 95 in fail-safe mode, simply press the F5 key when your workstation begins the boot process. In some instances, Windows 95 will detect a booting problem and present you with the choice to boot in fail-safe mode. It will do this whenever you reboot the workstation while it is loading Windows 95.

When Windows 95 loads in this mode, you will not be able to use all of your attached devices such as a network interface card or a modem. (See Figure B-2.)

However, you will be able to open the control panel and change any of the settings that may be causing the boot trouble.

Problem: Boot Failure

In many cases, using fail-safe boot will enable you to undo configuration changes that cause Windows 95 to boot improperly. However, in some instances, you may not be able to deduce the cause of your problems.

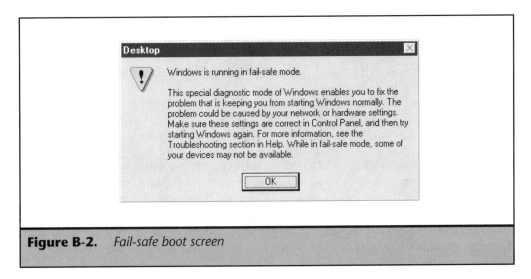

Figure B-2. *Fail-safe boot screen*

Solution: Try Alternative Boot Techniques

In cases where it is difficult to determine the cause of booting troubles, you should invoke the Windows 95 Startup Menu. This menu will let you choose a number of different ways to boot Windows 95. This menu should appear automatically if a previous boot process did not complete properly, but you can invoke it manually by pressing F8 while booting your workstation. Doing so will open a menu with the following options:

> Normal
> Logged (\BOOTLOG.TXT)
> Safe Mode
> Safe Mode with Network Support
> Step by Step Confirmation
> Command Prompt Only
> Safe Mode Command prompt only

Each selection is designed to help you solve particular boot problems. You can therefore save a great deal of time by familiarizing yourself with the purpose and features of each.

Normal

If you suspect that a previous boot failure was merely an aberration and that it will not happen again, select this option. It will simply start Windows 95 normally.

Logged (\BOOTLOG.TXT)

This option will let you run through your AUTOEXEC.BAT and CONFIG.SYS files one line at a time, choosing whether or not to process each statement in these files. Windows 95 then creates a hidden file called BOOTLOG.TXT in the root of the boot drive (usually C:), logging the success or failure encountered during each step of the boot process.

To view this file, you must first locate it using the ATTRIB command by typing the following at a command prompt:

```
ATTRIB BOOTLOG.TXT /S
```

The **/S** option will instruct ATTRIB to look for the file in all of your hard disk's subdirectories. Once you have located the file, you can edit it with any text editor. Don't be alarmed if this file looks long and complex. It merely tracks the success of each statement executed by Windows 95 during the boot process. (See Figure B-3.)

Therefore, you can use this file to locate problems simply by looking for statement failures. For example, if you notice that a video driver does not load successfully, you

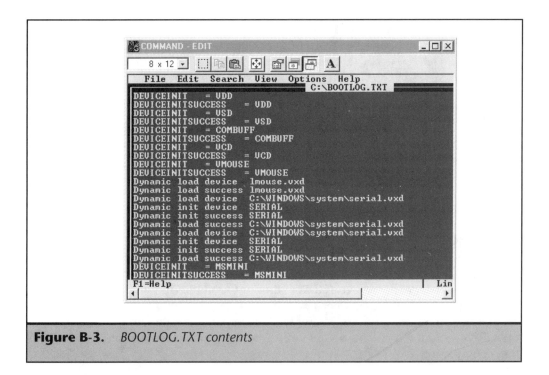

Figure B-3.   *BOOTLOG.TXT contents*

can reboot Windows 95 in fail-safe mode and replace that driver with one that will work properly.

    If you are unable to fix a problem using this method, do not worry. Save this file to disk and contact Microsoft's technical support department for further help.

Safe Mode
Similar to the fail-safe mode, this option simply bypasses all of the configuration files that might be responsible for your computer's problems. For example, it will not load any of the network drivers, modem drivers, or special Terminate and Stay Resident (TSR) drivers. You can then review your computer's settings, removing any conflicting or problematic devices manually.

Safe Mode with Network Support
This acts just like Safe Mode, except it makes your network devices available, which is beneficial if you have installed Windows 95 from a network.

Step by Step Confirmation
Press SHIFT-F8 to start Windows 95 in Step by Step mode. This is an excellent way for you to locate configuration problems. It allows you to review each device statement before it is loaded, choosing whether or not Windows 95 should execute the statement.

For example, if the system registry (which contains all of your user-specific information) does not appear to work properly, you can bypass it alone. This technique will let you verify that a suspect driver is at fault by process of elimination. You can also create a BOOTLOG.TXT file for further configuration review.

Command Prompt Only

Selecting to start only the command prompt will let you perform many low-level repairs that are impossible during the normal operation of Windows 95. You can press SHIFT-F5 to start this mode as well. This is a very useful tool in locating troubles because it, like the previous option, lets you select which devices to load. You can therefore quickly and easily eliminate suspect devices one by one without having to load the entire Windows 95 operating system.

Safe Mode Command Mode Only

This selection will give you a quick command prompt that is very useful in situations requiring repeated boot processes punctuated with editing chores. For example, if you need to repeatedly edit your AUTOEXEC.BAT or CONFIG.SYS files, this option will give you the quickest time between boot attempts.

In case you have used the Windows 95 DriveSpace application to compress your hard drive, do not worry. This option will ask you if you want to load DriveSpace's disk compression driver.

Networking Troubleshooting

Despite Windows 95's Plug and Play architecture and built-in support for Internet packet exchange/sequenced packet exchange (IPX/SPX) and transport control protocol/Internet protocol (TCP/IP), you may experience problems connecting your Windows 95 workstation to other computers and online services.

This section will address the most frequently encountered networking issues using general illustrations designed to give you tools with which you can solve your particular problems.

Problem: Applications Do Not Function Over More Than One Network Segment

If you use applications such as the peer to peer talk program (called Chat), with the NetBIOS protocol, you will find that your applications function properly only while you communicate with computers that are a part of your own local network segment (subnet). This is caused by NetBIOS's inability to route across different network segments. On a Novell Inc. NetWare network, for example, utilizing Microsoft Corp.'s Windows for Workgroups client workstations (which generally rely upon NetBIOS), only machines within each segment can communicate. It is the same for Windows 95 workstations using Novell's NetBIOS Open Datalink Interface (ODI) network driver. You may be able to communicate with a workstation located on a different subnet using an application that is IPX/SPX-centric, but you cannot communicate with that same workstation using an application that is NetBIOS-centric.

Solution: Add NetBIOS Support to IPX/SPX

The best way to overcome this limitation is to let a protocol that is routable transport the NetBIOS protocol from subnet to subnet. Novell's IPX/SPX protocol is able to do just that by tunneling NetBIOS packets within IPX/SPX packets. Routers that connect one subnet with another subnet see only an IPX/SPX packet's routing information, completely ignoring the NetBIOS information housed within the IPX/SPX packet. For more information about the Novell's NetBIOS tunneling, please refer to Appendix A, "Networking Protocols."

To enable NetBIOS to run within IPX/SPX packets, open the Control Panel window from the Settings menu and double-click the Network icon. This will open the network configuration dialog box. Here, select the IPX/SPX protocol selection and click the Properties button, which will open a dialog box containing three tabs labeled Bindings, Advanced, and NetBIOS. (See Figure B-4.) Select the NetBIOS tab and place a check mark in the box next to "I want to enable NetBIOS over IPX/SPX." This will allow IPX/SPX to tunnel NetBIOS packets.

Unfortunately, you cannot accomplish the same task over the TCP/IP protocol. Only the IPX/SPX protocol comes with this ability. That is not due to a fault within the TCP/IP protocol but to the increasing discontinuation of the NetBIOS protocol. Novell supports the NetBIOS protocol because there are a great number of applications written to communicate explicitly over the NetBIOS protocol. This is because it is quite easy to write to and because it provides a simple way to create peer-to-peer network connections. However, very few newer applications are written to its standards because of its inability to route.

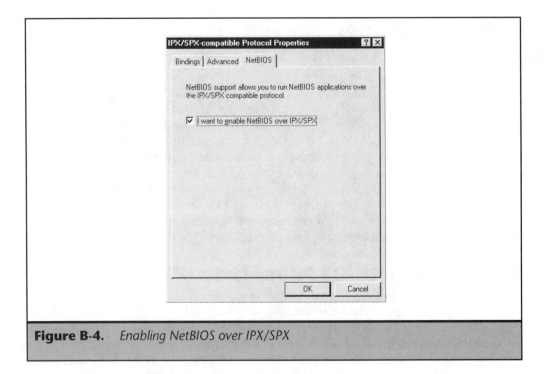

Figure B-4.   *Enabling NetBIOS over IPX/SPX*

Problem: Remote Access Server (RAS) Does Not Work

The Windows 95 RAS allows you to securely connect with many machines, such as Windows for Workgroups, Windows NT, and other Windows 95 workstations, and it is very simple to install. However, after connecting to another machine, you may notice that although the connection seems to have been established correctly, you are unable to work on the host machine.

Solution: Ensure That Device Sharing Is Enabled on Host Machine

This is a very easy problem to solve. However, its cause is not apparent. This is because during the RAS installation routine, you were asked to set up every aspect required to establish a remote connection except one: sharing. If sharing is not enabled on the host machine, you will not be able to see its hard drive, printer, or network volumes from your remote access client.

To install sharing on a Windows 95 host machine, simply double-click the My Computer icon, highlight your hard drive, and click the right mouse button. This will activate a pop-up menu. Click the Sharing option (see Figure B-5), opening the sharing dialog box. Here, you should click the radio button labeled Shared As: and enter a name for the drive as it should appear to the remote access user.

The Access Type you choose should depend upon the amount of security you desire. If you are the only remote user, you should click the radio button labeled Full. Otherwise, choose the level of security you need (either Read-Only or Depends on Password). When you have finished, you should see a change in the icon representing your hard drive. Instead of a simple hard drive icon, you should see a box being held by an outstretched hand.

To enable device sharing on other hosts such as Windows NT and Windows for Workgroups, you should consult documentation specific to those operating systems.

Problem: Internet Service Connection Does Not Work Properly

Once you have established a dial-up account with an Internet access provider with the protocols included with Windows 95, you can access the Internet as a Point-to-Point protocol (PPP) client. However, to set up a PPP service on your workstation you must make a great number of modifications to your network configuration and your remote access software. If you forget any steps, your connection will not work at all.

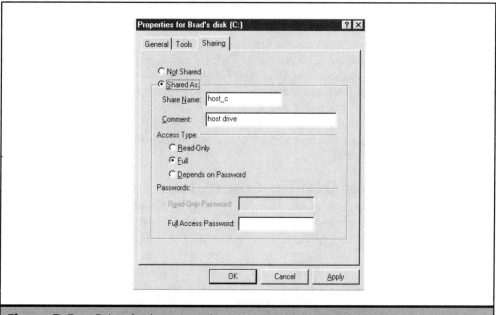

Figure B-5.   *Drive sharing properties*

Solution: Follow an Internet Connection Check List

To install Internet support on your Windows 95 machine, utilize the following check list:

Gather Internet Provider Information

To connect to the Internet via PPP, you must obtain information from your Internet access provider that will let your networking software communicate with the provider's host server. You should obtain your workstations Internet protocol (IP) address (if needed), the IP address of the host machine to which you wish to connect, the IP addresses of the Domain Naming System (DNS) servers you will need, and the IP addresses of a mail server (if needed).

Install Dial-up Adapter Support

After you have gathered the appropriate information, you must install the networking software. First you must add a modem driver, if you have not already done so, by double-clicking the Add New Hardware icon within the Control Panel window. Follow the directions within the Hardware Installation Wizard.

When you are done, double-click the Network icon within the Control Panel window and enter the configuration information gathered in the previous step. For example, once you have opened the Network icon, highlight the Microsoft TCP/IP protocol selection and enter the Internet access provider's information. (See Figure B-6.)

Once you have entered this information, all you will need to do is ensure that the newly created dial-up adapter is bound to the TCP/IP protocol. To do this, select the Microsoft Dial-up Adapter item from the Network dialog box, click on Properties, and select the Bindings tab. You should see an option for Microsoft TCP/IP within the box. Here, ensure that this item has a check mark next to it. If you do not bind a protocol to your dial-up adapter, you will never be able to make a connection because your modem will only try to speak over standard terminal emulation protocols, not networking protocols like PPP.

Select the Proper Dial-Up Connection Type

The only remaining items for you to check can be found within the Dial-up Networking program. To access this service, click the Start button, the Programs item, the Accessories item, and finally on the Dial-Up Networking item. If you have not already created an Internet session, double-click the Make New Connection icon and follow the Installation Wizard, entering a name for the connection and your access provider's host telephone number. When you have finished, select the New Connection icon and then click the right mouse button, activating a pop-up menu.

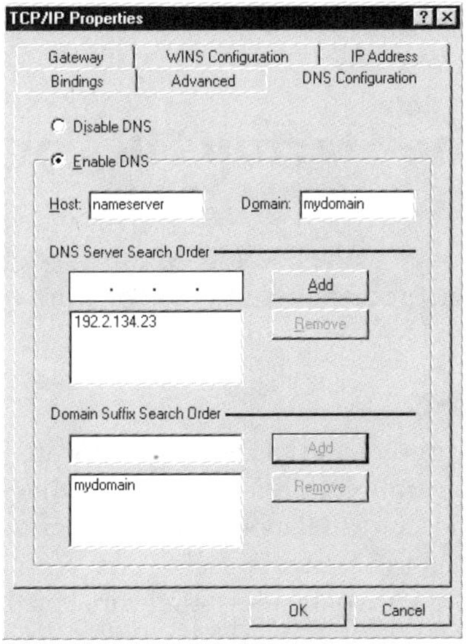

Figure B-6. *TCP/IP remote access information*

Here, click Properties and then click Server Types. Ensure that the type of Dial-Up server is labeled PPP: Windows 95, Windows NT 3.5, Internet. Click the OK button and then click the Configure button. Here, you must select the Options tab and then place a check mark next to the Bring up terminal window after dialing selection. This is necessary because without it, you will not be able to enter your account information like your name and your password once you establish a connection.

Once you have followed these steps, you should be able to connect to the Internet without any problems. If you experience further difficulties, however, contact your Internet service provider directly.

Problem: Network Interface Card Driver Does Not Load

Installing Windows 95's networking support is made simple because it comes with the drivers required to run many network interface cards. It can even automatically install these drivers. However, it cannot detect hardware conflicts between your interface card and any other add-on cards. Therefore, even though a network installation may appear to go smoothly, when you boot Windows 95 for the first time, you may see a command line error message indicating that the device driver for your network interface card could not be loaded.

Solution: Check the Startup Files and the Control Panel for Conflicts

If you receive an error message while booting Windows 95, the first thing you should do is determine whether the problem lies in your software configuration or your hardware settings.

Hardware Conflict

If you suspect a hardware conflict, the easiest way to locate the problem is to use the Windows 95 network configuration utilities. First, click the Start Button, then click the Settings option, click the Control Panel item, and finally double-click on the Network icon. This will open the Network dialog box. Note, some adapters that have software settings will not display a Resource tab. For these adapters, you must consult the adapter's documentation. From here, highlight the adapter card from the Configuration window and click the Properties button, opening the adapter configuration screen. Here, click the Resources tab and look at the input/output (I/O) address range and Interrupt (IRQ) fields. (See Figure B-7.)

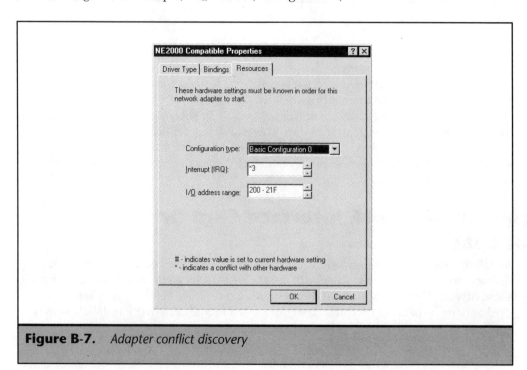

Figure B-7. *Adapter conflict discovery*

If there is a conflict with any other device such as an internal modem, video adapter, or another network interface card, you will see an asterisk next to the conflicting value. For example, if you have an internal modem that has a hardware setting of IRQ 4, and your network adapter is also set to IRQ 4, an asterisk will appear next to the value 4 in the IRQ field. The same principle applies to the I/O address range.

To fix this situation, you should try different IRQ and I/O values until the asterisk disappears. Once you have found a combination that does not conflict with any other hardware, you should first save the correct configuration, noting the IRQ and I/O values. Then, you must modify the hardware settings on your network interface card. Depending upon the make and model of your card, this will require you to either run a configuration program or remove the card and change the jumper settings by hand.

Software Conflict

If your hardware appears to be configured correctly, the next place you should look for trouble is within the software settings for the adapter and the protocols used by the adapter. As with the previous solution, double-click the Network icon from the Control Panel window. Once here, ensure that you have both a network interface card and a supporting protocol installed and configured. If you are not sure whether this has been done, refer to Chapter 4, "Installation Overview."

If everything appears to be in proper order, the problem most likely lies within your AUTOEXEC.BAT file. It is from here that you actually load the network drivers. To check this file, open an MS-DOS window and change to the root of your hard drive disk. Here, open the AUTOEXEC.BAT file with the MS-DOS editor that is included with Windows 95. For example, to open the file, you would type

```
EDIT C:\AUTOEXEC.BAT
```

Inspect the contents of this file, paying particular attention to the statements relating to network drivers. What appears within this file will depend upon a number of variables such as whether or not you have chosen ODI or Network Driver Interface Specification (NDIS) drivers, for example. If you have chosen to install ODI drivers, you should see a set of commands similar to the following:

```
LSL
NE2000
IPXODI
NETX
ODIHELP
NETSTART
```

With either ODI or NDIS drivers, if you have chosen to retain your original device drivers in lieu of Windows 95's 32-bit client drivers, you should ensure that you are referring to the same network interface card driver from the AUTOEXEC.BAT file as you are from the Network configuration screen.

The most common problem here stems from an incorrect reference. For example, if you have changed network adapter cards in the past and neglected to remove the old network driver, you may be referencing it instead of the new, correct driver.

General Troubleshooting

This section covers the most troublesome topics not covered in the other areas of this appendix. Therefore, its contents will be organized alphabetically rather than topically to make the varied contents more accessible. As with the other sections in this appendix, all problems and solutions will act as general, deductive stratagems from which you should be able to infer answers for your particular problems.

Problem: Windows 95 Slows During Disk Operations

Although Windows 95 is capable of preemptive multitasking (running more than one application simultaneously), it may appear to slow to a crawl in some situations when you run two applications at the same time. For example, if while you format a floppy disk from the Windows 95 Explorer you also open a solitaire game, you may notice that it takes an inordinate amount of time for solitaire to load and deal the cards. Because Windows 95 retains some 16-bit architecture for backward compatibility, some simultaneous program execution combinations will slow your workstations substantially, such as the format command and the solitaire game.

Solution: Run Disk Utilities from the Command Line

If you find this behavior unbearable, you can counter such anomalies by running file and disk utility commands from an MS-DOS box. This practice will bypass the overhead associated with the Windows 95 interface, removing one more step between the command and the operating system. Of course, the only commands that can effect your general productivity within Windows 95 are those that demand a great deal of consistent processor time, such as the format command. Most commands will actually complete before you are able to switch to another program.

Problem: Unwanted Banner and Blank Form Printing Under NetWare

When you install a NetWare network printer for the first time, Windows 95 assumes that you want to use a banner to identify your print job and a blank form at the end of your print job to further differentiate it from other print jobs. However, although this is an important tool for companies utilizing a large ratio of computers to printers, it is not always a welcome policy as it wastes paper.

Solution: Disable Banner and Form Feed Options Under NetWare

To solve this problem, you can do one of two things. You can simply change the default configuration for your printer through the Printer control panel, or you can change the capture setting used by NetWare's print redirector. Certainly the former solution is preferable; however, it is not always possible because some printer definitions simply do not contain the appropriate settings. In these cases, it is necessary for you to change the settings directly within Novell at the command line.

Control Panel Modifications

The Windows 95 control panel offers an easy way to disable banners and form feed pages through its menu-driven interface. First, open the Control Panel from the Settings selection on the Start menu, then double-click the Printers folder icon. This will open a folder containing the printers you have installed (note that you will have to make these changes to each installed printer).

Open the printer's settings by clicking with the right mouse button on the printer and then clicking the Properties selection at the bottom of the pop-up menu. This will open the Properties configuration screen for your printer. Click the Details tab and then remove the check marks next to the Banner and Form Feed check box items. That is all there is to it. (See Figure B-8.)

Command Line Modifications

If, however, your printer definition does not support such settings, you must perform the same configuration changes from the command prompt. The easiest way to do this is to open an MS-DOS box from the Programs menu and type the following at the command prompt:

```
CAPTURE L=1 S=FileServer Q=PrintQue NB NFF
```

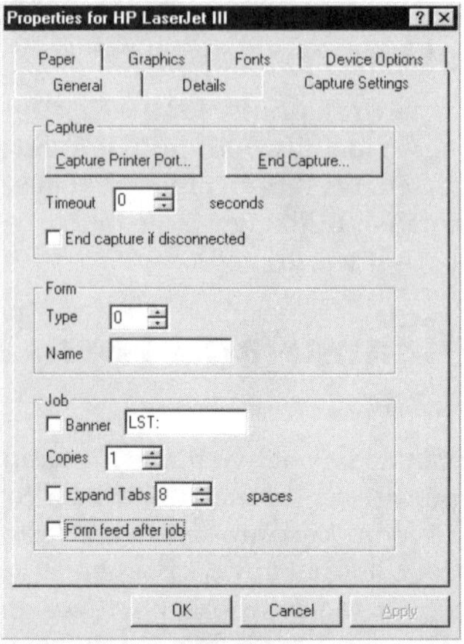

Figure B-8. *Disabling banner and form feed options*

Of course, to execute this command, you must have the NetWare PUBLIC directory in your path or you must execute the command from that directory. The two command line options that turn off the banner and form feed features are the NB and NFF options, respectively. With the **S=FileServer** option, you should replace the name FileServer with the name of the NetWare file server supporting the print server you wish to use. Likewise, you should replace the PrintQue name with the name of the queue you want to print through.

Problem: Windows 95 Will Not Work with Windows NT

Although you can maintain both Windows NT and Windows 95 on the same hard drive, dual-booting between the two operating systems, neither operating system will function properly if you install both in either the same directory or in a single hierarchy (different subdirectories within a single directory).

Solution: Install Separately

Because the default directory for both operating systems is labeled C:\WINDOWS, you must ensure that they are both installed in completely separate directories. If you do not, the currently active operating system may attempt to reference programs and drivers from the other operating system. This occurs because each operating system contains files with identical names but incompatible content. If the incorrect version of a requested file is referenced first because it falls first in the PATH statement located within the AUTOEXEC.BAT file, some programs will not run at all.

To solve this problem, ensure that each operating system has its own directory. An ideal directory structure that will ensure that no cross-referencing problems occur is as follows:

    C:\WINDOWS.95
    C:\WINDOWS.FWG
    C:\WINDOWS.NT

These directories should house Windows 95, Windows for Workgroups, and Windows NT, respectively.

If you have installed or configured multiple disk drives or disk partitions, you can simply maintain each operating system on separate partitions or disk drives. This is the most simple corrective technique. However, if you have only one disk or only one partition, you cannot install two partitions without destroying all of the data on your hard disk.

Index

Symbols and Numbers

* (asterisk)
    in adapter settings, 186, 187
    in Resources Properties
      settings for network
      adapters, 99
    in Resources tab display of
      I/O address ranges and
      IRQs, 290
\\ (backslashes), in the universal
    naming convention (UNC), 109,
    195
$ (dollar sign) in share names, 149
# (pound sign) in Resources

Properties settings for network
    adapters, 99
16-bit real-mode drivers, compared
    to 32-bit protected-mode, 91-92
32-bit network driver support, 92
32-bit networking architecture, 52
32-bit protected-mode drivers,
    compared to 16-bit real-mode,
    91-92
32-bit Virtual Device Driver (VxD).
    See VxD
802.2 frame type, 208
802.3 frame type, 208

LAN TIMES Free Subscription Form

○ Yes, I want to receive (continue to receive) LAN TIMES free of charge.   ○ No.

I am ○ a new subscriber ○ renewing my subscription ○ changing my address

Signature required _____ Date _____

Name_____

Title _____ Telephone _____

Company _____

Address _____

City _____

State/County _____ Zip/Postal Code _____

Free in the United States to qualified subscribers only

International Prices (Airmail Delivery)

Canada: $65 Elsewhere: $150

○ Payment enclosed ○ Bill me later

Charge my: ○ Visa ○ Mastercard ○ Amer. Exp

Card number _____

Exp. Date _____

All questions must be completed to qualify for a subscription to LAN TIMES. Publisher reserves the right to serve only those individuals who meet publication criteria.

1. Which of the following best describe your organization?

(Check only one)
○ A. Agriculture/Mining/Construction/Oil/Petrochemical/Environmental
○ B. Manufacturer (non-computer)
○ C. Government/Military/Public Adm.
○ D. Education
○ E. Research/Development
○ F. Engineering/Architecture
○ G. Finance/Banking/Accounting/Insurance/Real Estate
○ H. Health/Medical/Legal
○ I. VAR/VAD Systems House
○ J. Manufacturer Computer Hardware/Software
○ K. Aerospace
○ L. Retailer/Distributor/Wholesaler (non-computer)
○ M. Computer Retailer/Distributor/Sales
○ N. Transportation
○ O. Media/Marketing/Advertising/Publishing/Broadcasting
○ P. Utilities/Telecommunications/VAN
○ Q. Entertainment/Recreation/Hospitality/Non-profit/Trade Association
○ R. Consultant
○ S. Systems Integrator
○ T. Computer/LAN Leasing/Training
○ U. Information/Data Services
○ V. Computer/Communications Services: Outsourcing/3rd Party
○ W. All Other Business Services
○ X. Other _____

2. Which best describes your title? (Check only one)
○ A. Network/LAN Manager
○ B. MIS/DP/IS Manager
○ C. Owner/President/CEO/Partner
○ D. Data Communications Manager
○ E. Engineer/CNE/Technician
○ F. Consultant/Analyst
○ G. Micro Manager/Specialist/Coordinator
○ H. Vice President
○ I. All other Dept. Heads, Directors and Managers
○ J. Educator
○ K. Programmer/Systems Analyst
○ L. Professional
○ M. Other_____

3. Which of the following best describes your job function?

(Check only one)
○ A. Network/LAN Management
○ B. MIS/DP/IS Management
○ C. Systems Engineering/Integration
○ D. Administration/Management
○ E. Technical Services
○ F. Consulting
○ G. Research/Development
○ H. Sales/Marketing
○ I. Accounting/Finance
○ J. Education/Training

○ K. Office Automation
○ L. Manufacturing/Operations/Production
○ M. Personnel
○ N. Technology Assessment
○ O. Other _____

4. How many employees work in your entire ORGANIZATION?

(Check only one)
○ A. Under 25   ○ E. 1,001-5,000
○ B. 25-100   ○ F. 5,001-9,999
○ C. 101-500   ○ G. 10,000 and over
○ D. 501-1,000

5. Which of the following are you or your clients currently using, or planning to purchase in the next 12 months? (1–Own; 2–Plan to purchase in next 12 months) (Check all that apply)

Topologies	1	2
A. Ethernet	○	○
B. Token Ring	○	○
C. Arcnet	○	○
D. LocalTalk	○	○
E. FDDI	○	○
F. Starlan	○	○
G. Other	○	○

Network Operating System	1	2
A. Novell Netware	○	○
B. Novell Netware Lite	○	○
C. Banyan VINES	○	○
D. Digital Pathworks	○	○
E. IBM LAN Server	○	○
F. Microsoft LAN Manager	○	○
G. Microsoft Windows for Workgroups	○	○
H. Artisoft LANtastic	○	○
I. Sitka TOPS	○	○
J. 10NET	○	○
K. AppleTalk	○	○

Client/Workstation Operating Sys.	1	2
A. DOS	○	○
B. DR-DOS	○	○
C. Windows	○	○
D. Windows NT	○	○
E. UNIX	○	○
F. UnixWare	○	○
G. OS/2	○	○
H. Mac System 6	○	○
I. Mac System 7	○	○

Protocols/Standards	1	2
A. IPX	○	○
B. TCP/IP	○	○
C. X.25	○	○
D. XNS	○	○
E. OSI	○	○
F. SAA/SNA	○	○
G. NFS	○	○
H. MHS	○	○

6. Is your Organization/Clients network... (Check all that apply)

- ○ A. International
- ○ B. National
- ○ C. Regional
- ○ D. Metropolitan
- ○ E. Local
- ○ F. Other _____

7. What hardware does your department/client base own/plan to purchase. (Check all that apply)

	Owns	Plan to purchase in next 12 months
A. Bridges	○	○
B. Diskless Workstations	○	○
C. Cabling System	○	○
D. Printers	○	○
E. Disk Drive	○	○
F. Optical Storage	○	○
G. Tape Backup System	○	○
H. Optical Storage	○	○
I. Application Servers	○	○
J. Communication Servers	○	○
K. Fax Servers	○	○
L. Mainframe	○	○
M. Network Adapter Cards	○	○
N. Wireless Adapters/Bridges	○	○
O. Power Conditioners/UPSs	○	○
P. Hubs/Concentrators	○	○
Q. Minicomputers	○	○
R. Modems	○	○
S. 386-based computers	○	○
T. 486-based computers	○	○
U. Pentium-based computers	○	○
V. Macintosh computers	○	○
W. RISC-based workstations	○	○
X. Routers	○	○
Y. Multimedia Cards	○	○
Z. Network Test/Diagnostic Equipment	○	○
1. Notebooks/Laptops	○	○
2. DSU/CSU	○	○
99. None of the Above	○	○

8. What network software/applications do you/your clients own/plan to purchase in the next 12 months? (Check all that apply)

- ○ A. Network Management
- ○ B. Software Metering
- ○ C. Network Inventory
- ○ D. Virus Protection
- ○ E. Menuing
- ○ F. E-mail
- ○ G. Word Processing
- ○ H. Spreadsheet
- ○ I. Database
- ○ J. Accounting
- ○ K. Document Management
- ○ L. Graphics
- ○ M. Communications
- ○ N. Application Development Tools
- ○ O. Desktop Publishing
- ○ P. Integrated Business Applications
- ○ Q. Multimedia
- ○ R. Document Imaging
- ○ S. Groupware
- ○ Z. None of the above

9. What is the annual revenue of your entire organization or budget if non-profit (Check only one)

- ○ A. Under $10 million
- ○ B. $10-$50 million
- ○ C. $50-$100 million
- ○ D. $100-$500 million
- ○ E. $500 million-$1 billion
- ○ F. Over $1 billion

10. How much does your organization (if reseller, your largest client's company) plan to spend on computer products in the next 12 months? (Check only one)

- ○ A. Under $25,000
- ○ B. $25,000-$99,999
- ○ C. $100,000-$499,999
- ○ D. $500,000-$999,999
- ○ E. $1 billion

11. Where do you purchase computer products? (Check all that apply)

- ○ A. Manufacturer
- ○ B. Distributor
- ○ C. Reseller
- ○ D. VAR
- ○ E. System Integrator
- ○ F. Consultant
- ○ G. Other _____

12. In which ways are you involved in acquiring computer products and services? (Check all that apply)

- ○ A. Determine the need
- ○ B. Define product specifications/features
- ○ C. Select brand
- ○ D. Evaluate the supplier
- ○ E. Select vendor/source
- ○ F. Approve the acquisition
- ○ G. None of the above

ICS1639

---

fold here

LAN TIMES

McGraw–Hill, INC.

P.O. Box 652

Hightstown NJ 08520-0652